The Family Table

A Capital Lifestyles Book—Capital ideas for health and beauty, decorating your home and your garden, and entertaining your friends with style. Other titles include:

A Chicken in Every Pot: Global Recipes for the World's Most Popular Bird by Kate Keyhoe

Best Dressed Southern Salads: Sumptuous Salads from Key West to Washington, D.C. by Vicky Moon

Gathering in the Garden: Recipes and Ideas for Garden Parties by Shelley Snow and Elaine Husband

It's Just a Dinner Party: The Modern Approach to Entertaining with Style and Ease by Ron and Julie Malloy

Mangia Bene! The Italian-American Family Cookbook by Kate DeVivo

Sabroso! The Spanish-American Family Cookbook by Noemi Cristina Taylor

Quest for the Holy Grill: 50 Crummy but Good Restaurants within Rambling Range of Washington, D.C. by Donovan Kelly

The 7-Day Color Diet: The New Way to Health & Beauty by Mindy Weisel

The Asian Diet: Get Slim and Stay Slim the Asian Way by Diana My Tran

The Vietnamese Cookbook by Diana My Tran

What Goes With What for Parties: Planning Made Easy by Bo Niles

The Family Table

WHERE GREAT FOOD, FRIENDS, AND
FAMILY GATHER TOGETHER

Christy Rost

CAPITAL
BOOKS, INC.

CAPITAL BOOKS, INC.
22841 Quicksilver Drive
Sterling, Virginia

CAPITAL BOOKS, INC.

P.O. Box 605

Herndon, Virginia 20172-0605

ISBN 1-931868-47-6   (alk.paper)

Library of Congress Cataloging-in-Publication Data

Rost, Christy.
  The family table : where great food, friends, and family gather together / Christy Rost.
        p.cm.

"A Capital lifestyles book."
Includes index
  1. Cookery. I. Title.
  TX714.R675 2003
  641.5–dc21

                             2003007606

Printed in the United States of America on acid-free paper that meets the American National Standards Institute Z39-48 Standard.

Book Design: Suzanne Stanton Chadwick, Chadwick Design Incorporated

First Edition

10 9 8 7 6 5 4 3 2 1

To Randy, whose love and support

have made this book a reality.

To my grandmothers,

Kathryn Hewston and Henrietta Schnoes,

who inspired my love of baking,

and are dearly missed.

And, to my mother and father,

Jinx and Bob Schnoes,

who taught me by their loving example

that life is to be celebrated daily

around the family table.

Contents

Acknowledgments

*T*his book has been a spiritual, as well as a personal journey, and I have been touched by many who aided and inspired me along the way. I had no idea when I began this project how much I would come to depend on my sweet husband, Randy, to hold our lives together while I spent endless weeks and months developing recipes and writing text. Randy inspired, tasted, and critiqued recipes, gave much-needed hugs, cooked our everyday meals, washed dishes, walked the dog, and generally kept our household running during my final months and weeks of writing. Thank you, my love, for I could never have completed this book without your endless support and cheerful willingness to take over everyday tasks.

My deepest thanks to Evan Fogelman, my literary agent, who believed in me from the beginning, even when wallpapering my office with rejection letters seemed a real possibility. Evan never gave up, and from time to time he reminded me a that a publisher would one day recognize what he had seen in me years before. Thank you for your unwavering faith.

Every now and then, we meet people with unselfish, loving hearts who take us under their wings and change our lives. I have been fortunate to meet three, and every day I cherish their friendship, support, and guidance. Martin Yan, host of PBS's long-running cooking show, *Yan Can Cook*, has shown me what it is to be a mentor. Martin "adopted" me at a crucial time in my journey, when I had just chosen to continue an uncertain culinary path over a more lucrative career opportunity. He told me I would one day have a great culinary career and encouraged me to believe in myself and make the most of my talents.

Martin taught me how to give a great presentation, how important it is to spend time with each and every audience member, and how to help others along the way. He encouraged me to write a book and offered to develop a recipe for my first cookbook as if to say, "Look! I believe in Christy. You should, too." I am humbled and most grateful for his eloquent foreword to *The Family Table*. Thank you, Martin. May I be a mentor to an up-and-coming culinary professional as you have been to me.

Another man who took me under his wing is my dear friend David Davis, director of public relations for the elegant Hotel Adolphus in Dallas, Texas. David arranged my first network television appearance, where I learned I had a gift for working with the camera. David, thank you from my heart for all the opportunities you have created for me, for the warmth and friendship Randy and I always find waiting for us at The Hotel Adolphus, and for allowing us to make you part of our family.

My third angel is Carol Ritchie, a gifted cooking instructor who gave me my first opportunity in front of a television camera on her long-running Texas cooking show, *Cookin' with Carol*. Five years ago, Carol asked me to start a new television cooking show with her in Fort Worth, Texas, and my cable television show, *Just Like Home*, became a reality. Carol, thank you for teaching me how to plan and produce a show, demonstrate a twenty-minute recipe in an eight-minute segment, and artfully continue speaking with nary a glance when a Pyrex bowl falls to the floor while the cameras are rolling. You gave me my start in *Just Like Home*, then graciously departed to allow me to make it my own. You kept me grounded and encouraged me throughout this writing process. You're the best!

Special thanks and hugs go to many others who played a significant role in the ultimate production of *The Family Table*. To Judy Karpinski of Capital Books, who recognized the importance of this book's mission to strengthen families and foster deeper bonds of love by bringing people back to the family table. And, to my editor, Noemi Taylor, who was there to answer my questions, offer reassurance, and coordinate production of the beautiful volume you hold in your hands.

To Eric Little, my friend, wine expert, and author of Eric's Wine Notes for *The Family Table*. His gifted prose and expansive knowledge of wines and spirits have added tremendous richness to the text, provided an easily understood introduction to wine pairings, and reasserted our belief that serving wine in moderation with meals teaches children that wine enhances enjoyment of a meal and is not to be abused.

To my dear friends who, together with Martin Yan, enthusiastically contributed a recipe to *The Family Table*: fellow Registered Nurse, vegetarian cookbook author, restaurateur, and all-around cheerleader, Claire Criscuolo; cookbook author, PBS television host, and radio host, Lauren Groveman, whose family-centered message is dear to her heart and mine; and William Koval, gifted executive chef of The Hotel Adolphus in Dallas, Texas, and preparer of special culinary treats to warm my heart. And to Nathalie Dupree, cookbook author, restaurateur, PBS host, and expert in Southern cooking and entertaining, who inspired one of my recipes and offered needed support and advice. Thank you all from the bottom of my heart.

To René Sotelo, manager of World Market at Old Town in Dallas, Texas, and to her friendly associates. World Market has been a sponsor of my local cable television cooking/lifestyle show, *Just Like Home*, since the beginning. Thanks to René, many of the accessories pictured in *The Family Table* were generously provided to add richness to the text.

To Marj Waters, publisher of *The Park Cities News* in Dallas, Texas, who gave me my first writing job as a food editor almost twelve years ago. To television host, Debra Duncan, of *Good Morning Texas*, and, later, of *The Debra Duncan Show*, who called me a "natural" in front of the camera and encouraged me in my pursuit of teaching others how to entertain effortlessly.

To radio host and dear friend, Jim White, and his lovely and vivacious wife, Vicki.

Vicki's stroke of genius led to Jim's invitation three years ago to join him regularly on his North Texas radio show. His joie de vivre and encouragement have helped me to reach this goal.

To my good friend, John Bittrick, senior manager of planned gifts for PBS. Our chance meeting several years ago during a PBS dinner event developed into a friendship I cherish. Your enthusiasm and belief in my family-centered message have sustained me more than you know.

To my friends who have given selflessly of their time and energy to assist me in the studio and my kitchen: Gail Heinonen, Betty Merwin, Marilyn McElroy, Debbie Springer, Kathy Perry, and Janet Boynton. Without their talent, ideas, and enthusiasm, this book could not have been written. They have prepped ingredients, hauled equipment, washed dishes, arranged flowers, set tables, assisted with photo shoots, prayed for my success, and cheered, cheered, cheered me on. Special hugs and love to you all.

And to three very special friends, angels every one, who were there in the early days, and continued to be there for me, almost like sisters and most certainly as soulmates: Dyan Anderson, Vickie Hecht, and Nancy Upson. I am so blessed to have had your support and love throughout the years, and particularly during the days of writing *The Family Table*.

To television co-hosts Chuck and Jenni Borsellino, producer Trish Ragsdale, and associate producers Dan Parker and Leslie Davis of FamilyNet Television's *At Home–Live!* Your prayers and belief in my family-centered message have given me inner strength and a deeper assurance that the mission to write *The Family Table* and spread its loving message was inspired and sustained by God.

To the rest of my family, who have tasted recipes and offered undying support and love, but especially to our sons, Timothy and Bob. Their technical assistance in producing this manuscript, promotional videos, and my website have opened up an entire new world to me, and their humor has kept me laughing in the midst of long hours of cooking and writing. Timothy and Bobby, you have given me your time and talent in the spirit of unselfishness and enthusiasm for my work, and I am truly blessed to be your mother.

To my dear, sweet parents, Jinx and Bob Schnoes, who set a far-reaching example of sharing daily food around the table and whose pride in their daughter knows no limits. To Randy's mother, Pat Rost Shilstone, who has always regarded me as her own daughter and reminded Randy and our sons how fortunate they are to have a wife and mother who cooks for them (bless you, Mom).

To my sweet sisters, Lynn, Nancy, and Judy, who have kept the faith and the lines of communication operating at breakneck speed. Despite our geographical distance, when I needed love, support, or family anecdotes for my text, within minutes, the word was spread, and my phone would start ringing. Sweet Tarts Forever!

And to God, who inspired the idea for this book and revealed it as my mission—to bring families and friends back to the family table in celebration of life's moments, both great and small— that we may be drawn closer in love to our families, our friends, and those with whom we work, and that this love will ultimately bring us all closer to our Creator.

Special
Acknowledgment

One of the elements that distinguishes *The Family Table* from other cookbooks is its extensive wine notes, thanks to the wine expertise and comprehensive, yet easy-to-read writing style of my friend and culinary colleague, Eric Little.

With more than fourteen years in the wine industry, Eric Little has been the wine consultant for my television cooking/lifestyle show, *Just Like Home*, since its inception. Eric has judged the prestigious *Dallas Morning News* Wine Competition, has planned and hosted more than two hundred wine dinners, has written countless wine lists for restaurants, and writes about wine for several magazines.

Eric's training as a chef in several top-rated Texas restaurant kitchens, and his amazing ability to remember the characteristics of wines he has tasted, has contributed to the expertise with which he pairs wine and spirits with food. But it is Eric's ability to explain the world of wine, complete with history, technical descriptions, and interesting anecdotes, and in terms everyone can understand, that makes Eric's Wine Notes a valuable addition to *The Family Table*.

Foreword

Since her first days at *The Park Cities News* in Dallas, Texas, Christy has helped Texans and Americans in all aspects of home entertaining and just plain everyday life. She uses diverse media to share her talent and passion for bringing family and friends to the dinner table. Christy has a genuine desire to help people, as evidenced by her Registered Nurse degree, charity work, and collaboration with the American Heart Association. This book only continues her magnificent job of educating people on how to nurture the self through bringing others together.

I first met Christy during a two-city cooking/entertaining class we co-presented for a large department store. Realizing her passion and enthusiasm, I invited her to participate in the production of the *Yan Can Cook* program at KQED in San Francisco. She contributed her culinary skills and talent to the team during all phases of production. Few have what it takes to be successful in today's mass media, particularly television. I saw that spark and excitement in her and have been encouraging her to develop her own television show and to publish a cookbook that would showcase her love and passion for food. Finally, here it is. I couldn't be more pleased with the excellent job she and her associates have done.

During a recent dinner conversation in Christy's beautiful home, we were touching on the subject of today's family. It seems many of today's families are a bit disconnected and hardly share the family table and eat together. Throughout human history, meal and celebration times have been a catalyst for mental and emotional bonding, social structures, and passing down traditions. When mealtime bonding is missing, the family unit weakens.

From cover to cover, Christy's voice speaks from the pages with clarity and precision, honesty and conviction. Her recipes are concise and easy to follow. She finds a place for the flavors of grandmas and celebrity chefs alike. The way she divides the book's content is user-friendly. Her personal touch with the material is evident in her section introductions and recipe notes. Her dedication to the family asserts itself in her something-for-everyone approach. Her collaboration with Eric Little on the fabulous wine pairings proves that wine doesn't have to be a source of fear and, in certain cases, it belongs on the table nearly as much as salt and pepper. The Entertaining at Home section is the cure for those who get so overwhelmed with pomp and circumstance that they forget to enjoy being with their guests.

I was delighted to discover the premise of Christy's book, because I, too, share her desire to bring people together. In fact, most of my business is done over a meal and a cup of tea. Each and every time we sit around the table, it is a celebration. Christy's *Just Like Home* television series and *The Family Table* both draw from her prolific career to illustrate how people can share their homes and convey their own style with elegance and ease. I am honored to have a place at Christy's family table, as there is always a place for her at mine. And remember, if Christy can entertain, so can you.

Martin Yan
Yan Can Cook

Introduction

Whether we dine as a family or set a few extra places for others to join us, gathering around the table provides us the opportunity to celebrate the most important things in life—love, family, good health, and good friends. Now more than ever, coming together as a family gives us the opportunity to recognize our blessings and renew our commitment to each other. Never has this been more important than since our nation's tragic events on September 11, 2001.

As we continue the process of healing and deal with our nation's newfound vulnerability, it becomes more important than ever to feed our souls. At home, we have the power to do this every day by gathering our family and friends around the table to share a meal. This is particularly important for our children, who gain reassurance from the simple act of being together. The importance of sitting down together for meals cannot be overstated, for it fosters love, understanding, sharing, and connectedness. As parents or friends, it provides us an opportunity to nurture others and, in turn, to nurture ourselves.

When we feel apprehensive and vulnerable, comfort and family closeness are paramount and reaching back into our "food memories" often makes us feel better. In *The Family Table*, you will find a wealth of comfort foods you grew up with, such as Surprise Meat Loaf, Old Chicago Minestrone, Spaghetti with Meat Sauce, Roast Beef with Henrietta's Brown Gravy, Cinnamon French Toast, Buttermilk Cornbread Muffins, and All-American Apple Pie.

You will also discover many new recipes, created with easily found ingredients and designed with families, large and small, in mind. Look for Tomato Galette, Beef Bourguignon, Homemade Pizza, Thick and Creamy Tortilla Soup, Mexican Rice with Fideo and Roasted Corn, Sweetheart Brownies with Raspberry Coulis, and Bananas Foster. These recipes are easy enough to offer often as part of family meals.

When my husband and I lived in Paris with our two small sons, we loved the French approach to meals. Whether in the city or the countryside, the French have transformed dining into an art form. I can still picture the many occasions we dined with French friends, their tables laden with an array of regional fare, platters of cheese, bottles of wine, and the best bread I have ever tasted. Children joined adults at the table for the meal, then departed to play games as the adults lingered around the table, sometimes for hours, happily conversing and sipping wine while finishing the cheese.

It was the relaxed atmosphere of those meals, even the formal ones, that so impressed me and forever changed my approach to family meals and entertaining. I rediscovered the joy of simple foods, shared with friends and extended family, and the sheer happiness of sitting around a table after the meal, deep in conversation and laughter. Anyone as fond of entertaining, but as short on time as I, will love *The Family Table*'s Entertaining at Home section, because I believe the focus of entertaining should be more on the guests and less on the event. This section is devoted to recipes and suggestions that make entertaining fun and easy, but oh-so-distinctive.

I am passionate about family meals; they are part of the glue that holds our family together and keeps it close. They are the way our family celebrates triumphs large and small, the forum at which we discuss current events, school projects, and family vacation plans. It was at the dinner table that I learned to use the computer. After months of listening to our sons trade information about "operating systems" and Internet sites with their father, I realized it was time for me to jump in and become computer literate, if only to be able to contribute to the dinner conversation. Little did I suspect that I would one day be sitting at that same table discussing development of my own website.

For years, we have used family meals as a testing ground for new recipes I have developed. Not only is everyone free to offer an opinion about each new dish, they often contribute ideas for improving flavor or texture and confer the sought-after "Family Seal of Approval" when a dish is proclaimed perfect just the way it is. But the best part of these meals is the "Name This Recipe" sessions. From the outlandish to the hilarious, from silly to serious, each recipe is eventually awarded a title for use in cooking classes, newspaper articles, books, or television shows. When dinner is this much fun, no wonder they keep coming back for more!

For some families, sitting down together for a meal occurs primarily during the holidays, but in our home family meals have always been a daily ritual. Naturally, there were times when our sons' school activities necessitated feeding them an early meal by themselves, but for the most part we have always dined as a family, making necessary adjustments to the dinner hour to accommodate everyone's changing schedules. I regard this flexible approach to dinnertime as an affirmation that each member of the family is important, and that mealtime just isn't the same when someone is "missing."

Besides flexibility, the key to preserving the family meal is an arsenal of family-friendly recipes. Inspired by my television cooking/lifestyle show, *Just Like Home*, the recipes in *The Family Table* are designed to assist busy families and couples in getting nutritious, delicious meals on the table day after day, night after night. Even singles will find this book useful in preparing today's popular cocktails, quick and easy appetizers, and meals for last-minute get-togethers as well as celebrations with friends and family. And for those moments when we all crave a touch of home, *The Family Table* is ready with nostalgic homestyle recipes that transport us back to a time when we were nurtured by the love of family and friends around the table.

It should be pointed out that my use of the word "family" is meant in its broadest interpretation, for I believe our friends are part of our family. Whether married with children, a couple, or single, our families include the neighbors next door and across the street, the people we work with, and those we routinely encounter as we go about our daily lives. All of us can enrich our lives, and the lives of others, by inviting them to join us around the table for a meal.

Because wines pair so beautifully with food and enhance the enjoyment of meals, I have collaborated with good friend and wine expert Eric Little to present wine suggestions with many of the recipes in this book. A classically trained chef and wine consultant for *Just Like Home*, Eric has produced well over two hundred wine dinners, and is frequently called on to judge wine competitions. Eric's educated palate and lyrical prose, combined with his enviable ability to catalog, recall, and describe "wine memories," have resulted in a comprehensive guide to enjoying and learning about wines.

Everyone can feel like a wine expert without worrying about serving the wrong wine, because the wines are already paired with the appropriate recipe for optimal enjoyment. Not only that, but Eric explains why the wines were selected, what flavors to look for, characteristics of the recipe, and how the nuances of the food and wine complement each other. While the wines are generally well-priced, several suggestions are given for each recipe, in order of least to most expensive, so enjoying wine with everyday meals is practical and economical. Cost is designated by $ signs, and the following price guideline is used: $ indicates under $10, $+ indicates $10–$13, $$ is $13–$18, and $$$ is over $20.

Like most chefs, I prepare simple meals for my family. I combine the freshest ingredients I can find in my supermarket, the local farmers' market, and my herb garden to create uncomplicated meals bursting with flavor and eye appeal. No stacking or pyramids of ingredients on my table—just artistically arranged platters of fresh, wholesome, homestyle recipes my family and guests crave.

The Family Table is a practical volume of recipes for today's home cook that emphasizes the beauty of simple foods, local ingredients, reasonably priced wines from around the world, and the joy of dining together as a family.

I have been cooking since I was twelve. When I cook, it is a tribute to those who came before me as I share their recipes and traditions with my own family and friends. Both of my grandmothers were great cooks, and the love with which they fed their families inspired my love of the kitchen. My mother, who prepared delicious meals every day for our family of six, gave me the freedom and encouragement to experiment with cooking and indulge my passion for creating beautiful desserts. My mother, an avid gardener, and I still exchange bits of "kitchen wisdom" resulting from her latest harvest of seasonal produce.

Food provides both physical and emotional sustenance when it is shared at the table. It allows those who prepare it to nurture those who eat it. Dining with others, whether family or guests, gives us a feeling of connectedness with and love for those around us. Children learn the art of conversation, manners, and sharing while dining with others, and they learn an appreciation for good food and that wine is meant to enhance the food enjoyed during a meal.

In *The Family Table*, tempting recipe selections range from all-American favorites to Caribbean, Chinese, French, Italian, Japanese, and Mexican cuisine. I have provided my favorite, easy-to-follow recipes suited to everyday meals as well as recipes ideal for weekends, for entertaining, and for such holidays as Christmas, New Year's Eve, Valentine's Day, Easter, Halloween, and Thanksgiving.

I believe in well-balanced meals that provide the flavors we love, the nutrients we need to stay healthy, "something sweet" to satisfy our cravings, and ease of preparation that guarantees we have time to cook for ourselves and those we care about even on busy days. This cookbook takes this formula for well-balanced meals, combined with recipes that are delicious and doable, and empowers all of us to gather our loved ones around "the family table."

I am honored that several of my dear friends, who happen to be celebrity chefs and authors, have contributed a favorite family recipe for this book, and it gives me great pleasure to introduce them to you: Master Chef Martin Yan, star of the long-running PBS cooking series, *Yan Can Cook*, restaurateur and vegetarian cookbook author Claire Criscuolo; cookbook author, award-winning radio host, and PBS chef Lauren Groveman; and Executive Chef William Koval of the historic and elegant Hotel Adolphus in Dallas, Texas. One of my recipes in the Entertaining at Home section was inspired by Southern entertaining expert, cookbook author, and PBS chef Nathalie Dupree. In each case, my friends place great value on cooking for their families and friends and they were anxious to share much-loved recipes in this volume.

May these, and all the recipes in *The Family Table,* bring you and your loved ones closer together as you share many memorable meals around your table.

Entrées

Sandwiches

Side Dishes

Desserts

Everyday Meals

*A*s each day draws to a close and evening settles in, the warmth of sharing a meal with my husband and family fills my heart. Although our two sons are away much of the time now, either working or attending school, throughout their childhoods we enjoyed evening meals as a family nearly every night. This is a tradition my husband and I happily continue.

I am passionate about family meals. During the week, my schedule can be pretty hectic and often does not let up on the weekend. There are articles to write, recipes to develop, cooking classes to prepare, and television shows to plan. In between, I work in my gardens, take voice lessons, prepare meals for those who need a bit of loving attention, and spend precious time with family and friends. With this kind of schedule, family meals offer a much-needed respite during the week to connect with my family and nurture my body and spirit.

Looking back on my childhood, family meals were a natural part of everyday life. It was a foregone conclusion that my three sisters and I would appear in the kitchen at a specified hour for dinner with Mom and Dad. The camaraderie that developed around the table night after night, year after year, I am convinced, is partly responsible for the close relationships my sisters and I still enjoy so many years later.

Mealtime didn't begin the moment we sat down at the table, however. My grandmother, Kathryn Hewston, did not teach my mother anything about cooking before she was married. Mom had to learn on the job, so she was determined that all her daughters would learn to cook while they were growing up. Besides, as my mother, Jinx, said recently, "What they say about getting through to a man—it works!" Looking back on it, it certainly worked for me!

Each girl was responsible for assisting in meal preparation in one form or another, depending on our ages and abilities. Lynn, the oldest, was usually responsible for the salad, while my job tended to be whipping potatoes with the handheld electric mixer. It was always a bit of a challenge since the electric plug had an exasperating habit of detaching from the mixer in the middle of the process. Nancy, who is three years younger than I, usually poured milk into glasses and set the table, while Judy, fondly called "the caboose" by our father, was assigned random tasks as needed.

Mealtimes were steeped in tradition. Dinner was always preceded by prayer, and on those rare occasions when Grandmom Henrietta and Granddad Sebastian Schnoes visited, it always ended with prayer. It is rather amusing that when canvassing Lynn, Nancy, and Judy about their memories of meals at home, each of them referred to Granddad's insistence on the after-meal prayer. Sebastian would get irritated if we didn't say the prayer correctly, and we all recalled jostling for possession of my First Communion pink salt and pepper shakers, because the after-meal prayer was printed in gold on the back. Maybe that explains why, after all these years, I still have them.

My father, Robert, always carved the meat at the table and served the entrée. One by one, we would pass our plates until everyone was served. The remainder of the meal was served family style, involving endless passing of bowls and platters around the table. Woe to the unsuspecting one who forgot to accept the butter dish carefully, as the recipient often ended up wearing butter on his or her thumb! Yes, there were many practical jokes during those years, which is why I still think of family meals with a smile.

Because we moved every few years, often hundreds of miles, my sisters and I depended on each other for friendship to ease the awkwardness of making new friends in an unfamiliar neighborhood. Those everyday family dinners provided a continuity otherwise missing in our young lives. We celebrated everything at that table: new shoes, good report cards, a loose tooth, snow days, new boyfriends, and my father's announcements of yet another corporate transfer.

Today, I continue the tradition that was so much a part of my childhood. Our everyday meals are simple, wholesome, and depend heavily on comfort foods. In this section, I include those recipes to inspire you, the home cook, to gather your family around and celebrate daily life. Each of the family-friendly recipes is tailored for quick assembly, allowing you to get a wholesome meal on the table in a realistic amount of time. Some go straight from the skillet to the table, while others require simmering or roasting—ideal when there are children to pick up from after-school activities, homework assignments to review, or a few moments of peace and quiet to share with a loved one.

Recipes are grouped into subsections. You will find an enticing array of entrées, side dishes, salads, breads, and desserts, tailor-made for weekday meals. Head notes accompanying each recipe may contain personal memories associated with the dish, ideas for table décor, or serving suggestions.

As a result of living in Paris, France, while our sons were small, Randy and I learned that wine isn't just for special occasions. As the French have done for generations, we often enjoy a glass of wine with our dinner, even during the week. Thanks to my good friend and wine expert, Eric Little, three reasonably priced wine suggestions accompany every entrée, so you, too, can relax over a homestyle meal and perfectly paired glass of wine as you celebrate the joys of everyday life.

We enjoy the elegance of the interplay of flavors in this recipe. The proportion of meat to starch is less than is commonly found in our beef-loving culture, and the sauce is savory and bold. We find that any of the medium-bodied, supple-tannin blends work well. In addition, the larger the selection, the better we drink for the dollar.

Keeping in mind the subtleties of the dish, we found Super-Tuscans especially synergistic. Super-Tuscan is a term coined to describe the awesome Cabernet Sauvignon/Sangiovese blends coming out of Toscano. However, we know a few Tuscan old-timers who still spit when passing the Cabernet vineyards. Despite a two-hundred-year presence, Cabernet is still referred to as "that damn foreign grape"!

$ **Campo de Borja "Borsao" Old-Vine Grenache/Tempernio blend** (Navarre, Spain)

$+ **Fattoria d'Ambra "Carmignano" Super-Tuscan** (Toscano, Italy)

$$$ **Rodney Strong "Symmetry" Red Meritage** (Alexander Valley, California)

Beef and Mushrooms in Wine Sauce

This rich, tasty beef dish goes together quickly for everyday meals, but is so elegant you may wish to serve it when hosting guests.

INGREDIENTS:

2 pounds beef chuck roast

3 tablespoons flour

Salt and pepper, to taste

3 tablespoons olive oil

½ cup red wine

½ cup beef consommé

¼ teaspoon Worcestershire sauce

1½ cups sliced white mushrooms

1 tablespoon chopped fresh parsley

Select a very lean boneless chuck roast. Slice the beef into 2-inch-wide strips. Place flour, salt, and pepper in a large plastic food storage bag, then close and shake it to mix. Add the beef strips to the flour mixture and shake well to coat.

Meanwhile, preheat a large skillet over medium heat until hot; add oil. Transfer the beef strips to the skillet, raise the heat to medium-high, and stir-fry about 3 minutes until beef is rare. Transfer beef to a serving bowl; cover to keep warm.

Reduce heat to medium. Deglaze the pan with wine, stirring to loosen bits of beef. Add consommé, Worcestershire sauce, and mushrooms, stirring until the mixture thickens slightly. Return the beef to the skillet, cover, and simmer over low heat 5 minutes, stirring occasionally. Serve over spaetzle, noodles, or rice and garnish with chopped parsley.

Recipe serves 4 to 6.

Entrées

Beef Fajitas

Add a touch of fun to family meals with this classic Tex-Mex dish!

INGREDIENTS:

1 pound skirt steak, trimmed

2 tablespoons tequila (optional)

2 tablespoons olive oil

4 cloves garlic, minced

Juice of 1 large lime plus
    juice of ½ lime for garnish

½ teaspoon ground cumin

¼ teaspoon kosher salt

¼ teaspoon black pepper

¼ teaspoon red pepper flakes

1 green bell pepper

1 red bell pepper

1 yellow bell pepper

1 large onion

1 cup sour cream

1 20-count package flour tortillas

Place skirt steak on a large platter or in a small roasting pan and set aside. In a small bowl, stir together tequila, olive oil, garlic, lime juice, cumin, salt, pepper, and red pepper flakes and pour the mixture over skirt steak. Cover with plastic wrap, place in the refrigerator, and marinate 10 minutes, or up to 1 hour.

Preheat grill. Slice peppers and onion and set aside.

When the grill is hot, grill the marinated skirt steak 4 minutes on each side and the peppers and onions until they are crisp-tender. Discard the remaining marinade.

When the steak is done, slice it across the grain into thin slices and place on serving platter. Squeeze additional lime juice over it and top with grilled vegetables.

Serve fajitas in warm flour tortillas topped with sour cream.

Recipe serves 4 to 5.

This classic treat suggests a Zinfandel, with its crushed berries and plum flavors, or a Carmeniere — dark, smoky cherries and chocolate. In addition, we must not forget the traditional pairing with Negra Modelo, a dark ale developed by German immigrants in Yucatan, Mexico, after World War I. The community eventually was absorbed into the vibrant culture surrounding it, leaving only a heritage of brewing great beers.

$ Negro Modelo
(Mexico)

$+ Santa Rita RSV Carmeniere
(Chile)

$$ Alexander Valley Winery "Sin Zin"
(California)

Beef Tip Kabobs with Teriyaki Ginger Sauce

Fire up the grill for this summertime favorite. Tender beef is threaded onto skewers with colorful vegetables, then glazed with a sweet teriyaki sauce.

INGREDIENTS:

- 3 pounds beef tip roast or sirloin steak, trimmed
- 2 green bell peppers
- 2 red bell peppers
- 2 zucchini squash
- 2 yellow squash
- 1 large onion
- 1 pint cherry tomatoes

Basting Sauce:

- 1 tablespoon olive oil
- 3 large cloves garlic, minced
- 2 tablespoons minced onion
- ¾ cup light soy sauce
- 3 tablespoons ketchup
- 2 tablespoons molasses
- 2 tablespoons brown sugar, packed
- 2 drops Worcestershire sauce
- ¾ teaspoon grated ginger root

Slice the beef into 2-inch cubes and set aside. Slice peppers, squash, and onion in chunks to fit onto skewers, then cover and refrigerate while preparing the basting sauce.

Heat a medium saucepan over low heat and add the oil. Sauté garlic and onion in the hot oil until soft, about 3 minutes. Stir in soy sauce, ketchup, molasses, brown sugar, Worcestershire sauce, and grated ginger. Bring the mixture to a boil over low heat and simmer 30 minutes, stirring occasionally, until the sauce thickens.

Preheat the grill. Thread the beef cubes onto metal skewers alternately with the vegetables. Place skewers on a hot grill and baste with the sauce. Turn them every few minutes, basting often, until meat is cooked to desired doneness.

To serve, place kabobs on couscous or rice on a large serving platter.

Recipe makes 6 to 8 kabobs.

Entrées

Glazed Barbecued Short Ribs

These oven-barbecued ribs are cooked in a roasting pan lined with foil to make cleanup a snap. Molasses and brown sugar in the barbecue sauce create a finger-licking, tasty glaze on the ribs as they cook. If desired, toss these ribs on the gas grill for 10 minutes before serving for that outdoor grilled taste.

INGREDIENTS:

4 to 5 pounds short ribs

1 tablespoon olive oil

¾ cup chopped onion

3 cloves garlic, minced

1 cup ketchup

3 tablespoons soy sauce

2 tablespoons balsamic vinegar

2 tablespoons brown sugar, packed

1½ tablespoons molasses

Heat a medium saucepan over medium-low heat just until hot and add oil. Stir in chopped onion, sautéing until it begins to soften. Stir in garlic and cook one minute.

Stir in ketchup, soy sauce, balsamic vinegar, brown sugar, and molasses. Reduce heat to low and simmer sauce 20 minutes, stirring occasionally.

Preheat the oven to 325 degrees. Place the ribs in a large roasting pan lined with foil, brush some of the barbecue glaze over them, and place them in preheated oven. Cook 50 to 55 minutes, basting occasionally with glaze, until the ribs are almost cooked through.

If desired, transfer the ribs to a preheated gas grill and cook 5 minutes on each side, basting with the remaining barbecue glaze. If you're not finishing the ribs on the grill, raise the oven temperature to 350 degrees, and cook them 10 to 20 minutes more until they are cooked through and the glaze has caramelized.

Recipe serves 6 to 8.

In this recipe we begin with fat-rich, melt-in-your-mouth beef. This is counterbalanced by the salty soy and tart vinegar. These tart/salty flavors are mellowed in turn by the sweet ketchup, brown sugar, and earthy molasses. The underlying pungency of the garlic and caramelized sweetness of the onions add depth—a sort of subsonic boom, felt more than heard, in this decadently delicious dish.

We believe the structure of a crushed berry-bomb, old-vine, high-alcohol Zinfandel is downright magical when paired with these flavors. Then again, we feel a Carmeniere from Chile to be a match made in heaven. Hmmmm. Let's have both!

**$ Santa Emma
Carmeniere Reserve**
(Maipo Valley, Chile)

$+ Geyser Peak Zinfandel
(Sonoma, California)

$$ Jessie's Grove Zinfandel
(Lodi, California)

Such clean, powerful flavors in this deceptively simple dish...salty soy, sweet nutty sake, pungent aromatic ginger, lean rich beef...the obvious choice is a good sake (served chilled—tradition says only to heat sake when it's chilly outside, and not necessarily one of the finer sakes at that), but we feel tradition is a good starting point, not an iron-clad rule. There are no rules of color in our world; light-colored meat (chicken, whitefish) does not demand white wine, dark meat (tuna, beef, lamb) does not require red wine. The synergistic pleasures of the table—good food, good wine, good conversation—require only the balance of components, the knowledge to position strong flavors in contrast to each other and subtle flavors where they can be heard despite the raucous song of ginger and soy.

Beef Sukiyaki

I first enjoyed this dish while spending a summer in Japan as a foreign exchange student. Though it may sound rather exotic, this traditional Japanese stir-fry makes a quick and easy weekday dinner. To save time, steam the rice while slicing the beef and vegetables.

INGREDIENTS:

1 pound boneless beef tenderloin

1 package firm tofu

1 package bean threads (*sai fun*)

1 tablespoon olive oil

1 bunch green onions, cut in 1-inch pieces

1 small onion, sliced

1 carrot, sliced thinly at an angle

1 8-ounce can sliced bamboo shoots

4 Portabellini mushrooms, sliced

1 recipe Beef Sauce

Steamed rice

Beef Sauce:

2 cups beef broth

¼ cup soy sauce

¼ cup sake wine

3 slices peeled fresh ginger

Freeze the beef 30 minutes until it's slightly firm, then slice it into paper-thin 2-inch slices and set aside. Drain the tofu, and slice it into 1-inch cubes; set aside.

Soak the bean threads in a bowl of cool water 15 minutes, then rinse, drain, and set them aside.

Entrées

Prepare the beef sauce. In a medium saucepan, combine broth, soy sauce, sake wine, and ginger slices. (To peel ginger easily, scrape the surface with the bowl of a spoon, then slice.) Heat the sauce over medium heat until it's hot; then reduce the heat to low and cook for 10 minutes.

Heat a large wok over medium heat and brush its surfaces with oil. Immediately add half the beef and cook 30 seconds to brown. Turn the meat over and push it to one side of the wok. Add half the sliced vegetables and enough hot beef sauce to cover the bottom of the wok to a depth of ¾ inch. Cook the vegetables 2 to 3 minutes. Gently stir in the tofu and drained bean threads; add additional hot broth as needed. Cook 1 to 2 additional minutes more, or until tofu is cooked through.

Transfer to platter over rice. Cook remaining half of beef and vegetables; serve immediately.

Recipe serves 4.

The obvious choice is a good sake, served chilled unless the weather is cold.

An Alsation Gewürztraminer would be a daring choice. Bone dry, crisp, with all sorts of citrus and spice, with an underlying melon and apricot tapestry that would frame this dish with a subtle grace. With a bow to the old school, we suggest a red; an Australian blend of Shiraz (Syrah), Cabernet Sauvignon, maybe a splash of Mourvedre, or Grenache!

$+ Cabnernet/Shiraz/ Grenache Blend— Leasingham; Penfolds (southeast Australia)

$+ Gewürtztraminer— Dolf & Irion; Hugal (Alsace region, France)

$$ Dai Ginjo Sake— Momokawa; Shoshikubai (Japan)

Cast Iron Panfried New York Strip Steak

There used to be a casual restaurant located near us in Dallas, Texas that served great panfried steaks. They were tender and juicy, with a buttery flavor I loved. Now, you can enjoy this same delicious steak at home, and it is ready in fewer than 10 minutes!

INGREDIENTS:

2 1-inch-thick New York strip steaks

½ teaspoon coarse salt for pan, plus 2 teaspoon coarse salt for steaks

¼ teaspoon freshly ground black pepper

2 tablespoons clarified butter (3 tablespoons butter yield 2 tablespoons clarified butter)

2 slices Maître d'Hôtel Herb Butter

Preheat a large cast iron skillet over medium heat until hot. Season the steaks with salt and pepper.

To clarify butter, microwave it in a small bowl 2 minutes at 50 percent power until it has melted. Spoon off the white solids from the top of the melted butter and discard, then put 2 teaspoons of the clarified butter into the hot skillet and sprinkle with coarse salt.

Place the strip steaks in the skillet immediately. Cook 2 minutes until brown; then turn and cook 2 more minutes. Add 1–2 additional teaspoons of clarified butter to the skillet. Turn the steaks and cook them 2 minutes more on each side, for a total of 8 minutes' cooking time for medium-rare. Check the steaks for desired degree of doneness.

Serve immediately. If desired, top each steak with a slice of Maître d'Hôtel Herb Butter.

Recipe serves 2 to 4.

Entrées

Maître D'Hôtel Herb Butter

I keep a roll of this compound butter in my freezer, so I can slice what I need. Made from unsalted butter, lemon juice, and fresh herbs, a slice of Maître d'Hôtel Herb Butter provides a sophisticated, creamy finish as it slowly melts on steaks, chops, and seafood.

INGREDIENTS:

1 cup unsalted butter, softened

2 tablespoons chopped fresh herbs, such as parsley, dill, or tarragon

1 ½ tablespoons fresh lemon juice

Using a food processor or the back of a wooden spoon, mix herbs and lemon juice into the softened butter. Spoon the mixture onto plastic wrap or parchment paper and form it into a cylinder, using the plastic wrap or parchment to shape it.

Twist the ends closed and chill until the butter is firm.

To serve, unwrap and slice the butter into ¼-inch-thick slices. Garnish steaks, chops, or fish with a slice of herb butter just before serving.

Herb butter stays fresh in the refrigerator 2 weeks, or wrap well and freeze up to several months.

Recipe makes approximately 20 servings.

Southwestern Casserole

Serve this spicy Tex-Mex casserole straight from the skillet on busy nights, or spoon into a casserole dish, top with shredded cheese, and bake. Great for parties, too.

INGREDIENTS:

1½ pounds ground chuck

1 small onion, chopped

2 cloves garlic, minced

1¼ cups medium or hot picante sauce

1 8-ounce can tomato sauce

1 15-ounce can kidney beans, rinsed and drained

¼ cup shredded Longhorn Cheddar cheese

⅓ cup crushed tortilla chips

½ cup shredded longhorn Cheddar or Monterey Jack cheese

1 20-count package warm flour tortillas

1½ cups shredded lettuce

1 cup sour cream

Sauté ground beef and onion in a large skillet over medium heat until the meat is brown. Drain the fat, reduce the heat to low, and add minced garlic; sauté 1 minute. Pour in picante and tomato sauce and stir to mix. Stir in kidney beans, ¼ cup of the shredded longhorn cheese, and crushed tortilla chips.

Cook the mixture until it's bubbly. Serve immediately in flour tortillas or spoon into a casserole dish, sprinkle with additional cheese, and cover. Bake at 350 degrees for 30 minutes, or until it's hot and bubbly.

To serve, spoon Southwestern Casserole into warm flour tortillas; top with shredded lettuce, cheese, and sour cream.

Recipe serves 6.

Taco Salad

Use leftover Southwestern Casserole to create incredibly easy and tasty taco salads for a quick lunch or dinner.

INGREDIENTS:

1 recipe Southwestern Casserole, reheated

1 head romaine lettuce

2 green bell peppers, chopped

2 red bell peppers, chopped

½ cup sliced black olives

2 ripe avocados, peeled and sliced

½ cup regular or lowfat sour cream

½ cup shredded longhorn Cheddar cheese

½ cup shredded Monterey Jack cheese

Picante sauce

Tortilla chips

The classic pairing is, of course, Corona or Negro Modelo beer. We need either the crispness of cold beer or something acidic, such as lemonade or a Pinot Grigio to cut through all those yummy, concealed fats. Avoid red wines containing noticeable tannins, because the vegetal components of this salad could bring out some bizarre flavors in the wine.

$ **Corona** or
Negro Modelo Dark Ale
(Mexico)

$ **Cavit Pinot Grigio**
(Friuli, Italy)

$$ **Livio Felluga**
Pinot Grigio
(Friuli, Italy)

Rinse, spin dry, and slice romaine lettuce crosswise. Transfer the lettuce to a large, shallow salad bowl. Spoon hot Southwestern Casserole over lettuce and top with bell peppers, olives, and sliced avocado. Garnish with a large dollop of sour cream and sprinkle with cheeses.

Serve with picante sauce and tortilla chips.

Recipe serves 6.

Surprise Meat Loaf

My husband, Randy, started asking for surprises in his meat loaf years ago. The tradition has evolved from a simple center of melted cheddar cheese to this more sophisticated surprise of Monterey Jack cheese, jalapeños, and a Southwest-inspired sauce.

INGREDIENTS:

1¼ pounds ground chuck

1 pound ground pork

1 cup chopped onion

2 large cloves garlic, peeled and minced

1 teaspoon kosher salt

1 teaspoon Spice Island fines herbes

½ teaspoon freshly ground black pepper

¼ teaspoon red pepper flakes

2 eggs, slightly beaten

2 slices fresh wheat bread, torn into small pieces

6 ¼-inch-thick slices Monterey Jack cheese

2 sliced jalapeños

1 recipe Southwest Chili Sauce

Wear gloves or wash your hands well after handling jalapeños to prevent skin and eye irritation.

Entrées

Preheat the oven to 375 degrees. In a large bowl, combine ground chuck, pork, onion, garlic, salt, fines herbes, black pepper, and red pepper flakes. In a small bowl, pour beaten eggs over torn bread; stir gently to moisten the bread.

Using your hands, mix the moistened bread into the meat mixture. Transfer half of the meat mixture to a 9-inch loaf pan, pressing the mixture gently into the bottom of pan. Top with slices of cheese and jalapeños. Spoon the remaining meat mixture over the jalapeños, pressing to shape the loaf.

Cover with foil and bake 45 minutes; remove the foil and drain off excess fat. Replace the foil and bake 30 minutes more. Uncover, drain, and spread Southwestern Chili Sauce mixture over the meat loaf. Return it to oven, uncovered, and bake an additional 15 minutes, or until a meat thermometer registers 155 degrees.

Remove meat loaf from oven; let stand 10 minutes before slicing.

Recipe serves 6.

Southwest Chili Sauce:

⅔ cup chili sauce

½ teaspoon cumin

½ teaspoon garlic powder

3 drops Worcestershire sauce

Stir all ingredients together in a small bowl, cover, and set aside 5 minutes to allow flavors to develop.

Syrah is the first grape varietal mentioned in written history, 2300 years ago in the Persian village of Shiraz in North Africa. Assumed to have migrated up the trade route known as the "Silk Road," Syrah was cultivated in the southern mountains of Rhône, France, at least 2000 years ago.

$+ St. Cosme Côte du Rhône
(Rhône, France)

$$ Zaca Mesa Syrah
(Santa Barbara, California)

$$$ Leasingham Classic Clare Valley Shiraz
(Australia)

We have noticed a number of easygoing cooks who become quite passionate when the subject of chili comes up. Rarely does any recipe for this alchemist's pot of gold escape "tweaking" by the time dinner rolls around. So, have fun and take time to savor the process as much as the end result.

Tradition calls for a cold beer as you begin the cooking process, and with some recipes, half the beer is for the chef, and half is for the chili. At serving time, either a well-hopped ale, especially good at cooling a chili-seared palate, or a fruity, low-acid red are good choices.

$ Red Hook India Pale Ale
(Woodinville, Washington)

$ J Lohr "Wildflower" Valdiguié
(California)

$ Louis Jadot Beaujolais Village
(Burgundy, France)

Jinx Schnoes's Chili

I traditionally make this "Texas" version of my mother's Northern-style chili on Halloween, one of the busiest nights of the year. I can whip up a batch and have dinner on the table in 30 minutes. Though I add a heavier dose of chili powder and even some Tabasco, this is still Mom's chili. It's tasty and hearty, and with a simple green salad, dinner is ready.

INGREDIENTS:

2¼ pounds ground chuck

1 medium onion, chopped

4 cloves garlic, minced

2 28-ounce cans Italian-style peeled tomatoes

2 15-ounce cans dark red kidney beans, drained and rinsed

3 tablespoons flour

2 tablespoons chili powder, or to taste

¼ cup water

Salt and freshly ground black pepper, to taste

Several dashes Tabasco (optional)

Grated longhorn Cheddar or Monterey Jack cheese, for garnish

In a Dutch oven over medium-high heat, brown meat with onion until the ground chuck is completely cooked and the onion is soft; drain the fat.

Reduce the heat to medium and stir in garlic; cook 1 minute. Stir in tomatoes and their juice, then cover and cook 5 minutes to soften them. Using a large spoon, chop the tomatoes into bite-size pieces. Stir in drained kidney beans.

While tomatoes are softening, place flour in a small bowl. Add chili powder and stir well to mix. Whisk in water to form a smooth, thick slurry, pour it into chili, and stir.

Reduce the heat to low, cover, and cook 10 minutes. Season chili to taste with salt, freshly ground pepper, and Tabasco, if desired.

Serve chili in soup mugs or bowls. Garnish with grated cheese.

Recipe serves 8.

Roast Stuffed Chicken

Afternoon activities call for this quick and easy dish. Pop it in the oven; then return home to a fragrant, comforting meal.

INGREDIENTS:

1 4- to 4½-pound chicken

¾ teaspoon salt

5 slices dry wheat bread, sliced or torn into ½-inch cubes

¼ cup chopped celery

3 tablespoons minced onion

1½ teaspoons dried rubbed sage

1 teaspoon dried thyme leaves, rubbed between hands

1 egg

¼ cup milk

1 tablespoon butter, softened

1 teaspoon Lawry's Pinch of Herbs

¼ teaspoon cayenne pepper

Preheat oven to 425 degrees. Remove the packaged parts from inside the chicken cavity; rinse the cavity well and dry it with paper towels. Season the inner cavity with salt and set aside.

In a medium bowl, stir together the bread cubes, celery, onion, sage, and thyme. In a small bowl, beat egg with milk, then pour into the bread mixture and toss well with your hands to moisten bread. Add a little more milk if the mixture is too dry.

Stuff the chicken cavity loosely with the bread mixture. Tie the legs together with kitchen string, place the chicken in a roasting pan, and rub the skin with butter. In a small bowl, stir together the Lawry's seasoning and cayenne pepper and sprinkle it over the chicken. Cover chicken loosely with a tent of foil.

Place chicken in a preheated 425-degree oven for 30 minutes; then reduce the temperature to 350 degrees and continue roasting another 1¼ hours, or until a chicken leg moves freely in its socket and chicken juices run clear when the skin is pierced with a fork. Remove the foil during final 15 minutes of roasting to brown the skin.

Recipe serves 4 to 6.

Elegance is found not only in fabulous culinary art, but also in the simple done properly. James Beard regarded roast chicken as an elegant dish suitable for any occasion, although he preferred a bit of pink in the juice.

Here, we have four flavor components—crisp skin (fats), tender meat, pungent herbs and onions. We could go in two different directions: the dry elegance of an Alsacatian Gewürtztraminer or a light red wine. A good Pinot Noir from Oregon or a Burgundy would work particularly well, drawing out the sweetness of the meat and embellishing it with dark berry and tart cherry flavors.

$$$ Zind-Humbrecht Gewürtztraminer, Dry
(Alsace region, France)

$$$ Sokol Blosser Pinot Noir Estate
(Willamette Valley, Oregon)

$$$ Jadot Morey St. Denis
(Burgundy, France)

Images of summer picnics, checkered tablecloths fluttering in a gentle breeze, and the laughter of children are evoked instantly when we think of this dish. We find a crisp white, perhaps frizzante (slightly sparkling), to be a delicious choice, providing it contains sufficient acidity to cut through any oil.

A Moscato evokes honeydew melon, ripe peaches, and mandarin orange. Or select a floral, melon, and citrus Sauvignon Blanc.

$ **Martin & Wrylick "Allegro" Moscato** (Paso Robles, California)

$ **R H Phillips Sauvignon Blanc** (Dunningan Hills, California)

$$ **Iron Horse T Bar T Sauvignon Blanc** (Napa, California)

Almost Fried Chicken

Home cooks often ask for recipes that will reduce fat in their diets. I always share this dish because it tastes like fried chicken without the fat of deep frying. Skinless chicken pieces are dipped in a seasoned coating, then baked in the oven. One hour later, juicy, crunchy "fried" chicken is ready to enjoy.

INGREDIENTS:

3 cups corn, wheat, or bran flake cereal

½ cup cornmeal

⅓ cup bread crumbs

2 tablespoons flour

1 tablespoon freshly grated Parmesan cheese

1 teaspoon salt

½ teaspoon freshly ground black pepper

¼ teaspoon garlic powder

¼ teaspoon dried basil

¼ teaspoon fines herbes

1 egg

¼ cup lowfat milk

1 4-pound whole chicken, cut into pieces

2 tablespoons olive oil

Preheat oven to 350 degrees. Pour cereal into a large bowl and crush the flakes with the heel of your hand. Stir in cornmeal, bread crumbs, flour, Parmesan cheese, salt, black pepper, garlic powder, basil, and fines herbes, mixing well.

In a shallow bowl, whip egg with a fork and stir in milk; set aside.

Remove the skin from the chicken pieces, rinse chicken, and dry it with paper towels. Dip the chicken into the egg mixture; then roll it in the crumb mixture until it's well coated. Transfer to a baking pan that has been drizzled with olive oil.

Bake the chicken in preheated 350-degree oven, uncovered, 50 to 60 minutes until it is cooked through.

Recipe serves 6.

Chicken with Peppers

For late-summer meals when it's too hot to spend time in the kitchen, or for a quick and satisfying meal any time of year, this colorful entrée is fresh-tasting and satisfying. Chopped, fresh cilantro gives it just a hint of Southwest flair, or substitute your favorite fresh herb.

INGREDIENTS:

4 boneless chicken breasts

1 tablespoon olive oil

2 large green bell peppers

1 large red bell pepper

2 cloves garlic, minced

Coarse salt and freshly ground black pepper

2 tablespoons chopped fresh cilantro

Rinse chicken breasts and pat them dry with paper towel. Heat a large skillet over medium heat until it's hot, then add olive oil, swirling it to coat the bottom of the pan. Add chicken with the meatier side down.

Sauté the chicken 5 minutes, turn it over, and sauté 5 minutes more. While the chicken sautés, slice peppers into strips, discarding seeds.

Transfer the chicken to a platter and keep it warm. Reduce the heat to low, add peppers and garlic, and sauté until peppers are crisp-tender. Season with salt and ground black pepper.

Return the chicken to skillet and sprinkle it with cilantro. Cover and cook 3 to 5 minutes until chicken is cooked through. Transfer chicken to a serving platter and surround with peppers.

Recipe serves 4.

In this dish, we have three main components: tender chicken breast, pungent garlic and cilantro, and sweet pepper. The flavors are modest and require a wine that will not overshadow their simple, yet elegant interplay.

We find a dry Rosé enchanting both in its bright raspberry and peppery flavors, and in the rose-hued color that can appear to the wine novice to be an unsophisticated, cheap sugar bomb. Of course, these refreshing wines are all bone-dry—no sugar at all!

$ Bonny Doone Vin Gris Cigare Volant (Santa Cruz, California)

$ Domaine Sorin (Côte du Provence, France)

$$ Iron Horse T Bar T "Rosato di Sangiovese" (Alexander Valley, California)

Some dishes arrive tableside with great fanfare—robust and potent flavors seizing your full attention. Others arrive quietly with a subtle perfume and elegant layers of flavor. This is such a dish, and it requires a wine that enhances its essence —pungent shallots, earthy, silken-textured mushrooms, melt-in-your-mouth chicken breasts, and sweet butter— without overwhelming its delicate flavors.

Chicken Scaloppine

In this recipe, the chicken's delicate, crisp coating and creamy mushroom sauce combine for an elegant Italian restaurant favorite that is easy to prepare at home. Because the chicken breasts are pounded very thin, they take only minutes to cook.

INGREDIENTS:

4 boneless, skinless chicken breast halves

1¼ cups flour

1 teaspoon salt

½ teaspoon ground black pepper

3 tablespoons olive oil, divided

¼ cup dry white wine

½ cup chicken broth

1 tablespoon minced shallot

3 cups sliced white mushrooms (about ½ pound)

1 to 2 tablespoons butter, cold

Parsley for garnish

Preheat the oven to its lowest setting. Rinse the chicken breasts and pat them dry with paper towels. Place the chicken breasts on a cutting board between 2 sheets of plastic wrap and pound them to ½-inch thickness with a meat mallet; trim the edges and set aside.

Combine flour, salt, and pepper in a plastic zipper bag and shake it to mix. Heat a nonstick skillet over medium-low heat; add 2 table-spoons of olive oil. As the skillet heats, coat a chicken breast with seasoned flour to cover. Place the chicken breast in hot oil, then repeat with second chicken breast.

Entrées

Sauté the breasts 2½ to 3 minutes, or until golden brown, then turn them over and sauté them until the other side is golden, about 3 minutes. Remove them from the skillet, place on a warm serving platter, and put them in the oven. Add the remaining oil to skillet; coat the remaining breasts with the flour mixture and sauté. Reserve the remaining seasoned flour for later use. Transfer cooked breasts to a serving platter and keep them warm.

Deglaze the pan with white wine and chicken broth, scraping up brown bits. Cook 2 minutes; then add shallot and mushrooms. Cook several minutes, until mushrooms are tender, and reduce the heat to low.

Cut cold butter into quarters and drop them into the flour mixture. Then stir the butter one piece at a time into the mushrooms to thicken the sauce. Spoon the mushroom sauce over the chicken scaloppine, garnish with chopped parsley, and serve.

Recipe serves 4.

The traditional Napa Valley Chardonnay is frequently served as an apéritif, but in this case, it has sufficient acidity to counterbalance the sweet butter and admirable restraint in its use of oak.

$$ Edna Valley Chardonnay
(Edna Valley, California)

$$$ St. Clement Chardonnay
(Napa Valley, California)

$$$ Chalk Hill Estate Chardonnay
(Sonoma, California)

Martin Yan's Sweet and Sour Chicken

Martin Yan, Master Chef, author, celebrated host of PBS's Yan Can Cook, *and very dear friend, created this family-friendly, guest-worthy recipe especially for* The Family Table. *Thanks to Martin's philosophy that Chinese cooking should be made simple and accessible to all home cooks, you will find this mouthwatering sweet and sour chicken dish is easy enough to prepare during the week.*

Here we find tender chicken, pungent garlic and tangy ginger, sweet peppers and onions, salty soy, and loads of sweet/tart flavors in the sauce and pineapples. We require a wine with a hair more sweetness than the dish. A Riesling is ideal, but we can also pair with a Gewürtztraminer's spicy lusciousness, or even an old-world Chenin Blanc.

These wines contain sweet fruit balanced by good acidity, and have something left over to handle the salty soy. Enjoy this masterpiece of elegant, layered flavors. We love this guy!

INGREDIENTS:

Marinade:

½ cup cornstarch

1 egg, slightly beaten

Chicken Stir-fry:

¾ pound light or dark meat chicken, cut into 1-inch cubes

Vegetable oil for deep frying

½ teaspoon minced garlic

½ teaspoon minced fresh ginger

½ green bell pepper, seeded and cut into 1-inch dice

½ red bell pepper, seeded and cut into 1-inch dice

½ yellow onion, cut into 1-inch dice

½ cup Martin Yan's Sweet and Sour Sauce or store-bought sweet and sour sauce

1 cup fresh or canned pineapple chunks

Stir the cornstarch and egg together in a bowl until blended. Toss the chicken gently in the marinade to coat and let stand 10 minutes.

Pour enough oil into a deep skillet to fill 2 inches, and heat it to 360 degrees. Deep-fry the chicken, a few pieces at a time, turning occasionally, until golden brown, 3 to 4 minutes. Scoop the chicken from the oil with a slotted spoon and drain on paper towels. Reserve the oil.

Entrées

Heat a wok over high heat until hot. Add 1 tablespoon of the reserved oil and swirl to coat the sides of the wok. Add the garlic and ginger and stir-fry until fragrant, about 20 seconds. Add the bell peppers and onions and stir-fry until tender-crisp, 2 to 3 minutes.

Pour the sweet and sour sauce into the wok and stir to coat the vegetables. Slide the chicken into the wok, add the pineapple, and toss until heated through and evenly coated.

Scoop the contents of the wok onto a warm platter and serve immediately.

Recipe serves 4 as part of a multicourse meal.

$ **Dr. Pauly-Bergman Riesling Bernkasteler Badstube Spätlese**
(Rhine, Germany)

$ **Firestone Gewürztraminer**
(Sonoma, California)

$ **Domaine Pichot Vouvray**
(Loire, France)

Martin Yan's Sweet and Sour Sauce

INGREDIENTS:

¾ cup ketchup

3 teaspoons Worcestershire sauce

6 tablespoons sugar

3 tablespoons soy sauce

2 tablespoons fresh lime juice

Combine all ingredients in a medium bowl and mix well. Cover and refrigerate until ready to use. Sauce will last up to 2 weeks refrigerated.

Recipe makes about 1 cup.

There are times when our palates are intensely focused on the exotic sensation of a culinary masterwork. Then there are times when the world seems a cold wasteland and we feel positively fussy. These are the times nothing is as nurturing, as satisfying, as that liquid gold known as chicken noodle soup or this dish that transforms the soup into a casserole.

Ordinarily, with the rich stock foundation, vegetable infusion, and bland pasta, we gravitate towards a lower-acid, buttery, white wine such as Viognier, or a Santa Barbara Chardonnay. However, adding cream and cheese, not to mention sherry, to the equation, changes our solution to a high-acid white such as a white Rhône or a Burgundian-style Chardonnay. Here, we can have it all by selecting the intensely aromatic Chardonnay, with good acidity and rich complexity found in Arcadian's "Sleepy Hollow" Chardonnay.

$ **Chateau de Beaucastel "Coudoulet" White Rhône** (Rhône, France)

$$ **Arcadian Chardonnay "Sleepy Hollow"** (Santa Barbara, California)

$$ **Treana Marsanne/Viognier Blend** (Paso Robles, California)

Deluxe Chicken Noodle Bake

This is my favorite recipe to take to friends who are ill or who need a helping hand. The mixture of bite-size chicken pieces, soft noodles, and creamy sauce touched with sherry is the perfect combination when the situation calls for comfort food. It's also an easy way to use up leftover chicken or turkey.

INGREDIENTS:

. . . .

1 12-ounce package wide egg noodles

2 tablespoons olive oil

1 tablespoon butter or margarine

½ cup diced onion

2 to 3 stalks celery, sliced

½ cup diced carrot

1 10¾-ounce can cream of chicken condensed soup

1½ cups milk

1 cup sour cream

3 tablespoons sherry

3 cups cubed cooked chicken

½ cup green peas

Salt and pepper, to taste

½ cup grated cheddar or Monterey Jack cheese

Cook egg noodles al dente according to package directions; drain and set aside.

Preheat oven to 350 degrees. Heat a large saucepan or Dutch oven over medium-low heat; add olive oil and butter or margarine. Sauté onion, celery, and carrot in hot oil until tender, about 7 minutes. Stir in chicken soup, milk, sour cream, and sherry, stirring until sauce is smooth and thick.

Stir in reserved noodles, chicken, and peas and season with salt and pepper. Pour the mixture into a large ovenproof casserole, sprinkle with grated cheese, and cover tightly with a lid or foil.

Bake at 350 degrees 40 to 45 minutes until the casserole is hot and bubbly.

Recipe serves 6.

Entrées

Chicken and Wild Mushroom Frittata

Somewhat like a quiche without a crust, this meal-in-one frittata may be made with fresh, poached chicken breasts or last night's leftover chicken. Serve it for a quick dinner or an elegant but easy brunch.

INGREDIENTS:

3 tablespoons butter

⅓ cup chopped onion

1 cup sliced white mushrooms

½ cup sliced assorted wild mushrooms

2 cups shredded, cooked chicken breast

1 cup fresh spinach leaves, washed, dried, and trimmed

Salt and freshly ground black pepper

10 eggs

3 tablespoons water

½ cup shredded cheese, such as Monterey Jack or Havarti

Preheat oven to 350 degrees.

Heat a 10-inch ovenproof skillet over medium heat; add butter. When the butter has melted, swirl it around the bottom of the pan. Add onion and sauté 2 minutes to soften. Add all mushrooms and sauté 1 minute, then stir in the chicken and spinach. Cook the mixture several minutes, until spinach just begins to wilt. Season with salt and pepper.

While the chicken is cooking, whip eggs, water, and additional salt and pepper with a fork until the mixture is light. Pour it into the skillet over the mushroom-chicken mixture. Cook 1 minute to set egg mixture; then transfer the skillet to the preheated oven.

Bake the frittata 15 minutes, or until it is almost set. Sprinkle with shredded cheese and bake 3 to 5 minutes more, until the cheese is melted and a knife inserted into the center comes out clean. Remove from the oven, slice, and serve immediately.

Recipe serves 6.

This dish is composed of a number of textures and flavors—the silky egg whites with chicken, the earthy mushrooms, the flavorful spinach, and the buttery cheese. Let's start with the strongest flavor. Spinach occasionally brings out undesirable astringent and bitter vegetal flavors in some red wines, so to play it safe, a full-bodied Chardonnay is a good choice.

The classic choice for the mushrooms in this dish is a Pinot Noir; however, the delicate egg mixture can be overshadowed easily, so good acidity helps. It also counterbalances the rich butterfats. We'll go with a sparkling wine! This naturally produced sparkling blend of Pinot Noir, Chardonnay, and, sometimes, Pinot Meunier is considered the classic pairing in France. And if Champagne brings a note of festivity to our meal, so much the better!

$ Cordinuu Cuvée Raventos (Spain)

$$$ Roederer Estate Sparkling (Anderson Valley, California)

$$$ Billecart-Salmon Rosé (Champagne, France)

With this delicate medley of three flavors and two textures, we need a straightforward wine that will allow the palate to savor each flavor fully, to add a quiet citrus chord that keeps the butter on key. We find the bone-dry, simple elegance of a Muscadet (not a sweet wine from the Muscat grape—this is a completely different varietal) delightful with this delicacy. A noted choice is a dry Savennières out of the vineyards of Loire— a well-bred, gentleman bringing tiny apricots, graham crackers, and tart mandarin oranges to the table.

The traditional pairing is a German Riesling that has developed lush flavors of nectarine and lime blossom, and sometimes a little peach. Auslese is the latest, most mature (and sweetest) harvesting designation short of the intense, wonderful dessert and ice wines.

$ Chateau de la Ragotière Muscadet de Sèvre et Maine "Vieilles vignes"
(Loire, France)

$$ Dr. Weins-Prüm, Riesling "Wehlener Sonnenuhr"
(Mosel-Saar-Ruwer, Germany)

$$+ Domaine des Baumard Savennières "Tre Selection"
(Loire, France)

Panfried Golden Trout

My husband and I have been vacationing in Colorado since our honeymoon, and one of my favorite mountain dinners is panfried trout. The sweet flavor of golden trout really comes through in this simple dish. Ask your fishmonger to butterfly it for you.

INGREDIENTS:

2 golden trout, butterflied (½-pound each)

2 tablespoons butter

Salt to taste

2 lemon wedges (optional)

Rinse butterflied trout and pat it dry with paper towels; set aside.

Heat a large skillet over medium heat; add butter and swirl to coat pan. When the butter is melted, place the trout in pan, closed. Cook the outside 2 minutes, turn over, and cook 2 additional minutes.

Open trout to the butterfly position. Cook 2 minutes, skin side down, then season it with salt, carefully flip it over with a spatula, and cook it 2 minutes more, or until the interior is golden brown and the fish is done.

Transfer the trout to a serving plate and serve with lemon wedges, if desired.

Recipes serves 2.

Orange Roughy with Caper Dill Beurre Blanc

Fresh herbs and capers, dressed in an elegant sauce, add panache to mild-flavored orange roughy. This recipe is everyday easy, but try it the next time you want to serve an impressive seafood meal to guests.

INGREDIENTS:

1 pound orange roughy fish fillets, 2 large or 4 small fillets

Salt and pepper

1 tablespoon olive oil

1 tablespoon minced shallots

¼ cup dry white wine

1 tablespoon tarragon vinegar

⅛ teaspoon white pepper

⅔ cup heavy cream

5 tablespoons cold unsalted butter, sliced into 5 pieces

1½ tablespoons chopped dill

1 tablespoon capers, drained and rinsed

Wash the fish fillets and pat them dry with paper towels. Season them with salt and pepper. Heat a large skillet over medium heat; add olive oil and fish fillets. Sauté the fillets 4 to 5 minutes until lightly browned. Then turn them over with a spatula and sauté until done, about 8 minutes.

Meanwhile, in a medium saucepan, combine minced shallots, wine, tarragon vinegar, and white pepper. Bring to a boil over medium-high heat and reduce by half. Reduce the heat to medium, add cream, and reduce the mixture by half.

Reduce heat to very low. Stir cold butter into the cream mixture, one piece at a time, until the beurre blanc is creamy and thick. Do not allow mixture to boil or the butter will separate. Stir in dill and rinsed capers and keep mixture warm, stirring frequently.

Transfer fish fillets to serving plates, spoon caper dill sauce over them, and serve.

Recipe makes 4 servings.

This delicate white fish in a rich beurre blanc is pierced dramatically by the sour/tart combination of dill and capers. Choosing a wine that can stand up to the dynamic duo, without concealing everything else, is a challenge.

Two French wines present themselves. Muscadet, from the Loire, is not to be confused with Muscat, a sweet orange-blossom-scented white wine. This crisp, bone-dry white is a favorite when dining on white fish in the coastal areas of France. The second wine would be the classic pairing of an Alsatian Riesling. Approximately every hundred years since 1600, France and Germany have taken turns capturing Alsace, creating a region that exhibits the cultures of both. The wines of this region are German, but they are vinified in a bone-dry French manner. The landscape is neatly Germanic, but the cuisine is delightfully French. These wines are very long-lived and complex, yet delicate.

$ **Hugel Riesling**
(Alsace, France)

$ **Chateau de Raggottier Muscadet**
(Loire, France)

$$ **Josmeyer Riesling**
(Alsace, France)

Grilled Salmon Steaks with Tropical Fruit Salsa

With the year-round availability of salmon and a wide variety of fruit from the tropics, this summertime treat may be enjoyed whenever the urge strikes to fire up the grill.

INGREDIENTS:

4 salmon steaks, 1 inch thick

2 tablespoons butter

3 tablespoons olive oil

1 tablespoon fresh lemon juice

1 tablespoon fresh lime juice

2 tablespoons dry white wine

1 tablespoon chopped fresh cilantro

¾ teaspoon lemon pepper seasoning

1 teaspoon minced fresh ginger

1 recipe Tropical Salsa

Rinse the salmon and pat it dry with paper towels. In a small saucepan, combine butter, oil, lemon and lime juices, wine, cilantro, lemon pepper, and ginger. Heat the mixture over medium-low heat until it is hot, but not boiling, stirring occasionally.

Preheat the outdoor grill. Brush the salmon steaks with warm marinade and place them on the grill. Cook 9 to 11 minutes, turning twice. Brush the salmon steaks with marinade every few minutes while cooking. Serve with Tropical Salsa.

Entrées

Tropical Salsa:

1¼ cups diced cantaloupe

1 ripe mango, peeled and diced

1 large ripe peach, diced

1½ teaspoons freshly squeezed lime juice

1 teaspoon raspberry vinegar

⅛ teaspoon allspice or nutmeg

Dash of salt

Combine ingredients in a medium bowl. Toss well, cover, and refrigerate 30 minutes or longer to allow flavors to blend. Serve with grilled salmon.

Recipe makes 4 servings.

for the popular Pinot Noir pairing would be a wine with some oomph! The terroir of low-yield, small estates such as Ponzi or Panther Creek shines through this deep ruby nectar, adding depth and complexity to the dark cherry, semisweet chocolate, and dried cranberry fruit of this surprisingly voluptuous red.

$$ Equis (by Wild Horse) Viognier
(Paso Robles, California)

$$$ Ponzi Estate Pinot Noir
(Willamette Valley, Oregon)

$$$ Guigal Condrieu
(Viognier at its best)
(Rhône, France)

This dish has as many faces as a talented actress, with the sweet onions, rich beef, acidic tomatoes, pungent garlic, fresh oregano, and hard cheese. Only the cook—and Christy—knows what flavor combination will take center stage.

That said, we do know some things to be true. Fresh is always better, grandmothers make the best cookies, and Barbera d'Asti always tastes great with Spaghetti and Meat Sauce.

Spaghetti with Meat Sauce

A perennial family favorite, this dish is popular with kids of all ages and uses ingredients usually found in the pantry. This is comfort food at its best!

INGREDIENTS:

1¼ pounds lean ground beef

3 tablespoons olive oil, divided

1 cup diced onion

5 cloves garlic, peeled and minced

2 28-ounce cans Italian peeled Roma tomatoes

1 8-ounce can tomato sauce

2 tablespoons fresh oregano, chopped

1 tablespoon dried oregano

1½ teaspoons coarse salt

1 teaspoon sugar

¼ teaspoon ground black pepper

½ cup grated Parmesan cheese

Additional grated Parmesan cheese for garnish

Prepared spaghetti

Entrées

$ **Prunotto Barbera d'Asti "Fiulot"**
(Piamonte, Italy)

$ **Condado de Haza "Ribera"**
(Del Deuro, Spain)

$$ **Pepi Barbera**
(North Coast, California)

Heat a large Dutch oven over medium-high heat and brown crumbled ground beef until it is cooked thoroughly; drain the fat. Transfer the cooked beef to a large bowl; set aside. Wipe out the Dutch oven with a paper towel and turn the heat to low.

Add 2 tablespoons of the olive oil to the Dutch oven. Sauté onions in oil until soft, then stir in garlic and sauté 1 minute.

Process tomatoes through a food mill to remove their seeds; pour milled tomatoes and tomato sauce into Dutch oven. Season with fresh and dried oregano, salt, sugar, and black pepper; stir in grated cheese.

Raise the heat to medium, cover, and bring sauce to a low boil. Reduce heat to low, uncover, and simmer the sauce at least 15 minutes. Meanwhile, bring a large pot of water to a boil and cook the spaghetti according to the directions on the package.

When the spaghetti is al dente, drain it in a colander, reserving ½ cup of cooking water. Do not rinse the pasta. Add 1 tablespoon olive oil to reserved cooking water; swirl pot to mix. Return drained spaghetti to pot and toss to coat the pasta with the olive oil mixture.

Transfer the spaghetti to a large pasta or serving bowl; top with meat sauce. Serve with additional grated Parmesan.

Recipe serves 8.

Quick Marinara Sauce

I always make this sauce when I'm short on time. It's wonderful over pasta or chicken.

INGREDIENTS:

3 tablespoons olive oil

1 medium onion, chopped

4 to 5 cloves garlic, minced

6 medium Roma tomatoes, chopped

½ teaspoon sugar

Freshly ground black pepper, to taste

1 15-ounce can tomato sauce

1 tablespoon dried oregano

1 tablespoon chopped fresh basil

Heat a large saucepan over medium-low heat; add olive oil and chopped onion. Sauté onion several minutes until it is soft and translucent; stir in garlic and cook 1 more minute. Add tomatoes; raise the heat to medium and cook several minutes until tomatoes soften, stirring often. Season with sugar and ground pepper. Stir in tomato sauce.

Reduce the heat to low. Add herbs, rubbing oregano between your hands to release its flavor. Simmer the sauce 15 to 20 minutes. Correct the seasonings and add a little salt, if needed.

If desired, purée the sauce with a handheld blender for smoothness. Serve over pasta, chicken, or eggplant Parmesan.

Suggested Serving Size: ¾ cup sauce.

Recipe makes 4 to 5 cups sauce.

Entrées

Farfalle with Chicken and Sun-Dried Tomatoes

This colorful, tasty pasta salad is wonderfully refreshing on a warm spring or summer night. Add a fruit salad and crusty bread for a complete meal.

INGREDIENTS:

- 1 16-ounce package farfalle or bow tie pasta
- 3 tablespoons water
- 1 tablespoon olive oil
- 1 cup broccoli florets
- 4 pound sugar snap peas
- 4 cups cooked, shredded chicken (2 whole chicken breasts)
- 1 red bell pepper, chopped
- 1 green bell pepper, chopped
- ¼ cup drained sun-dried tomatoes, packed in oil
- 2 teaspoons Dijon mustard
- 3 tablespoons white wine vinegar
- ½ cup olive oil
- 2 tablespoons snipped chives
- Salt and freshly ground black pepper, to taste

Cook pasta al dente according to package directions, drain, and toss with 3 tablespoons water mixed with 1 tablespoon olive oil. Drain and pour into a large mixing bowl. Cool 20 minutes.

Blanch broccoli florets and sugar snap peas in ½ inch boiling water for 1 minute. Drain and transfer to a bowl of ice water to stop the cooking process. Stir the broccoli and snap peas into pasta along with the chopped bell peppers and sun-dried tomatoes.

In a medium bowl, whisk together mustard, vinegar, olive oil, chives, salt, and pepper. Pour this vinaigrette over the pasta and toss well to mix. Cover and refrigerate until ready to serve.

Recipe serves 8.

The fresh and lively flavors covering the ivory pasta are a succulent treat. However, innocent-appearing sweet peppers can turn previously friendly wine into an unpleasant stranger, with disagreeable flavors.

Our first step is to go low-acid for contrast. Next, we need jammy, ripe berries that can get along with the peppers. We don't want to stir up the broccoli—it's safer to take the low-tannin road this time.

We're left with a soft, luscious red wine with ripe cherry and dark berries, low tannins, and not very much oak barrel time. That sounds very much like a Chianti? Now you know exactly what to look for in the Chianti or Sangiovese (the name of Chianti's grape varietal) you bring to the table.

$ Rocca Della Macie Chianti Classico
(Toscano, Italy)

$$ Atlas Peak Sangiovese
(Napa, California)

$$$ Fontodi "Vigna de Sorbo" Chianti Classica Riserva
(Toscano, Italy)

Fettuccine Rustica

I love to savor this simple, uncomplicated entree with a glass of wine at the end of a hectic day. The saltiness of the pancetta and black olives, together with the creamy texture and flavors of the pasta and mushrooms, provide complexity in this simple dish.

INGREDIENTS:

1 12-ounce package fettuccine

3 tablespoons olive oil

3 ounces Pancetta, diced

1 shallot, minced

3 large cloves garlic, minced

3 tablespoons dry white wine

¼ cup of the pasta cooking liquid or more, as needed

¼ cup chicken or vegetable broth

3 cups sliced white mushrooms (about ½ pound)

1 zucchini, halved lengthwise and sliced

½ cup black olives, halved lengthwise

2 tablespoons chopped parsley

Grated Parmesan cheese

Cook pasta in 3 quarts salted water until al dente. Drain, reserving ¼ cup of the cooking liquid; set aside and keep the pasta warm.

Meanwhile, heat a skillet over medium heat; add olive oil. Stir in pancetta and shallot. Cook, stirring occasionally, until the pancetta renders its fat and the shallot is soft. Stir in minced garlic; cook for 1 minute.

Deglaze the pan with wine, scraping up any bits stuck to bottom of skillet. Stir in ¼ cup of cooking liquid and the chicken or vegetable broth; add mushrooms and zucchini. Cook until the liquid is reduced by one third and mushrooms and zucchini are soft.

Stir drained pasta, olives, and parsley into skillet; toss to mix. Cook 2 minutes, stirring constantly, until pasta is hot. Add a bit more broth, if necessary. Transfer the pasta to a large serving bowl and serve with Parmesan cheese.

Recipe makes 4 main dish or 6 side dish servings.

Wild Mushroom Linguine

Vermouth's natural acidity provides a nice contrast to the cream and mushrooms in this simple pasta dish.

INGREDIENTS:

8 ounces white button mushrooms, sliced

6 ounces baby Portabella mushrooms or 1 large Portabella mushroom, sliced

1 to 2 ounces oyster mushrooms, coarsely chopped

2 tablespoons olive oil

1 leek, white part only, diced

1 medium shallot, minced

3 cloves garlic, minced

¼ cup Martini & Rossi Dry Vermouth

1 cup chicken or vegetable broth

1½ teaspoons cornstarch

¼ cup heavy cream

Salt and pepper to taste

2 tablespoons chopped parsley

1 package linguine, cooked al dente

Grated Parmesan cheese, for garnish

Clean and slice mushrooms; set aside. Remove dark gills from underside of Portabella mushroom. Heat a large skillet over medium-low heat; add olive oil. Sauté leek and shallot until translucent; add garlic and sauté 1 minute. Stir in mushrooms and sauté until they begin to soften.

Deglaze the pan with vermouth. In a small bowl, whisk a small amount of chicken or vegetable broth into cornstarch until smooth; add to skillet. Stir in heavy cream.

Season with salt and pepper; stir in parsley. Cook several minutes until mushrooms are soft and sauce is hot. Serve over hot linguine and garnish with Parmesan cheese, if desired.

Recipe serves 4.

Mushrooms, mushrooms, mushrooms...these tender morsels bring an earthy finesse to the rich, cream-laced broth, sweet-pungent garlic and onions, and the vermouth's hot intensity. The flavors are subtle and easily overshadowed, so we require a wine with comparable subtlety and a light, not dilute, body.

The classic pairing is a Pinot Noir. In Burgundy, where Pinot Noir first reached perfection, we frequently find mushroom aromas in the nose. Most Californian Pinots lack this "Burgundian nose"; however, Oregon's outstanding Pinots often make the classic, earthy mushrooms ideal for this pairing.

$$$ Girardin Santenay 1er Cru
(Burgundy, France)

$$$ Sokol Blosser Pinot Noir
(Willamette, Oregon)

$$$ Panther Creek Pinot Noir
(Willamette, Oregon)

We have a virtual party in this dish. The exuberant, spicy, and tart flavors need a wine with a bit of residual sugar to contrast the peppers. That doesn't mean you have to drink a syrupy, cloying blush. We can have our bit of chile-fighting sweetness, while making sure there is sufficient acidity to balance out the wine; in essence, to hide the sweetness from sight.

The noble Riesling, once the most sought-after white wine in the world, remains one of the great wines of the world. We also suggest a fun alternative: an Italian-style Moscato d'Asti, with its luscious honeydew melon and peach flavors. We prefer the style called "frizzante," which has about a third as many bubbles as in a bottle of Champagne, and those bubbles conceal the Rubenesque curves of the fruit sugars better than a Hong Kong tailor!

$ **Martin Weyrich Moscato d'Asti** (Paso Robles, California)

$$ **Argyle "Nuthouse" Riesling** (Willamette Valley, Oregon)

$$$ **Doctor Pauly-Bergweiler Riesling Spätlese Bernkasteler alte Badstube am Doctorberg** (Mosel-Saar-Ruwer, Germany)

Shark 'n' Bake

My husband and I enjoyed this Caribbean island favorite while visiting Trinidad. Shark fillets are deep-fried, placed on freshly baked rolls and topped with vegetables and spicy condiments. It's a Trinidad culinary tradition not to be missed! Here, I have substituted tuna fillets for shark. If tuna is unavailable, use another mild-flavored, firm fish.

INGREDIENTS:

4 tuna fillets

1½ cups shredded red cabbage

1½ cups shredded lettuce

1 cucumber, peeled and julienned

2 tomatoes, sliced

1 cup vegetable oil

½ teaspoon salt

½ teaspoon curry powder

¼ teaspoon cayenne pepper

Freshly ground black pepper

1¼ cups flour

Assorted salsas and pepper sauces

4 large potato rolls

Wash fish fillets and pat them dry with paper towels; set aside.

Arrange cabbage, lettuce, cucumber, and tomatoes in separate bowls; set aside. In a plastic zipper bag, combine flour, salt, curry powder, cayenne, and black pepper. Seal the bag and shake it to mix.

Heat a large skillet or wok over medium heat; add oil. Place two fish fillets in the flour mixture, seal the bag, and shake gently to coat fish. Carefully lower fish into hot oil and cook 2 minutes until it is golden brown; turn once and cook on the other side 1 to 2 more minutes. Remove fillets from skillet and drain on paper towel. Repeat this procedure with the remaining two fillets.

Place each on a potato roll and top with shredded cabbage, lettuce, cucumber, tomato, and sauces, to taste.

Recipe makes 4 sandwiches.

Sandwiches

Chicken Caesar Wrap

This tasty wrap is like a chicken Caesar salad in a sandwich.

INGREDIENTS:

6 to 8 thin slices grilled chicken breast

1 round Mediterranean flat bread or large flour tortilla

2 tablespoons lowfat bottled Caesar dressing

4 thin slices red onion

½ cup chopped romaine lettuce

3 slices red bell pepper, preferably grilled

3 slices yellow bell pepper, preferably grilled

1 tablespoon shredded Parmesan cheese

1 12-inch piece parchment or wax paper

Arrange the chicken strips in the center of the flat bread or flour tortilla. Drizzle with Caesar dressing. Top with onion, chopped lettuce, and bell peppers and sprinkle with Parmesan cheese.

Fold both sides of the flat bread or tortilla over the filling. Place the wrap on parchment paper, with the top of the sandwich at the upper end of parchment. Fold the paper lengthwise over the sandwich once, then fold up the lower edge of the paper twice to prevent drips. Wrap the remaining parchment lengthwise around sandwich until it fully encases sandwich.

Peel the parchment paper away as sandwich is eaten.

Recipe makes 1 sandwich wrap.

Teriyaki Steak Wrap

A delicious dinner or lunchtime sandwich using last night's leftover beef!

INGREDIENTS:

6 to 8 thin slices grilled sirloin steak

1 round Mediterranean flat bread

2 tablespoons Kikkoman teriyaki baste and glaze sauce

¼ cup bean sprouts

2 tablespoons chow mein noodles

1 12-inch piece parchment or wax paper

Arrange the steak strips in the center of flat bread. Drizzle with teriyaki base and glaze sauce and top with bean sprouts and chow mein noodles.

Fold both sides of the flat bread over the filling. Place the sandwich on parchment paper with the top of the sandwich at the upper end of parchment. Fold the paper lengthwise over the sandwich once, then fold up the lower edge of the paper twice to prevent drips. Wrap the remaining parchment lengthwise around the sandwich until the paper fully encases the sandwich.

Peel parchment paper away as sandwich is eaten.

Recipe makes 1 sandwich wrap.

Sandwiches

Grilled Fajita Pocket Sandwich

Make lunchtime away from home a Southwestern fiesta. Packed school lunches were never like this when I was growing up! An entire world of options exists for sack lunches beyond the standard P. B. and J. sandwich, whether you're packing lunch for your children or yourself.

This Grilled Fajita Pocket Sandwich uses last night's grilled skirt steak and is so enticing, just thinking about lunch will make your mouth water. A splash of fresh lime juice perks up the flavor of the meat, which is then tucked into pocket bread with thinly sliced bell peppers, red onion, and shredded lettuce. Dressed with prepared salsa, the sandwich is ready in time to catch your morning ride. Try it for a quick dinner, too.

INGREDIENTS:

1 cup leftover marinated, grilled skirt steak

Salt and freshly ground black pepper, to taste

2 teaspoons freshly squeezed lime juice

1 round pocket bread

⅓ cup thinly sliced green bell pepper

⅓ cup thinly sliced red bell pepper

1 thin slice red onion

¼ cup prepared salsa

Shredded lettuce

Slice skirt steak into thin slices, season with salt and ground black pepper, and drizzle with lime juice. Slice pocket bread in half, open the pockets, and tuck in the meat.

Top the meat with sliced bell peppers. Separate onion into rings, tuck them into the pockets, and top each sandwich with 2 tablespoons salsa. Garnish the sandwiches with shredded lettuce, wrap in them parchment paper or plastic wrap, and pack in lunches.

Recipe makes 2 sandwiches.

This vibrant, colorful diva stretches the scales with potent notes of salty feta, acidic tomato, pungent garlic, sweet peppers, and savory olives—all against a chewy backdrop of yeasty pita. This is a song few wines can harmonize with. It takes a wine that would perhaps be less than enjoyable when sipped daintily with tea sandwiches in polite company.

A Retsina from Greece is such a wine. If you've never tasted one in such company, then you've deprived yourself of a delightful experience. Another stout-hearted tenor is a New Zealand Sauvignon Blanc. Closer to home, we enjoy the handful of California Sauvignon Blancs with sufficient acidity and herbal components to hold their own.

$ **Geyser Peak Sauvignon Blanc** (Sonoma, California)

$ **Boutari Retsina** (Greece)

$$+ **Brancott Sauvignon Blanc RSV** (Marlborough, New Zealand)

Claire Criscuolo's Greek Pita Pizzas

I am honored and delighted to share this fun family recipe from my dear friend, Claire Criscuolo, author of several excellent vegetarian cookbooks. She and her sweet husband, Frank, own two acclaimed vegetarian restaurants, Claire's Corner Copia in New Haven, Connecticut.

Because Claire and I are both registered nurses, a special bond exists between us, as we shifted our attention from loving care of our patients' immediate physical and emotional well-being, to caring with love for the physical, emotional, and spiritual nourishment of our families and friends around our tables.

INGREDIENTS:

6 pita breads (use the thick Greek pita breads if you can)

1 tablespoon trans-fat–free margarine or butter, softened to room temperature

1 teaspoon dried oregano, divided

1 10-ounce bag prewashed baby spinach

½ red onion, thinly sliced

1 large tomato, diced

1 large clove garlic, finely minced

3 small bell peppers—one red, one yellow, and one green— cut into strips or diced

1 small bunch broccoli florets, separated

10 kalamata or Gaeta olives, pitted and coarsely chopped

6 pepperoncini peppers, cut in half lengthwise (sold in jars in the supermarket)

6 ounces feta cheese, drained and crumbled

2 tablespoons extra-virgin olive oil

1 tablespoon red wine vinegar

1 tablespoon freshly squeezed lemon juice

Salt and pepper to taste

Sandwiches

Preheat the oven to 350 degrees. Arrange the pita breads on two nonstick cookie sheets. Spread margarine evenly over the pita breads, using a butter knife or small rubber spatula. Sprinkle half the oregano evenly over the pita breads.

Bake in a preheated oven 5 minutes, then transfer the pita rounds to a large serving platter.

Meanwhile, in a large bowl, combine spinach leaves, onion, tomato, garlic, bell peppers, broccoli florets, olives, pepperoncini, and feta cheese. Toss gently to combine.

In a separate bowl, combine olive oil, vinegar, lemon juice, remaining oregano, salt (add only a little salt—the feta, olives, and pepperoncini are salty), and pepper to taste. Whisk to combine.

Pour the dressing evenly over the tossed salad mixture. Toss well to combine, using two wooden spoons, and taste for seasonings.

Divide salad mixture evenly over the pita breads and serve immediately.

Recipe serves 6.

New Orleans Muffuletta

When my husband, Randy, and I were students at The University of Texas at Austin, one of our favorite dates was a dinner at the Capitol Oyster Company in downtown Austin. There, I experienced my first muffuletta, a New Orleans sandwich tradition. The Capitol muffuletta was a 5-inch roll of thick sourdough bread, layered with Italian meats, provolone cheese, chopped tomatoes, lettuce, and the most divine green olive dressing. It created one of those food memories that have stayed with me through the years. Here is my Texas-size version.

INGREDIENTS:

1 9-inch boule, or round loaf, sourdough bread

1 red bell pepper

⅓ cup chopped green Spanish olives

⅓ cup chopped niçoise or kalamata olives

⅓ cup olive oil

1 tablespoon fresh lemon juice

1 tablespoon chopped Italian parsley

½ teaspoon dried oregano

Freshly ground black pepper, to taste

8 ounces sliced mortadella

3 ounces Sopressata salami

4 ounces sliced provolone cheese

¾ cup chopped ripe tomato

¼ cup fresh basil leaves, rinsed and dried

Pinch of coarse salt

Sandwiches

Slice the boule in half horizontally; tear out a bit of excess soft bread in the center and set aside. Grill or broil red bell pepper until its skin blackens. Place it in a plastic zipper bag, seal, and allow to steam until the pepper becomes soft. Peel the skin from the pepper, slice it in half, remove the seeds, and dice it; set aside.

In a medium bowl, stir together olives, diced red pepper, olive oil, lemon juice, parsley, oregano, and black pepper. Spoon half the olive mixture onto the lower half of the boule.

Top with sliced meats, provolone, chopped tomato, basil leaves, and salt. Spoon the remaining olive mixture over the sandwich and replace top half of bread.

Wrap the muffuletta tightly with plastic wrap and refrigerate 2 or 3 hours until the layers are secure and flavors meld. To serve, unwrap and place on a large cutting board. Slice the muffuletta with a serrated knife into quarters, or as desired. Serve immediately.

Recipe serves 4 to 6.

Couscous with Golden Raisins and Cranberries

This pretty side dish is one of my favorites, especially because it's ready in 15 minutes. I love the way the flavors of the sweet, golden raisins play off the tart fresh cranberries. For variation, substitute dried apricots, dates, or other favorite fruits.

INGREDIENTS:

1 tablespoon olive oil

1 tablespoon unsalted butter

2 tablespoons minced onion or shallot

1 clove garlic, minced

⅓ cup golden raisins

2 tablespoons chopped fresh cranberries

1 tablespoon chopped fresh parsley

2 cups chicken broth

¾ cup plain couscous

Heat a medium saucepan over medium-low heat; add olive oil and butter. When the butter has melted, swirl the pan to mix. Sauté onion or shallot in butter mixture until soft, about 2 minutes. Stir in garlic, raisins, cranberries, and parsley; sauté 2 minutes until cranberries start to soften and raisins plump a bit.

Pour in chicken broth, stir, and cover the saucepan. Bring the mixture to a boil, uncover, and stir in couscous. Cover and remove from heat; let stand 5 to 6 minutes until the couscous has absorbed the broth.

Using a fork, gently fluff the couscous and distribute the raisins and cranberries. Serve immediately or keep covered until ready to serve.

Recipe serves 4.

Side Dishes

Everyday Basmati Rice

Basmati Rice adds simple, delicious flavor to everyday meals. This aromatic rice becomes tender and even more savory when it is sautéed for a few minutes and then cooked in chicken broth.

INGREDIENTS:

1 tablespoon olive oil

1 tablespoon unsalted butter

1 cup basmati rice

1¾ cups lowfat chicken broth

½ cup water

1/8 teaspoon salt

1½ tablespoons chopped fresh parley

Heat a medium saucepan over medium-low heat. Add olive oil and butter, swirling the pan to melt butter. Stir in basmati rice and sauté for 2 minutes, stirring constantly.

Pour in chicken broth and water and season with salt. Raise heat to high and bring rice just to a boil. Reduce heat to low, cover, and simmer 15 to 20 minutes.

Add chopped parsley and fluff the rice with a fork to separate the grains. Serve immediately.

Recipe serves 4.

Quick Tex-Mex Rice

In less than 30 minutes, this versatile rice side dish is ready to complement Southwestern entrées, chicken, or grilled meats or fish. Yellow and green onions, fresh, chopped jalapeño, and cumin add flavor, while keeping preparation time to a minimum.

INGREDIENTS:

1½ tablespoons vegetable oil

3 green onions, white and green part, sliced

½ cup diced onion

1 large jalapeño

1 cup long grain rice

1¾ cups vegetable or chicken broth

¾ cup water

1½ tablespoons tomato sauce

¼ teaspoon cumin

1/8 teaspoon salt

Heat a medium saucepan over low heat; add oil and swirl to coat the bottom of the pan. Add sliced and diced onions, sautéing several minutes until onions are soft.

Remove stem and seeds from jalapeño and discard. Slice jalapeño in half lengthwise and remove any remaining seeds. Dice jalapeño and add to the saucepan along with the rice. Sauté rice 4 minutes, stirring constantly.

Stir in vegetable or chicken broth, water, tomato sauce, cumin, and salt. Raise heat to high and bring the rice mixture to a boil. Reduce heat to low, cover, and cook the rice 15 to 20 minutes until all liquid has been absorbed.

Stir the rice with a fork to separate the grains, then serve.

Recipe serves 6.

Side Dishes

Skillet Potatoes

As a side dish for breakfast or dinner, skillet potatoes have that down-home goodness that's hard to resist. No need to parboil the potatoes before frying; just slice them into small cubes and they practically cook all by themselves!

INGREDIENTS:

3 tablespoons olive oil

½ cup diced onion

5 cups peeled, cubed potatoes, cut into ½-inch cubes

¼ teaspoon salt

Freshly ground black pepper

Preheat a large skillet over medium heat. When the skillet is hot, add oil, swirl to coat bottom of the pan, and add onions. Sauté onions 1 minute.

Add potatoes to the skillet, forming a single layer on the bottom of the pan. Cook the potatoes 5 minutes without stirring until they brown lightly on bottom.

Cook the potatoes 10 to 15 more minutes, stirring every 2 to 3 minutes until they are golden brown on all sides and a sharp knife pierces them easily.

Season potatoes with salt and pepper during the final 2 minutes of cooking.

Recipe serves 4.

Caramelized Onions and Empire Apples

This vegetable side dish is wonderful with pork chops.

INGREDIENTS:

2 tablespoons olive oil

1 large onion, peeled and sliced

¼ teaspoon coarse salt

2 Empire or other soft cooking apples, cored and diced

¼ cup dried cherries

¼ cup golden raisins

Sauté onion in olive oil over medium-low heat until golden in color, stirring occasionally, about 15 minutes. Season with salt; stir to mix.

Stir in apples, dried cherries, and raisins. Cook 8 to 10 more minutes, until the apples are soft and the cherries and raisins have plumped. Serve immediately.

Recipe serves 4.

Side Dishes

Broccoflower and Cauliflower Sauté

During the week, I prefer vegetables that can be prepped and cooked in 15 minutes. This colorful combo is just the thing for a busy weeknight. If you have never tasted broccoflower, its flavor is a blend of, you guessed it, broccoli and cauliflower. When the pale green broccoflower florets are steamed for a few minutes with cauliflower, then sautéed with garlic, you have an attractive, tasty side dish.

INGREDIENTS:

½ head broccoflower

½ head cauliflower

1 tablespoon olive oil

1 tablespoon butter (optional)

2 cloves garlic, minced

Salt and freshly ground black pepper, to taste

Divide broccoflower and cauliflower into florets. Transfer them to a steamer basket in a large saucepan with ¾ inch of water. Cover and bring to a boil over high heat; reduce heat to medium and steam just until the vegetables are tender, about 3 minutes.

Preheat a large skillet over medium-low heat; add oil and butter and swirl to mix. Remove the steamed florets from the steamer basket and add them to skillet, along with garlic. Sauté 2 minutes, season with salt and ground pepper, and serve.

Recipe serves 4 to 6.

Pepper Medley

Colorful strips of red, green and yellow bell peppers are sautéed together quickly with zucchini and julienned carrots for a delicious change from everyday vegetables. Each time I serve this stir-fry when my husband's business colleagues come to dinner, they rave about it. I can't give a better recommendation than that!

INGREDIENTS:

1 large green bell pepper

1 large red bell pepper

1 large yellow bell pepper

1 zucchini squash

2 carrots

2 tablespoons olive oil

2 cloves garlic, minced

Salt and freshly ground black pepper, to taste

2 tablespoons freshly grated Parmesan cheese

Slice peppers into long, thin strips. Slice zucchini in half crosswise; then slice it lengthwise into thin strips. Peel and julienne the carrots.

Heat a wok or large skillet over medium heat. Add olive oil, peppers, zucchini, and carrots and stir-fry the vegetables just until crisp-tender. Add garlic, salt, and pepper; stir-fry additional 1 minute.

Transfer mixture to a serving platter and garnish with Parmesan cheese.

Recipe serves 4.

Acorn Squash with Brown Sugar Syrup

It's easy to enjoy acorn squash with a sweet, brown sugar syrup, even on the busiest nights. Steaming the squash face down in a small amount of water cuts the usual cooking time in half. Fill the soft centers with brown sugar and butter and steam a few more minutes to allow the sugar to melt. In just 20 to 25 minutes, it is ready to enjoy!

INGREDIENTS:

2 acorn squash

4 tablespoons packed brown sugar

4 tablespoons butter

Slice acorn squash in half lengthwise; scrape out the seeds and stringy pulp with a spoon. Place squash face down in a large skillet and add water to a depth of ¾ inch.

Cover the skillet tightly with a lid or foil and bring the water to a boil over high heat. Reduce the heat to medium-low and simmer the squash until its insides are soft, about 15 to 20 minutes, depending on size. As the squash steams, add additional water as needed.

Turn the squash upright. Fill each half with 1 tablespoon brown sugar and 1 tablespoon of the butter. Cover and steam several minutes until sugar and butter have melted.

Transfer squash to dinner plates and serve.

Recipe makes 4 servings.

Homestyle Applesauce

The aroma of the apples and cider as they simmer on the stove makes me feel warm all over. Serve this hot, with a garnish of cinnamon, on a cold winter night.

INGREDIENTS:

7 to 8 large Rome or other tart cooking apples (about 2 pounds)

1 cup apple cider or apple juice

2 to 3 tablespoons sugar

Ground cinnamon, for garnish

Wash, peel, core, and slice apples and place them, along with cider or juice and sugar, in a large saucepan. Cover and bring the mixture to a boil; reduce the heat to medium. Cook the apples, stirring occasionally, until they soften and begin to lose their shape, about 10 minutes.

Reduce heat to low and continue cooking until the applesauce is fairly smooth, with a few chunks of apple remaining, about 10 minutes. Stir the applesauce frequently to prevent scorching.

To serve, transfer the hot applesauce to a large serving bowl and sprinkle it with cinnamon. If desired, add cinnamon to the applesauce as it cooks.

Recipe makes 4½ to 5 cups applesauce.

Side Dishes

Hot Spiced Fruit

When the dinnertime menu needs a warm, fragrant, and last-minute easy dish, Hot Spiced Fruit is the ideal solution. It is made from canned fruits usually found in the pantry, and its blend of fragrant spices gives it that "touch of home" flavor. Best of all, this recipe transforms from homespun to elegant in a flash. Serve it in a silver footed casserole dish, and it's a delicious accompaniment to baked ham or pork roast.

INGREDIENTS:

1 29-ounce can sliced peaches in heavy syrup

1 29-ounce can pear halves in heavy syrup

1 15-ounce can unpeeled apricot halves

2 whole cloves

¾ teaspoon cinnamon

¼ teaspoon freshly grated nutmeg

⅛ teaspoon ground cardamom

In a large saucepan, stir together fruits and their syrups. Add cloves, cinnamon, nutmeg, and cardamom; stir well.

Cover and bring the mixture to a boil over medium heat. Reduce the heat to low and simmer 5 to 10 minutes, stirring occasionally.

Serve the fruit in small bowls or ramekins.

Recipe makes 6 to 8 servings.

Winter Fruit Compote

A hearty recipe that doubles as a side dish or dessert, this compote of dried fruits is wonderful when paired with poultry or pork. For dessert, serve it alone or over a scoop of rum raisin or French vanilla ice cream.

INGREDIENTS:

1½ cups water

¼ cup plus 2 tablespoons sugar

1 cup dried apricots

1 cup pitted prunes

⅓ cup dried cranberries

¼ cup dried cherries

¼ cup golden raisins

¼ cup Zante currants

2 pears, peeled, cored, and sliced

¼ cup apple juice

2 teaspoons cornstarch

In a large saucepan, stir together water and sugar. Cook over high heat, stirring with a wooden spoon, until the sugar dissolves, about 2 minutes.

Reduce heat to medium and stir in all the fruit. In a small bowl, whisk apple juice into cornstarch until smooth, then add the cornstarch mixture to the saucepan, stirring until the sauce thickens.

Reduce heat to low, cover, and simmer the fruit 10 to 15 minutes, stirring occasionally. Serve as an accompaniment to poultry or roasted pork or as a winter dessert.

Recipe serves 6.

Side Dishes

Baby Spinach Salad with Citrus Vinaigrette

The citrus dressing on this simple salad is refreshing all year long.

INGREDIENTS:

1 large bunch baby spinach, rinsed and stemmed

2 oranges, peeled and sliced

⅓ cup freshly squeezed orange juice

¼ cup extra virgin olive oil

1 teaspoon red wine vinegar

1 teaspoon Dijon mustard (preferably Maille)

1 teaspoon orange zest

Salt and freshly ground black pepper, to taste

Arrange spinach and sliced oranges in a large salad bowl.

In a small mixing bowl, whisk together orange juice, oil, vinegar, mustard, orange zest, and salt and pepper until well blended. Pour the mixture over the spinach salad and toss well.

Recipe serves 4.

Mixed Greens and Asparagus Salad

I grew up on tossed salads, but the "entertainer" in me loves the innate beauty of composed salads, even for everyday meals. I work with the ingredients I have on hand to create salads as beautiful to the eye as they are to the palate. I fixed this salad one evening for my brother-in-law, Mike Thompson, when he was visiting town on business. As I was putting the final touches on each salad plate, he took me completely by surprise by proclaiming it "a work of art."

INGREDIENTS:

16 asparagus spears, trimmed

1 small bunch romaine lettuce

1 small bunch green leaf lettuce

1 small bunch red leaf lettuce

¼ pound spring mix (mesclun)

¾ cup sliced white mushrooms

½ cup sliced radicchio

¼ cup sliced black olives

Coarse salt and freshly ground black pepper

Parmesan cheese, for garnish

Place asparagus spears in a large skillet with ½ inch water, cover, and bring to a boil. Reduce heat to low and simmer just until asparagus spears are tender, about 2 minutes, depending on their thickness. Drain and transfer the asparagus to a bowl of ice water to stop the cooking process; set aside.

Rinse and spin lettuces dry. Toss to mix, then arrange on individual salad plates. Rinse and spin spring mix; arrange on top of the lettuces. Arrange mushrooms, radicchio and black olives on the salads. Arrange 4 blanched asparagus spears side by side in the center of each salad. Then season with salt and black pepper and top with grated Parmesan and Vinaigrette d'Agnes.

Recipe makes 4 servings.

Side Dishes

Vinaigrette D'Agnes

Our good friends, Agnes and Olivier Guard, who live in Dijon, France, make this vinaigrette for salad almost every evening. While they never measured any of the ingredients, I watched carefully one evening, paper and pencil in hand, and estimated the amounts. Upon returning home to Texas, I was delighted to discover I had captured the flavor perfectly! Now you, too, can enjoy a little bit of France every day. This recipe doubles and triples beautifully.

INGREDIENTS:

1 teaspoon Dijon mustard (preferably Maille)

2 teaspoons red wine vinegar

¼ cup olive oil

1 tablespoon chopped fresh chives

Salt and ground black pepper, to taste

In a small mixing bowl, whisk mustard, vinegar, olive oil, chives, and salt and pepper together until the mixture is emulsified. Spoon over salad.

Recipe makes approximately ⅓ cup dressing.

Belgian Endive and Pear Salad with Roquefort Dressing

The splashes of red in the pears, red leaf lettuce, and dried cranberries of this arranged salad look beautiful against the creamy white Belgian endive. Originally designed to be served as individual salads, this would look impressive arranged on a large platter and can be doubled or tripled for a buffet dinner when entertaining.

INGREDIENTS:

Salad:

- 2 Belgian endives
- 1 head red leaf lettuce
- 2 ripe red Bartlett pears
- ½ cup sliced mushrooms
- ¼ cup coarsely chopped pecans or walnuts

- ¼ cup dried cranberries
- 1 green onion, green part only, sliced
- 1 wedge fresh lemon
- Roquefort Dressing

Arrange endive and leaf lettuce on 4 salad plates. Core and slice pears and arrange them between endive leaves. Top with sliced mushrooms. Sprinkle the salad with nuts, dried cranberries, and green onion. If you are making the salads ahead, rub the pears with a lemon wedge to keep them from turning brown.

Roquefort Dressing:

- 4 ounces Roquefort cheese (can substitute blue cheese), crumbled
- ½ cup mayonnaise

- ¼ cup buttermilk
- ⅛ teaspoon white wine Worcestershire sauce
- Freshly ground black pepper

In a medium bowl, crumble Roquefort with a fork. Stir in mayonnaise, buttermilk, Worcestershire sauce, and black pepper until mixture is creamy, with small lumps of cheese. Spoon over salads and serve.

Recipe makes 4 salads.

Side Dishes

Summer Fruit Salad with Citrus Yogurt Dressing

Summer meals and picnics are all about fresh foods that refresh and energize us. This is especially important on hot, sultry days. Summer salads should be light and colorful and packed with flavor. This fruit salad is made from cool melons, tropical fruit, and summer berries, and is accompanied by a light, lemony yogurt dressing. Add more fun to your summer meals and more fruit to your diet with this wonderful summer salad.

INGREDIENTS:

4 cups watermelon cubes

4 cups cantaloupe cubes

2 cups fresh halved strawberries

1 papaya, peeled, seeded, and cubed

1 cup fresh blueberries

2 8-ounce cartons lemon fruit-on-the-bottom yogurt

Zest of 1 orange

3 tablespoons freshly squeezed orange juice

2 teaspoons poppy seeds

Place fruit in a large serving bowl and stir to mix.

In a small bowl, stir together yogurt, orange zest, orange juice, and poppy seeds until smooth. Spoon the dressing over the fruit salad, toss if desired, and serve.

Recipe serves 8.

Buttermilk Cornbread Muffins

Casual family meals taste even better when a basket of oven-fresh cornbread muffins are on the table. Serve them with chili, gumbo, or your favorite soup.

INGREDIENTS:

1¼ cups flour

1 cup yellow cornmeal

2 tablespoons sugar

2 teaspoons baking powder

1 teaspoon baking soda

1 teaspoon salt

1 egg

1¼ cups buttermilk

3 tablespoons vegetable oil

Preheat oven to 400 degrees. In a large bowl, stir together flour, cornmeal, sugar, baking powder, soda, and salt; set aside.

In a small bowl, whisk together egg, buttermilk, and vegetable oil. Pour the buttermilk mixture all at once into the dry ingredients and stir just to combine ingredients.

Spray muffin tins with nonstick cooking spray or line each cup with a paper liner. Spoon the batter into the muffin tins, filling each cup ⅔ full.

Bake the muffins in a preheated oven 15 to 18 minutes, or until a cake tester inserted into the center of a muffin comes out clean.

Remove the muffins from the oven and transfer them to a wire rack or cloth-lined basket. Don't allow them to cool in the tins or they will become soggy.

Recipe makes 12 muffins.

Side Dishes

Blueberry Muffins

If you have trouble getting your family to the dinner table, bake a batch of these fragrant muffins. The aroma draws everyone to the kitchen like bees to honey.

For breakfast or dinner, these muffins, with their soft, cakelike interior and sweet blueberries, are all the reason anyone needs to slow down and savor the family meal.

INGREDIENTS:

2¼ cups flour

2 teaspoons baking powder

1 teaspoon salt

½ cup unsalted butter, softened

1 cup sugar

2 eggs

1½ teaspoons vanilla

¾ cup milk

1¼ fresh or frozen blueberries

1 tablespoon flour

1 tablespoon sugar

Preheat the oven to 400 degrees. In a medium bowl, stir together 2¼ cups flour, baking powder, and salt, until thoroughly mixed.

In large bowl of an electric mixer, cream the butter and sugar until light. Add eggs, beating well after each addition; stir in vanilla.

Stir flour mixture into creamed mixture, alternating with the milk. Toss blueberries gently with the remaining flour. Fold the blueberries into the batter.

Line muffin tins with paper liners or spray with nonstick cooking spray and fill them ¾ full. Sprinkle the top of the batter with sugar.

Bake the muffins in a preheated oven 18 to 20 minutes until they are golden brown and a tester inserted into the center comes out clean.

Remove the muffins from the oven and transfer them to a wire rack or lined basket; serve warm.

Recipe makes 14 to 16 muffins.

Apple Crisp

Warm from the oven, with a scoop of vanilla ice cream or a drizzle of milk or cream, apple crisp is a fragrant, heartwarming recipe that has been putting smiles on American family faces for generations.

INGREDIENTS:

3 pounds Granny Smith
  or other baking apples
  (about 8 medium)

⅔ cup sugar

2 tablespoons flour

1¼ teaspoons cinnamon

½ teaspoon nutmeg

¼ cup golden raisins

1 recipe Streusel Topping

Preheat the oven to 350 degrees. Wash, peel, core, and slice apples and layer the slices in a 10-inch casserole or soufflé dish.

In a small bowl, stir together sugar, flour, cinnamon, and nutmeg. Pour the mixture over apples and sprinkle with raisins.

Streusel Topping:

1 cup packed brown sugar

½ cup old-fashioned oats

2 tablespoons flour

1½ teaspoons cinnamon

3 tablespoons butter, melted

In a medium bowl, stir together brown sugar, oats, flour, and cinnamon. Pour in melted butter and stir with a fork to mix; the mixture will be crumbly. Sprinkle streusel mixture over the apples and raisins.

Bake the apple crisp in a preheated oven 50 to 55 minutes, or until juices bubble and apples are tender when pierced with a sharp knife.

Serve apple crisp warm or cold with cream or a scoop of vanilla ice cream.

Recipe makes one 10-inch apple crisp.

Desserts

Individual Deep Dish Apple Pies

I keep rounds of pie pastry in the freezer so I can whip up individual desserts on a whim. These apple pies, made individually in 4-inch ramekins, can be assembled in 20 minutes. Thaw the pastry earlier in the day; slice apples right into the ramekins and top with cinnamon sugar and small rounds of pastry. Pop them in the oven, and dessert is ready!

INGREDIENTS:

4 large baking apples

⅔ cup sugar

2 tablespoons flour

1½ teaspoons cinnamon

¼ teaspoon allspice

¼ teaspoon freshly grated nutmeg

Frozen homemade pie pastry, thawed

1 egg

1 tablespoon water

1½ teaspoons sugar, for garnish

Thaw pie pastry earlier in the day and keep it chilled.

Preheat the oven to 375 degrees. Peel, core, and slice apples directly into ramekins. In a small bowl, stir together sugar, flour, cinnamon, allspice, and nutmeg until well blended. Dividing the sugar mixture equally among the ramekins, sprinkle it directly onto the apples.

Roll out the pastry on a floured pastry cloth or floured surface. Cut it into 4 sections and top each ramekin with pastry. Trim and flute edges and slice several steam holes into the pastry with a sharp knife.

In a small bowl, whip egg and water with a fork to form an egg wash. Brush the egg wash over the pastry and sprinkle with sugar.

Place ramekins on a cookie sheet and bake them in a preheated oven 25 to 30 minutes until pastry is golden brown and filling is bubbly.

Remove from oven and cool 30 minutes. Serve deep dish pies warm with milk or cream, if desired.

Recipe serves 4.

Black Forest Gingerbread

Warm and spicy from the oven, this delectable cool-weather dessert makes any meal special. Serve it with a dusting of confectioners' sugar, a dollop of fresh whipped cream, or a spoonful of applesauce.

INGREDIENTS:

1¾ cups all-purpose flour

1 teaspoon baking soda

¾ teaspoon cinnamon

¾ teaspoon ginger

½ teaspoon salt

½ cup unsalted butter, softened

½ cup brown sugar, packed

1 egg

⅔ cup molasses

⅔ cup boiling water

Preheat oven to 350 degrees.

In a small bowl, stir together flour, baking soda, cinnamon, ginger, and salt; set aside.

In a large mixing bowl, cream butter and sugar until mixture is light. Add egg and molasses and beat until the mixture is creamy.

Add the flour mixture, alternately with boiling water, to the butter and sugar mixture, starting and ending with flour. Pour the batter into a greased and floured 9-inch round cake pan.

Bake 25 to 30 minutes, or until a tester inserted into the middle of the cake comes out clean. Remove to a rack to cool 20 minutes; then place the cake on a serving platter. Serve the gingerbread warm with a dollop of sweetened whipped cream, if desired.

Recipe makes one 9-inch cake.

Desserts

Sour Cream Blueberry Cake

Delicious in summer or winter, this light-as-a-feather cake is versatile enough to serve with morning coffee, afternoon tea, or as a satisfying dessert. Each summer, I buy extra blueberries to freeze, then I enjoy them in this cake throughout the year.

INGREDIENTS:

1⅓ cups sifted cake flour

¾ teaspoon baking powder

½ teaspoon salt

6 tablespoons unsalted butter, softened

⅔ cup sugar

2 eggs

1 teaspoon vanilla

½ cup sour cream

1 tablespoon milk

1¼ cups fresh or frozen blueberries

1 tablespoon flour

1 tablespoon confectioners' sugar, for garnish

Preheat the oven to 350 degrees. Grease and flour a 9-inch round cake pan and set aside.

In a medium bowl, stir together 1⅓ cups flour, baking powder, and salt and set aside.

In the large bowl of an electric mixer, cream butter and sugar until light and fluffy, about 8 minutes. Add eggs one at a time, mixing well after each addition. Stir in vanilla.

Gradually add dry ingredients to the creamed mixture, alternating with the sour cream and milk and stopping mixer to scrape sides of bowl.

In a small bowl, toss blueberries with remaining 1 tablespoon of flour to coat. Gently stir blueberries into the cake batter, then discard any remaining flour used to coat berries. Pour batter into the prepared cake pan and bake in a preheated oven 35 to 40 minutes, or until a tester inserted into the center comes out clean.

Remove the cake from the oven and set it on a wire rack to cool. When it is cool, dust it with sifted confectioners' sugar, if desired.

Recipe makes one 9-inch cake.

Cherry Berry French Country Tart

Once your family and friends taste this country tart, you may be tempted to throw away your pie pans! No need to fret about fluting the edges of this fruit pie. The yummy cherry and blueberry filling is spooned into a single layer of pie pastry, which is folded up around the filling in a free-form fashion. It's simple, yet elegant.

INGREDIENTS:

Pastry:

⅓ cup thinly sliced almonds

1⅓ cups flour

1½ tablespoons sugar

½ teaspoon salt

½ cup cold unsalted butter

3 tablespoons ice water

¼ teaspoon almond extract

Filling:

1 21-ounce can cherry pie filling

1½ cups fresh blueberries

2 tablespoons sugar

1 tablespoon flour

½ teaspoon cinnamon

2 teaspoons freshly squeezed
  lemon juice

1 tablespoon unsalted butter

1 egg

1 tablespoon water

1 tablespoon sparkling sugar or
  2 teaspoons granulated sugar

Desserts

Place almonds in the bowl of a food processor and process until they are finely ground. Add flour, sugar, and salt and pulse several times to mix.

Slice cold butter into 8 pieces and add it to the flour mixture. Process until the butter is pea-size. Add ice water and almond extract; process until pastry forms a ball. Do not overprocess. Remove the pastry from the processor, wrap it in plastic wrap, and refrigerate it at least 30 minutes.

In a large bowl, stir together cherry filling and blueberries. In a small bowl, mix sugar, flour, and cinnamon. Stir the sugar mixture into the berry filling, add lemon juice, and mix well.

Preheat the oven to 400 degrees. On a floured pastry cloth, roll the almond pastry into a 14-inch circle. Fold the pastry in half and transfer it to a baking sheet covered with parchment paper. Turn the edges of the paper up to catch any juices that may overflow during baking.

Spoon cherry-blueberry filling into the center of the pastry and dot with 1 tablespoon of butter. Gently fold the edges of the pastry up around the filling, overlapping them to form a round tart. Take care the pastry doesn't tear around the base of the tart or juices will escape during baking.

In a small bowl, mix egg and water with a fork. Brush egg wash over the pastry and sprinkle with sparkling sugar.

Bake the tart in a preheated oven 25 minutes, or until pastry is golden brown and filling is bubbly.

Recipe makes 1 tart.

Chocolate Chip Cookies

No family-style cookbook would be complete without this classic American cookie. My version is crisp around the edges with a soft interior.

INGREDIENTS:

2½ cups flour

1 teaspoon baking soda

½ teaspoon baking powder

¾ teaspoon salt

½ cup unsalted butter, softened

½ cup shortening

1¼ cups packed brown sugar

1 cup granulated sugar

2 eggs

1½ teaspoons vanilla

1½ cups semisweet chocolate chips

Preheat the oven to 350 degrees. In a medium bowl, stir together flour, baking soda, baking powder, and salt; set aside.

In the large bowl of an electric mixer, cream butter, shortening, and sugars until light. Add eggs and vanilla and beat until thoroughly mixed.

Using a large spoon, gradually stir the flour mixture into the creamed mixture until well blended. Stir in chocolate chips. Drop generous teaspoons of cookie dough onto lightly greased cookie sheets, leaving 2 inches between each one.

Bake in a preheated oven 11 to 13 minutes until cookies are golden brown. Remove them from oven, cool 1 minute, then transfer them to wire racks to cool.

Recipe makes 6 to 7 dozen (72 to 84) 3-inch cookies.

Desserts

Golden Brown Sugar Cookies

Brown sugar adds a hint of caramel flavor to the classic drop sugar cookie in this much-loved recipe. As an after-school snack with a glass of milk, or a treat to tuck into a lunch bag for the office, these light and crisp homemade cookies satisfy the urge for something sweet.

INGREDIENTS:

3 cups flour

1 teaspoon baking powder

¾ teaspoon salt

½ teaspoon baking soda

½ cup unsalted butter, softened

½ cup shortening

1½ cups granulated sugar

½ cup light brown sugar, packed

2 eggs

2 teaspoons vanilla

Granulated sugar, for garnish

Preheat the oven to 375 degrees. In a medium bowl, stir together flour, baking powder, salt, and baking soda; set aside.

In the large bowl of an electric mixer, cream butter, shortening, and sugars until mixture is light and fluffy. Add eggs and vanilla and beat until thoroughly blended.

Stir the flour mixture into the creamed mixture to form a soft dough. Drop small teaspoons of the cookie dough onto a lightly greased cookie sheet; they will spread as they bake, so leave ample space between them.

Bake in a preheated oven 8 to 9 minutes until cookies are golden brown. Remove them from oven, sprinkle with sugar, and cool 1 minute on cookie sheet. Transfer cookies to a wire rack to cool and store them in an airtight container.

Recipe makes 5½ dozen (66) 3-inch cookies.

Entrées
Sandwiches
Side Dishes
Desserts

Weekends

For as long as I can remember, I've looked forward to weekends with great anticipation. During my early school years, weekends meant freedom from classrooms and day trips in the car with my parents and sisters to the country, the mountains, or the beach, depending on where we lived at the time. We would pack yummy picnic lunches and venture out of town, sometimes with a destination in mind, and other times aimlessly just to see what we would discover along the way.

We visited a lot of farms in those days. Born and raised in Pittsburgh, Pennsylvania, my father always wanted to live on a farm. At the sight of "farm for sale" signs, we tramped through acres of crops, hip-high weeds, and small forests in pursuit of the perfect farm. We climbed fences in Pennsylvania and stone walls in Connecticut, talked with farmers and Realtors in several states, and stared in wonder at dilapidated Massachusetts farmhouses built in the 1800s and in desperate need of someone to love them.

I am happy to say that, at long last, my father got his farm. It was years after my sisters and I left home, but those weekend car trips eventually led to a lovely and historic Illinois farmhouse built over a stream during the years of Black Hawk Indian raids.

Since Randy and I were married, weekends have meant time for house projects, particularly during our early years when we renovated an old home in Houston, Texas. The weekend picnic lunches of my childhood gave way to stick-to-the-ribs, hearty meals that could be assembled and cooked quickly at the end of a busy day of home remodeling.

Weekends have also been a time to strengthen our connections with friends and neighbors by inviting them to join us for last-minute cocktails and hors d'oeuvres, backyard cookouts, potluck suppers, and block parties. A large pot of fragrant, homemade soup is an excuse to invite others for an informal meal of soup, salad, and bread, while the occasional winter weekend ice storm provides all the reason we need to put on a big pot of chili and gather around the hearth with a few neighbors.

Weekends are a time to slow down, savor the day, pamper oneself, and reconnect with family and friends. They provide opportunities to linger over a sumptuous breakfast or appreciate the special pleasures of Sunday brunch. Picnic lunches at the park, potluck suppers down the street, tailgate parties in the parking lot of a nearby college or professional football team, a poolside cocktail party or backyard barbecue with special friends. All of these pleasurable activities are memorable ways to spend weekends and each revolves around sharing the pleasures of the table with others.

In this section are recipes to make these and other weekend moments even more delicious. Start your weekend morning with a breakfast of Shirred Eggs with Maple Sausage and Gruyère, or enjoy a leisurely Champagne brunch featuring Onion and Spinach Tart. Gather your family for an old-fashioned Sunday dinner of Roast Beef and Henrietta's Brown Gravy, or fire up the barbecue pit for Grilled Teriyaki Pork Chops. Relax by the hearth on a chilly afternoon or cold winter night, warmed by mugs of Old Chicago Minestrone or feel like a kid again and decorate individual homemade pizzas with a choice of toppings.

Take pleasure in a glass of fine wine, either as an apéritif, or paired with many of the entrées presented in this section. As with each part of *The Family Table*, wine expert Eric Little has assembled an impressive array of wine suggestions to enhance your enjoyment of weekend meals. His text makes enjoyable reading as he reveals the fundamentals of wine pairing as well as interesting anecdotes to expand your knowledge of the world of wine.

I hope these recipes, wine suggestions, and family stories inspire each of you to slow down; recharge your physical, emotional, and spiritual self; reconnect with family and friends; and revel in the pleasures the weekend table has to offer.

Kathy's Berry Good Banana Smoothie

My niece, Kathy Thompson, shared this recipe with me. An accomplished gymnast, she depends on a diet of healthy foods to keep her flipping, jumping, and vaulting to success in competitions. This frosty, pink smoothie is a delightful companion to any breakfast and a terrific pick-me-up after school.

INGREDIENTS:

1½ ripe bananas

1 cup fresh or frozen strawberries

1 8-ounce carton vanilla yogurt

¼ cup orange juice

2 fresh strawberries, for garnish

Place all ingredients, except 2 fresh strawberries, in a blender. Purée until the mixture is thick and smooth. Serve in stemmed glasses with a fresh strawberry on the rim of each glass.

Recipe makes 2 smoothies.

Breakfast & Brunch

Classic Omelet

The secret to making a good omelet is constantly tilting the pan to facilitate complete cooking and a bit of wrist action when sliding the finished omelet onto a plate. Practice makes perfect, and the best part is, even the mistakes are absolutely delicious!

INGREDIENTS:

Assorted fillings, such as mushrooms, peppers, ham, salsa

2 eggs

Salt and freshly ground black pepper, to taste

2 to 3 tablespoons butter or clarified butter

3 tablespoons grated cheese, such as cheddar or pepper jack

In a small pan, sauté mushrooms, peppers, ham, or other fillings; set aside.

Preheat an 8- to 10-inch omelet pan over medium heat. In a small bowl, whisk eggs and seasonings until lightly beaten.

Add butter or clarified butter to the omelet pan, swirl to coat, and pour in egg mixture all at once. Push cooked edges of the eggs into the center the of pan, tilting it as necessary to allow the uncooked egg to run onto the pan surface. When no visible liquid egg remains, sprinkle center of the omelet with cheese and fillings.

Fold the omelet in half and slide it onto a plate, or fold one side of the omelet toward the center, and slide the omelet onto a plate; then tilt the pan so the remaining side folds over the fillings and the seam side is down.

Recipe makes 1 omelet.

Eggs Benedict with Hollandaise Sauce

Popular legend says that Eggs Benedict originated in New York City at Delmonico's Restaurant. This classic dish is well suited to a lazy weekend morning and lends an air of sophistication to Sunday brunch gatherings. For a perfectly decadent experience, enjoy Eggs Benedict with a glass of Champagne or a Mimosa.

INGREDIENTS:

1 tablespoon butter

4 slices Canadian bacon

4 eggs

Salt and pepper, to taste

1½ teaspoons white vinegar

2 English muffins

1 recipe Hollandaise Sauce

2 pitted and sliced black olives, for garnish

Hollandaise Sauce:

2 egg yolks

1 tablespoon water

1 tablespoon freshly squeezed lemon juice

5 tablespoons unsalted butter, cold, cut in 5 pieces

Salt and freshly ground black pepper, to taste

Pinch of paprika

Breakfast & Brunch

To prepare sauce, heat water in bottom of a double boiler just until hot, not boiling. In the top of the double boiler, but not over the heated water, whisk together egg yolks, water, and lemon juice; place over hot water. Stir the egg mixture until it is hot and bubbles begin to form around the edges of the pan. Gradually whisk in cold butter, one piece at a time, until a thick sauce is formed. If the mixture gets too hot and appears to be separating, remove it from the heat and whisk in additional cold butter until the sauce cools a little. Season the sauce with salt, pepper, and paprika. Remove the double boiler from the heat; set it aside and keep it warm.

In a medium sauté pan, melt butter over low heat. Add Canadian bacon and sauté gently while cooking the eggs.

To poach eggs, fill a shallow pan with 2 inches water, add vinegar, and bring to a low boil. Carefully crack 1 egg into a small bowl and slip it into boiling water; repeat quickly with the remaining eggs. Cook the eggs 2 to 3 minutes until whites are set and the yolks are cooked, but still runny. Remove them from the pan with a slotted spoon; season with salt and pepper.

Meanwhile, split English muffins with a fork and toast them until golden brown. To serve, place 2 English muffin halves on each plate and top each with a slice of Canadian bacon and a poached egg. Spoon warm Hollandaise Sauce over the eggs and garnish with sliced black olives.

Recipe serves 2.

Shirred Eggs with Maple Sausage and Gruyère

This breakfast and brunch recipe always elicits sighs of sublime satisfaction and smiles of delight from my cooking class students, camera crew, and family. The day I developed the recipe, I went door-to-door asking neighbors to taste it. One bite and I could tell I had a hit on my hands from the smile on each and every face.

INGREDIENTS:

¼ pound maple-flavored bulk sausage, cooked and crumbled

2 eggs

Salt and freshly ground black pepper, to taste

4 tablespoons heavy cream

¼ cup grated Gruyère cheese

Preheat the oven to 325 degrees.

Spray two ramekins with nonstick vegetable cooking spray. Spoon cooked sausage into the bottom of the ramekins. Crack 1 egg into a small bowl, then carefully slip it on top of the sausage. Repeat with other ramekin. Season with salt and pepper.

Bake the eggs 10 minutes. Spoon 2 tablespoons cream over each egg and sprinkle it with grated cheese. Bake the eggs 3 to 8 minutes more until they are set and the cheese is melted.

Recipe makes 2 servings.

Buttermilk Pancakes

From the time I was a child, pancakes on weekend mornings have been a special treat. When I married Randy, I discovered not everyone makes them round. For years, Randy has delighted our sons, and the biggest kid in our family—me—with pancakes made into animal shapes and letters of the alphabet. Create your own morning fun with these light and fluffy buttermilk pancakes.

INGREDIENTS:

2 cups flour

1½ tablespoons sugar

1 teaspoon baking soda

¾ teaspoon salt

¼ teaspoon baking powder

2 eggs

2½ cups buttermilk

1 tablespoon vegetable oil

¼ teaspoon vanilla

Lightly grease the top of a griddle with vegetable oil and heat over medium-low heat.

In a large bowl, stir together flour, sugar, baking soda, salt, and baking powder until well mixed. Add eggs, buttermilk, vegetable oil, and vanilla and stir until all of the dry ingredients are well mixed and only a few small lumps remain.

Ladle the batter onto the griddle to form 4½-inch-round or animal-shaped pancakes. When bubbles form on top of the batter, flip the pancakes over and cook until they are golden on the bottom.

Serve immediately or transfer the pancakes to a warm platter, cover with foil, and place in a warm oven until ready to serve. Serve the pancakes with warm maple syrup, fruit preserves, or Hot Blueberry Conserve (page 91).

Recipe makes 16 4½-inch pancakes.

German Apple Pancake

The memory of a light, puffy pancake enjoyed in a pancake house on Green Bay Road in Wilmette, Illinois, inspired this recipe for German Apple Pancake. It was cooked in a well-seasoned iron skillet, and the glistening, sweet top crust was rich with apples and cinnamon. For breakfast or a hot-from-the-oven delectable dessert, delight guests and loved ones with my version of this mouthwatering deep dish pancake.

INGREDIENTS:

Batter:

1 cup flour

2 teaspoons sugar

¼ teaspoon baking powder

¾ cup milk

3 eggs

1 teaspoon vanilla

3 tablespoons unsalted butter

Sifted confectioners' sugar,
   for garnish

Warm maple syrup

Topping:

1 tablespoon unsalted butter

1 cup peeled, chopped apples

2½ tablespoons sugar

1 teaspoon cinnamon

¼ teaspoon freshly
   grated nutmeg

Breakfast & Brunch

Preheat oven to 425 degrees.

Melt 1 tablespoon unsalted butter in a small skillet, and add apple slices. Sauté over medium-low heat until the apples are soft, 4 to 5 minutes, and set aside.

In a small bowl or cup, stir together sugar, cinnamon, and nutmeg; set aside.

Place a 10-inch iron or ovenproof skillet, or 9-inch cake pan, in the oven to preheat while mixing the batter. In a medium bowl, stir together flour, sugar, and baking powder. Whisk in milk, eggs, and vanilla until the batter is well blended and only a few small lumps remain. Stir in sautéed apples.

Remove the skillet from the oven. Melt 3 tablespoons of unsalted butter in it, then pour in the batter all at once. Top with reserved cinnamon sugar mixture.

Return the skillet to the oven. Bake the German pancake 15 to 20 minutes until top crust is puffy and a cake tester inserted into the center has only small crumbs clinging to it.

Cool the pancake 5 minutes, then loosen it from the pan and transfer it to a serving plate. Dust with sifted confectioners' sugar and serve with warm maple syrup.

Recipe makes one 10-inch German pancake
(approximately 4 servings).

Cinnamon French Toast

Here is a delicious way to start any day. Thick slices of French bread are dipped in a rich egg, milk, and cinnamon mixture and cooked until they're golden brown. Serve with a dusting of powdered sugar, warm maple syrup, and fresh fruit or hot blueberry conserve, and you can now enjoy a pancake house-style breakfast without leaving home!

INGREDIENTS:

4 eggs

1 cup milk

½ teaspoon cinnamon

16 ¾-inch-thick slices French bread, sliced at an angle

2 tablespoons margarine (divided)

1 tablespoon sifted confectioners' sugar, for garnish

Warm maple syrup

1 recipe Hot Blueberry Conserve, for garnish

In a large bowl, whip eggs with a fork, add milk, and whip until the mixture is well blended. Stir in cinnamon. Soak half the bread slices in the egg mixture 2 minutes, then turn them over and soak them 1 more minute.

Meanwhile, preheat a griddle or large skillet over medium-low heat. When the griddle is hot, melt 1 tablespoon of margarine on the griddle and tilt to coat.

Place egg-soaked bread slices on the griddle, cook 1½ to 2 minutes until the bottom of the French toast is golden brown. Turn the slices over and cook 2 more minutes, or until bottoms are golden brown and French toast is cooked through.

Cook remaining egg-soaked French bread and serve with a dusting of sifted confectioners sugar, warm maple syrup, and Hot Blueberry Conserve, if desired.

Recipe serves 4.

Hot Blueberry Conserve

For a special breakfast treat, spoon Hot Blueberry Conserve over French toast or pancakes. Conserve is also delicious on toasted English muffins, bagels, ice cream, pound cake, and other desserts.

INGREDIENTS:

2 cups fresh or frozen blueberries

¼ cup sugar

3 tablespoons water

In a medium saucepan, stir together blueberries, sugar, and water. Cook over medium heat until mixture begins to boil; reduce heat to low.

Simmer the blueberry mixture 7 to 8 minutes, stirring frequently, until the sugar dissolves and the mixture thickens.

Transfer the conserve to a serving bowl; it will thicken as it cools. Spoon it over Cinnamon French Toast or Buttermilk Pancakes.

Recipe makes approximately 2¼ cups.

We have two directions to go in this pairing, depending on your mood. This savory tart breaks down into sweet onions, buttery cheese, silky custard, and a bit of pungent/piquant from the cayenne, spinach, and onions.

Our favorite pairing is Champagne or sparkling wine. We like the festive air and the smiles these tiny bubbles seem to inspire. Its tart acidity works beautifully, and the yeasty, apple flavors play well with the pastry. Then again, a dry Riesling or Alsace works quite well, too.

$ Freizenet Carta Nevada (Spain)

$$ Chateau St. Michelle/Dr. Loosen "Eroica" (Columbia Valley, Washington)

$$$ Champagne Deutz (Reims, France)

Onion and Spinach Tart

Perfect for a springtime weekend brunch or cool-weather dinner, this savory tart is filled with a creamy cheese and fresh spinach filling that satisfies year round.

INGREDIENTS:

Pastry:

1¼ cups flour

½ teaspoon salt

6 tablespoons cold unsalted butter

3 to 4 tablespoons ice water

Filling:

1 tablespoon olive oil

1 tablespoon unsalted butter

1 large onion, sliced

1¾ cups shredded Swiss cheese

1 cup fresh spinach, rinsed and stems removed

3 eggs

⅔ cup half-and-half

¼ teaspoon cayenne pepper

¼ teaspoon salt

⅛ teaspoon freshly ground pepper

Breakfast & Brunch

Preheat the oven to 375 degrees.

To make the pastry, place flour and salt in the bowl of a processor and pulse to mix. Slice butter into 6 pieces and add to flour. Pulse until butter is pea-size. Add 3 tablespoons ice water; process until pastry forms a ball, adding additional water if mixture seems dry. Remove the pastry, wrap it in plastic wrap, and refrigerate 30 minutes.

On a floured surface or pastry cloth, roll out the pastry 2 inches wider than the tart pan. Fold the pastry in half, transfer to tart pan, and unfold it, fitting it into pan. Fold the edges of the pastry under to reinforce the sides of the tart and pinch off any excess pastry along rim. Cover the tart with plastic wrap and refrigerate it while preparing the filling.

Preheat a large sauté pan over medium heat; add olive oil, butter, and onion. Sauté until onion is soft, then transfer it to the bottom of the tart and top with shredded cheese and spinach.

In a small bowl, whisk eggs and half-and-half. Add cayenne pepper, salt, and pepper and stir. Pour the mixture over the cheese. Place the tart pan on a baking sheet and bake at 375 degrees 40 to 45 minutes, or until pastry is brown and filling is puffed and golden.

Remove the tart from the oven; set aside 10 minutes until the filling is set. Slice into wedges and serve.

Recipe makes one 11-inch tart (approximately 6 servings).

The textures of flaky, butter-rich pastry; soft, creamy-thick custard; and slightly chewy, sweet-pungent onions and the delicate acid-bite of fresh tomatoes—this is an "arche-type" combination that forms the basis for tens of thousands of recipes. We profess a certain fascination with culinary arche-types, the underlying "bones" of different recipes for a particular dish.

Hidden in this classic combina-tion of acid vs. butterfat/oil; pungent/tart vs. sweet/bland; textures both creamy and flaky-dry is a well-camouflaged wine lover's trap—the nutmeg-enhanced custard!

This soft-spoken, old-world spice is highly aromatic when freshly grated. Forget that powdered sawdust sold in the little tins. Its "warm" flavor is seldom experienced fully, except when it's used in eggnog at Christmas.

For pairing, we choose to mirror the sly but creamy custard's nutmeg turbo-charger with an Oregon Pinot Gris. A highly aromatic, slender-but-tough wine reminiscent of our beloved Alsace, we find Texas ruby red grapefruit, lime blos-soms, apricot, and nutmeg in a refined white wine.

Tomato Galette

I watched my friend, Agnes Guard, assemble a tart similar to this one while visiting her home in Dijon, France. Agnes served it as a first course, but it's equally divine served for brunch or as an entrée for a light dinner.

INGREDIENTS:

Pastry:

1¼ cups flour

½ teaspoon salt

6 tablespoons unsalted butter

3 to 4 tablespoons ice water

Place flour and salt into the bowl of a food processor and pulse several times to mix. Slice butter into 6 to 8 pieces and add to flour mixture. Pulse until butter is pea-size. Add ice water; pulse until pastry forms a ball, adding additional water as necessary.

Remove the pastry from the processor, wrap in plastic wrap, and refrigerate at least 30 minutes.

When the pastry is cold, roll it out on a floured pastry cloth or lightly floured surface. Fold it in half, transfer it to a 10-inch tart pan, and unfold it, fitting the pastry into the bottom of the pan. Fold the pastry edges under to reinforce the sides of the tart, then roll a rolling pin across the top of the tart pan to remove any excess pastry. Cover the galette shell with plastic wrap and refrigerate it while preparing the filling.

Breakfast & Brunch

Galette Filling:

1 tablespoon olive oil

1 tablespoon butter

1 large onion, sliced

1¾ cups grated Gruyère or Swiss cheese

2 eggs

1¼ cups milk

¼ teaspoon salt

⅛ teaspoon freshly ground black pepper

⅛ teaspoon freshly grated nutmeg

1 tomato, sliced

1 tablespoon chopped fresh Italian parsley

Preheat the oven to 400 degrees.

Heat a large skillet over medium heat; add oil and butter, swirling to mix. Add onion and sauté until it is soft and translucent. Transfer the cooked onion to the bottom of the tart shell and sprinkle grated cheese over them.

In a small bowl, whisk eggs and milk with a fork. Add salt, pepper, and nutmeg and stir to mix. Pour the mixture over the cheese.

Arrange tomato slices on top of the galette and place the tart pan on a sturdy baking sheet. Bake at 400 degrees 35 to 40 minutes, or until filling is set and pastry is golden. Remove galette from oven and sprinkle with Italian parsley. Allow to rest 10 minutes before slicing.

Recipe serves 6.

For a red, we ventured to Mendocino County to find Il Cuore's Rosso Classico. The willowy body of this rare beauty shows a restrained elegance redolent of crushed dark berries, sun-dried cherries, Damson plum, and spice (yes, nutmeg).

We believe that some of the Tempernillo/old-vine Grenache blends out of Navarro, Spain, would add to the party with flavors of rose petal, fresh red-berry jam, tart cherries, and dark chocolate. If you listen very carefully with your palate, you will perceive a spicebox and eucalyptus thread running beneath the more flamboyant flavors.

$ **Campo de Viejo "Borsao" Old-Vine Grenache/Tempernillo** (Navarro, Spain)

$ **Il Cuore "Rosso Classico"** (Mendocino, California)

$$ **King Estate Pinot Gris** (Willamette, Oregon)

Cinnamon Coffee Cake

The aroma of something cinnamony baking makes me feel relaxed and cozy. On weekends, nothing starts the day like warm coffee cake, with fresh fruit and a cup of tea. Try this tender cake with its spicy crumb topping for coffee with friends or an evening snack.

INGREDIENTS:

2¼ cups flour

2 teaspoons baking powder

¾ teaspoon salt

¼ teaspoon baking soda

½ cup unsalted butter, softened

1 cup sugar

2 eggs

1 teaspoon vanilla

½ teaspoon almond extract

1 cup milk

¾ cup packed brown sugar

½ cup oatmeal

1 tablespoon flour

1½ teaspoons cinnamon

1 tablespoon butter, melted

Preheat the oven to 350 degrees. In a medium bowl, stir together flour, baking powder, salt, and soda and set aside.

In the large bowl of an electric mixer, cream softened butter and sugar until light and fluffy, about 5 minutes. Add eggs, vanilla, and almond extract and beat well.

Add the flour mixture to the creamed mixture, alternating with the milk, starting and ending with the dry ingredients. Pour the batter into a greased and floured 9- by 13-inch pan.

In a small bowl, combine brown sugar, oatmeal, 1 tablespoon flour, cinnamon, and melted butter, mixing well with a fork or your fingers. Sprinkle this crumb topping over the batter and bake in a preheated oven 22 to 25 minutes, or until a cake tester inserted into the middle comes out clean.

Serve the coffee cake warm.

Recipe makes one 9- by 13-inch cake.

Irish Soda Bread

This traditional Irish loaf, studded with raisins and rich with butter, bears a traditional cross and a dusting of sparkling sugar on top. Warm from the oven with butter or jam, Irish Soda Bread is delicious any time of day. Serve this slightly sweet bread for breakfast, brunch, or afternoon tea.

INGREDIENTS:

2 cups flour

1 teaspoon baking powder

¾ teaspoon baking soda

½ teaspoon salt

3 tablespoons sugar

5 tablespoons unsalted butter, cold

⅔ cup raisins

¾ cup buttermilk

1 tablespoon unsalted butter, melted

1 tablespoon sparkling sugar or 2 teaspoons granulated sugar

Preheat the oven to 350 degrees. In a large bowl, stir together flour, baking powder, baking soda, salt, and sugar. Slice the cold butter into 5 pieces and cut it into the flour mixture with a pastry blender until it looks like coarse crumbs.

Stir in raisins and buttermilk, mixing just until all of the flour is incorporated; do not overmix. If the dough is too dry, stir in additional buttermilk, 1 teaspoon at a time.

Turn dough out onto a lightly floured surface; knead 1 to 2 minutes until its surface is smooth. Shape the dough into a round loaf and pat it with your fingertips until it's 1½ inches thick. Place the dough in a greased round 8- or 9-inch cake pan. With a very sharp knife, cut a cross ½ inch deep through the center of the dough.

Brush the top of the loaf with melted butter, sprinkle with sparkling sugar, and bake in a preheated oven 30 to 35 minutes until a cake tester inserted in the middle comes out clean. Serve the bread warm or at room temperature.

Recipe makes 1 loaf.

Barbecued Spareribs

On weekends, it's hard to beat a platter full of tasty, lick-your-fingers ribs. These pork spareribs, cooked slowly over low heat, are tender and juicy, with a smoky sauce that seals in the moisture. For spur-of-the-moment gatherings, keep extra ribs on hand in the freezer and double the sauce recipe. Cold or hot, rainy or sunny, the weather is always perfect for grilling.

INGREDIENTS:

1 5-to-6-pound rack pork spareribs

2 tablespoons vegetable oil

1 cup diced onion

3 large garlic cloves, minced

1 cup ketchup

⅓ cup chili sauce

2 tablespoons brown sugar

¼ teaspoon freshly ground
black pepper

1 tablespoon balsamic vinegar

1 tablespoon freshly squeezed
lemon juice

1 teaspoon Worcestershire sauce

¾ teaspoon Liquid Smoke

Coarse salt and freshly ground
black pepper

Preheat a medium saucepan over low heat. Add oil, swirl to coat the bottom of the pan, and add onion. Sauté the onion 5 minutes until soft; stir in garlic and cook 1 more minute.

Stir in ketchup, chili sauce, brown sugar, pepper, vinegar, lemon juice, Worcestershire sauce, and Liquid Smoke. Simmer the sauce 30 minutes, stirring occasionally.

Preheat the grill. Season the ribs with coarse salt and freshly ground pepper. When the grill is hot, adjust the heat to low and place the ribs right side down; cook 10 minutes. Turn the ribs over, baste with barbecue sauce, and cook them slowly, basting often with additional sauce. Ribs will cook a total of 1½ to 2 hours, depending on the size of the rack and temperature of the grill.

Recipe serves 6.

This most cherished of culinary pleasures has become firmly entrenched in our minds as the archetype "American casual" food.

The classic pairing is a beer: a good lager or, our preference, a pale ale. The important thing is that it have sufficient hops to slice through the fat-rich meat and clingy-intense sauce.

We sometimes venture off the beaten path and serve a dry rosé of good acidity. The delightful tart-cherry and luscious raspberry flavors are refreshing and fun.

A third choice is a Carmenére/ Cabernet Sauvignon blend. Bing cherries tango dramatically with dark-plum and cedar-studded semisweet chocolate. This larger-than-life combination rocks.

$ **Sierra Nevada Pale Ale**
(Grass Valley, California)

$ **Bonny Doone Vin Gris de Cigare Pink Wine**
(California)

$+ **Montes "Limited Selection" Cabernet/Carmenère "La Finca" Estate, Apalta District**
(Colchagua Valley, Chile)

Grilled Lemon Chicken

Casual weekends and grilling just naturally go together. For family meals or relaxed backyard gatherings with a few friends, this easy-does-it recipe uses items already in your spice cabinet and refrigerator.

INGREDIENTS:

5 pounds chicken pieces

¼ cup butter

3 tablespoons freshly squeezed lemon juice

½ teaspoon paprika

¼ teaspoon garlic powder

Coarse salt and freshly ground black pepper, to taste

Preheat the outdoor grill. Rinse and dry chicken pieces, removing any excess fat with a sharp knife. When the grill is hot, turn the heat to medium-low. Place the chicken on the grill skin side down, and cook 10 minutes.

Meanwhile, make the lemon sauce. In a small saucepan, melt butter over low heat. Add fresh lemon juice, paprika, garlic powder, and salt and pepper.

Turn the chicken over and baste it with lemon sauce. Cook it for a total of 35 to 45 minutes, depending on the thickness of meat and the temperature of the grill, turning frequently. Baste the chicken often until the final 10 minutes of cooking.

Recipe makes 6 to 8 servings.

Here we have aromatic, pure, uncomplicated flavors. The chicken features silky and crisp textures, low fat, and low acidity. Seems like an ideal time to crack open a bottle of Chardonnay!

$ Meridian Chardonnay
(Paso Robles, California)

$+ Edna Valley Chardonnay
(Napa, California)

$$$ Arcadian Estate Chardonnay
(Napa, California)

Grilled Chicken with Sweet Apricot Ginger Sauce

Fresh ginger and summer apricots add excitement to grilled chicken in this made-for-summer-weekends recipe. Serve it with grilled corn and a fresh fruit salad.

INGREDIENTS:

6 chicken breast halves,
  bone-in or boneless

w cup apricot nectar

2 tablespoons vodka

2 slices fresh ginger, 4-inch thick

Coarse salt and freshly
  ground black pepper

3 fresh apricots

2 to 3 teaspoons sugar

1 tablespoon butter

At least 1 hour before cooking, rinse the chicken and pat it dry with paper towels.

In a casserole or other dish large enough to accommodate the chicken, stir together the apricot nectar, vodka, and ginger slices. Add the chicken pieces to this marinade, cover, and chill for at least 1 hour.

Preheat the grill or light the coals. When the grill is ready, remove the chicken from the marinade, reserving the marinade for later use. Season the chicken with salt and freshly ground black pepper and grill it 20 to 25 minutes, turning frequently to prevent scorching.

While the chicken is grilling, pour the marinade into a small saucepan. Slice apricots and add them to the marinade, along with the sugar. Bring the mixture to a boil, reduce heat to medium-low, and simmer 10 minutes. Stir in butter.

When the chicken is tender and cooked through, arrange it on a serving platter. Spoon the sauce over it and serve.

Recipe serves 6.

We have three main components in this luscious dish—the tender chicken breast, the sweet, heady apricots, and the tangy ginger. Vodka is by nature a grain-neutral spirit—no flavor or aroma—and the alcohol evaporates long before serving, so it doesn't enter into the pairing equation. A Riesling (the flavors must be sweeter than the dish or the they will show their dark side), a Gewürztraminer, or even an Alsace Pinot Gris would show off this recipe properly.

$ Chateau St. Jean Gewürztraminer
(Sonoma, California)

$$ Chateau St. Michelle/Dr. Loosen "Eroica"
(Columbia Valley, Washington)

$$ Hugel Tokay Pinot Gris
(Alsace, France)

Grilled Teriyaki Pork Chops

Pork chops are so flavorful, they taste great grilled without marinade. But there's nothing like a really tender, juicy Teriyaki Pork Chop, especially when you feel like firing up the grill on the weekend. The teriyaki marinade can be assembled in less than 5 minutes, and the pork chops marinate from 1 hour to overnight. This recipe is designed for those who want the freedom to pursue weekend activities and still have dinner ready for family or guests in 30 minutes.

INGREDIENTS:

¾ cup soy sauce

¼ cup brown sugar, packed

2 cloves garlic, crushed

2 ½-inch pieces fresh ginger, peeled

6 1-inch-thick pork rib chops

In a large pan, stir together soy sauce, brown sugar, garlic, and ginger. Place rib chops in the marinade, turning once to coat both sides. Cover tightly and refrigerate at least 1 hour or overnight.

Preheat the grill. When it's hot, place the chops over coals and discard the marinade. Cook 5 minutes, turn the chops over, and cook 5 more minutes.

Grill the chops 5 to 7 more minutes, turning partway through the cooking time; serve.

Recipe makes 6 servings.

Building on a framework of slightly sweet, crisp pork, we add the troika of salty soy, pungent garlic, and the cleansing twang of ginger root. When accompanied by random swirls of smoke and seductive aromas, and the grill music crackling and sighing, this dish requires a slightly brazen wine.

Carmenère, the long-lost grape of Bordeaux, has beautiful boysenberry, blackberry, and ripe plum, a rich, smoky, character, and even a bit of vanilla from its contact with wood in the oak barrels of its youth.

Mourvedre, another good choice, has lush blackberry, blueberries, dark chocolate, and saddle leather supported by sturdy tannins that, with air contact, slowly melt into soft velvet. The whites that can sing on this stage are rare, but a good Alsace Pinot Gris could do it with Fred Astaire's grace.

$ Mont Gras
Carmenère RSV
(Maipo Valley, Chile)

$$ Cline Mourvedre
"Ancient Vine"
(Contra Costa County, California)

$$$ Hugel Gewürztraminer
(Alsace, France)

Grilled Leg of Lamb

For the grill master whose repertoire consists mainly of hamburgers, leg of lamb is an easy next step even novice cooks can manage. The key to success is marinating the lamb in a mixture of wine and olive oil before placing it on the grill, then cooking it slowly over low to medium-hot coals.

Grilled Leg of Lamb is an exciting variation on a popular springtime dish for weekend family meals and alfresco dining. Serve it with buttery, sautéed new potatoes, fresh asparagus, and seasonal fruit. Set up a table near the garden and decorate it with colorful place mats, small clay pots of fresh herbs, and candles in lanterns to protect them from breezes. Then enjoy a beautiful and relaxing moonlit evening, the real star of which is a succulent meal prepared with love.

INGREDIENTS:

1 6- to 7-pound leg of lamb

4 large cloves garlic

2 cups dry red wine

4 cup olive oil

3 tablespoons chopped fresh rosemary

1 tablespoon dried sage

1 tablespoon dried basil

2 teaspoon salt

4 teaspoon freshly ground black pepper

Entrées

Early in the day, or the day before, trim lamb of extra fat and cut ¾-inch-deep slits in the lamb. Peel and slice garlic into thin slices and insert into the slits. Transfer lamb to a large dish or casserole.

In a medium bowl, stir together the wine, oil, rosemary, sage, basil, salt, and pepper. Pour this mixture over the lamb, cover tightly, and refrigerate 6 hours or overnight, turning the lamb occasionally.

Preheat the grill. When the coals have died down to medium heat, remove the lamb from the marinade and place it over coals; reserve the marinade. Pour the marinade into a medium saucepan and bring it to a boil over high heat. Reduce the heat to medium-low and simmer sauce 10 minutes.

Cook the lamb, uncovered, about 1½ hours, turning occasionally, until an instant-read thermometer registers 150 degrees for medium-rare or 160 degrees for medium. Baste the lamb with the cooked marinade every 15 minutes during grilling.

When the lamb is cooked to desired doneness, remove it from the grill and place it on a platter. Cover it with foil and set aside 15 minutes.

Recipe serves 8 to 10.

Luckily, the United States produces some amazing "Bordeaux blends" in California and Washington, and the labels are in English. Called "Meritage," "Claret," or simply "Red Table Wine" they often have impressive names such as "Opus 1," or "Marlstone." These yummy blends of Cabernet Sauvignon and Merlot, or Cabernet Franc, Petite Verdiot, or Malbec (sometimes all of the above) are the proverbial "match made in Heaven" when served with this fantastic leg of lamb.

$$ Newton Claret
(Napa, California)

$$$ Beringer "
Alluvium Red"
(Knights Valley, California)

$$$ Merryvale "Profile"
(Napa, California)

Henrietta's Brown Gravy

Making really good gravy is an art, of which my grandmother, Henrietta Schnoes, was a master. Not knowing where my path would lead, I neglected to take careful notes, but I can still picture the way she painstakingly stirred potato water into the pan juices, scraping up all the brown bits to capture every bit of flavor. Grandmom's gravy was unfailingly dark, rich, and smooth.

I remember my first attempt to make gravy. Randy and I had been married only a few months, and we invited Paul and Margie Bohn, lifelong friends of my parents, to our tiny Houston apartment for dinner. Trying to keep things simple, I cooked a beef roast and whipped potatoes. All these years later, two images still come to mind. One, I had trouble timing everything so dinner would be ready all at the same time, and two, the gravy yielded less than a cup of thick, flavorless, brown glue. It certainly didn't begin to resemble the liquid magic my grandmother made so easily.

I became a student of gravy making, carefully watching my mother whenever we visited during the holidays, and keeping a careful eye on Grandmom's technique when my grandparents came to Texas. Each roast or turkey became a testing ground for my gravy-making skills and eventually I, too, learned the art.

Becoming a gravy master takes practice and an understanding of where the flavors originate. I roast meat and poultry at a high temperature during the first 20 or 30 minutes, because that yields darker, richer drippings. I realize now that my grandmother always made whipped potatoes with her roasts, not just because roast beef or pork tastes great with mashed potatoes and gravy, but because the potato cooking water adds flavor to gravy. I also learned from my mother that she and Grandmom always dropped a bouillon cube or two into the pan juices to compensate for diluting them with the potato water.

Entrées

This recipe is the product of years of making brown gravy for Sunday dinners and family celebrations as well as observing my mother and grandmother. With this recipe as a guide, who knows—you may be the next gravy master!

INGREDIENTS:

Pan drippings from roast meat

3 cups reserved hot cooking water used to boil potatoes for mashed potatoes

1 to 2 cups boiling water, depending on amount of pan drippings

2 bouillon cubes

½ cup flour

Cold water to make a slurry

Salt and freshly ground black pepper, to taste

Remove the roast meat from the roasting pan; set the roast aside on a cutting board, and cover it with foil while making gravy.

Spoon fat from the roasting pan and discard. Place the roasting pan over the stove burners and turn the heat to medium-low. Stir in the hot cooking water from the potatoes, scraping up the brown bits from the bottom of the roasting pan. Add boiling water and bouillon cubes and cook several minutes until bouillon dissolves, stirring occasionally.

Meanwhile, place flour in a medium bowl. Whisk enough cold water into the flour to create a smooth, creamy slurry the thickness of egg whites. Whisk the slurry, a little at a time, into the broth mixture, stirring constantly until the gravy begins to thicken. If mixture is too thick, stir in a little extra potato or tap water. If it's too thin, mix together additional flour slurry and whisk it into gravy.

Season the gravy with black pepper and a pinch of salt, if needed. Turn heat to low and keep the gravy hot, stirring occasionally, until ready to serve. Transfer the gravy to a pitcher or gravy boat.

Recipe makes 4 to 5 cups gravy.

We find that the simple dishes, properly prepared without watching the clock, are renewing to the spirit to prepare and delicious to eat. In some magical bit of sorcery, these uncomplicated recipes transcend an ordinary day, infusing the house with tantalizing aromas and the awareness that something special is in the works. Our kitchen becomes irresistible, drawing children, husbands, wives, dogs, and cats to the warmth of the hearth—kitchen magic at its best. Of course, a glass of good wine helps, too.

The choice of wine is uncomplicated as well. We have melt-in-your-mouth beef, a hint of sweet/pungent flavor, and a savory, rich gravy. We always enjoy a chance to drag out the big reds—the kind with tannin that would scare a lesser dish.

$$ "Mak" (Snowy River) Cabernet/Shiraz/Merlot (Coonawarra, Australia)

$$$ Treana Red Table Wine (Paso Robles, California)

$$$ Chappellet Cabernet Sauvignon (Napa, California)

Roast Beef

When I think of family meals with Grandad and Grandmom Schnoes, seated at their massive mahogany dining room table which was always draped in damask linens and facing the German cuckoo clock hanging high on the wall, I am reminded of the many times Grandmother Henrietta served roast beef with buttery whipped potatoes and the best gravy I have ever tasted. Those were comfort meals at their finest, and the warm memories I still carry from those simple gatherings inspire me to create the same meals for my family. Distinguished enough for Sunday dinner, but easy enough for weekday meals, serve roast beef the next time your family or friends need a hug.

INGREDIENTS:

1 3½- to 4-pound beef bottom round roast

1¼ teaspoons coarse salt

½ teaspoon freshly ground black pepper

5 cloves garlic, minced

Preheat the oven to 400 degrees. Place roast in a roasting pan and season with salt and pepper. Rub some of the garlic over the sides of the roast and sprinkle the remaining garlic over the top, pressing down to help the garlic adhere.

Roast the beef in a preheated oven for 25 minutes to brown bottom of meat; this ensures dark, flavorful drippings for gravy. Reduce the oven temperature to 325 degrees. Continue roasting the meat 1 to 1½ hours, until a meat thermometer registers 145 degrees for medium-rare or 160 degrees for medium. Remove the meat from the oven, transfer it to a cutting board, and cover it with foil to keep warm.

Remove the fat from the roasting pan and pour the remaining meat juices over sliced roast beef, or reserve for gravy.

Recipe serves 8.

Entrées

Brown Butter and Pecan Rocky Mountain Trout

This beautiful dish was inspired years ago by a meal Randy and I enjoyed at the Snake River Saloon in Keystone, Colorado, on our honeymoon. In this easy but impressive recipe, unsalted butter is browned in the oven to impart a nutty flavor, then a splash of Marsala wine is stirred in, along with pecan halves. When butterflied trout is baked in this sweet, toasty mixture, it tastes positively sublime.

INGREDIENTS:

2 freshwater trout, cleaned and butterflied

3 to 4 tablespoons unsalted butter

1 tablespoon Marsala wine

Coarse salt and freshly ground black pepper

⅓ cup pecan halves

Preheat the oven to 400 degrees. Rinse the trout and pat it dry with paper towels.

In a baking dish large enough to accommodate both trout, heat 3 to 4 tablespoons butter, depending on the size of the pan, in the oven until it begins to brown, about 5 minutes. Take care that it doesn't burn. Remove from the oven and stir in the Marsala.

Season the trout well with salt and freshly ground black pepper. Place the trout, white flesh side down, in the baking dish and add pecans to the brown butter surrounding it.

Cover the baking dish tightly with a lid or foil and bake in a preheated oven 10 minutes. Using a metal spatula, carefully turn the trout over so the skin side is down. Spoon some browned butter mixture over fish, cover, and return to oven 5 minutes, or until fish is done.

Transfer the trout to dinner plates, spoon the brown butter sauce over it, and garnish with pecans.

Recipe serves 2.

This recipe mixes the delicate flavors of trout with potent Marsala, sweet nutmeats, and sweet butter. Our wine must be a bit sweeter than the recipe, yet not a buttery Chardonnay, lest all that butter cloy the palate.

The traditional pairing is a Riesling, and with good reason. Until the accidental production of White Zinfandel by Bob Trinchero of Sutter Home (he was actually working on producing a richer Red Zinfandel at the time), German Rieslings were recognized as among the finest white wines in the world. Their fall from grace is to our benefit, however, because now a world-class bottle costs less than a quarter of a similar-quality Chardonnay or sparkling wine.

$ Hogue Riesling
(Columbia Valley, Washington)

$$ J. J. Prum Riesling
(Wehlener Sonnenuhr Spätlese, Mosel, Germany)

$$ Bonny Doon "The Heart Has Its Rieslings"
(Santa Cruz, California)

Beginning with a delicate white fish, we lay a foundation of pungent, tart, and piquant. Layered on this are soft, sweet butter and olive oil. Next we construct a similarly balanced, but much more finely sculpted layer of flavor—the sauce. Consisting of the slightly sweet, slightly piquant poblano, the acid tartness of fresh lime juice, and the pungent, classic duo of cumin and garlic, the addition of fish broth pulls the sauce together. It now has subtle nuances of aroma and flavor, plus textures to bring out the best in the fish.

When pairing a wine with this unusually constructed recipe, why not take a giant step outside the traditional. We need a white wine of subtle sophistication with enough silken body to enfold this trio of flavors. A bit of residual sweetness is needed, just enough to counterbalance the poblano's bit of piquancy.

Oven-Baked Cod Fillets with Sauce Verde

I prefer cooking fish in the oven because it stays so moist. Here, cod fillets enjoy a Southwestern spice rub before baking, and a mild, roasted poblano sauce is served alongside.

Roasting the poblano pepper is as easy as turning on your oven broiler, and the process can be done hours ahead. Then, in a matter of seconds, whip up the sauce in a blender. Voila—you have a flavorful fish dinner with a Texas flair.

INGREDIENTS:

2 pounds cod fillets

1 large or 2 small poblano peppers

1 teaspoon coarse salt

1 teaspoon dark chili powder

½ teaspoon lemon pepper

½ teaspoon garlic powder

¼ teaspoon ground cumin

2 tablespoons olive oil

1 tablespoon butter

1 recipe Sauce Verde

1 lemon, cut into wedges, for garnish

1 small bunch fresh cilantro, for garnish

At least 1 hour before serving, preheat the broiler. Place a pan on a lower oven rack to catch any juices that drip while you're roasting the poblano pepper. When the broiler is hot, place the poblano directly on oven rack under broiler, turning it with tongs as needed to blacken skin on all sides of pepper, about 20 to 25 minutes.

Remove the roasted pepper and place in a plastic zipper bag to steam and soften. Close the bag and set aside.

Entrées

To cook the cod, preheat the oven to 400 degrees. Rinse the cod fillets and pat them dry with paper towels.

In a small bowl, stir together salt, chili powder, lemon pepper, garlic powder, and cumin until well mixed. Sprinkle the fillets with the seasoning mixture and gently rub it in.

Place a baking dish in the oven with olive oil and butter. When the butter has melted, remove the dish, and swirl it to mix the oil and butter. Dip both sides of the fillets in the oil mixture and place them skin side up in pan.

Cover tightly with a lid or foil and bake the fillets in a preheated oven 10 minutes. Remove from the oven, turn the fillets over with a metal spatula, and return them to oven. Bake 5 to 10 minutes, depending on the thickness of the fillets. When they are done, prepare Sauce Verde.

Sauce Verde:

1 large poblano pepper, roasted

3 tablespoons broth from cooked fish

1 tablespoon freshly squeezed lime juice

1 large clove garlic, peeled and chopped

4 teaspoon salt

4 teaspoon ground cumin

Peel the blackened skin from the poblano pepper, split it open with a knife, and remove the stem and seeds. Place the pepper in a blender.

Add broth, lime juice, garlic, salt, and cumin and purée the mixture until smooth.

To serve, transfer fish to a serving platter, garnish with fresh lemon wedges and sprigs of cilantro, and pass the sauce.

Recipe serves 4.

A white of layered, subtle flavors such as those found in the rare whites of Rhône (we feel that these archaic, incredibly complex white blends are perhaps the most pleasurable of all white wines) or perhaps a California Meritage of some depth? Then again, we can say, "To heck with subtlety. How about a luscious Moscato?" An Italian-style "frizzante" (slightly sparkling) Moscato shows such straightforward honeydew melon and peach flavors, it provides an unadorned stage on which the cod can star.

$ Martin & Weyrich
Moscato "Allegro"
(Paso Robles, California)

$$$ Caymus "Conundrum"
(Napa, California)

$$$ Chapoutier Hermitage
Blanc "Chante-Alouette"
(Rhône, France)

Crab Cakes

I always think of my sweet mother-in-law, Pat Rost Shilstone, when I make crab cakes; they are one of her favorite quick-meal entrées. My version has just the right amount of "zip," thanks to the addition of Worcestershire sauce and Tabasco, but feel free to add additional Tabasco if you like your crab cakes really spicy.

INGREDIENTS:

½ pound fresh lump crab meat

1½ cups soft bread crumbs

1 egg

2 tablespoons mayonnaise

1 tablespoon freshly squeezed lemon juice

1½ teaspoons Dijon mustard

1 teaspoon Worcestershire sauce

¼ teaspoon Tabasco

1 tablespoon chopped fresh parsley

Salt and pepper to taste

½ cup plain or seasoned bread crumbs

2 tablespoons olive oil

At least 1 hour before cooking, stir all ingredients, except seasoned bread crumbs and olive oil, with a fork in a medium bowl. With your hands, form the mixture into 3-inch patties. Place the crab cakes on a platter, cover tightly, and refrigerate 1 to 8 hours.

Pour bread crumbs into a small dish. Dredge each crab cake in them.

Preheat a large skillet over medium-low heat; add olive oil, then crab cakes. Sautè the crab cakes approximately 3 minutes, or until golden brown; turn them over with a metal spatula and sauté them 3 minutes. Drain the crab cakes on paper towels and serve.

Recipe makes 4 to 5 3-inch crab cakes.

Beef Bourguignon

This classic French stew made with red wine takes about 25 minutes to prepare, then simmers unattended until you're ready to serve it. It's a perfect choice for a chilly autumn or winter evening.

Wine enhances a meal in many ways, bringing forward flavors both subtle and bold. In Christy's classic Beef Bourguignon, a historical aspect eases our wine choice. Countless generations of Burgundians fine-tuned this dish to enhance the two red wines they produced and drank—Pinot Noir and Cru Beaujolais (Gamay).

$+ Louis Jadot Pinot Noir
(Burgundy, France)

$$ Ponzi Pinot Noir
(Oregon)

$$$ Jean Marc Boillot, Volnay 1er Cru
(Burgundy, France)

INGREDIENTS:

3 pounds beef chuck roast, trimmed

3 tablespoons vegetable oil

1 large onion, chopped

3 cloves garlic, minced

2 tablespoons flour

1 10.75-ounce can beef consommé

1 cup water

1½ cups red wine

1 tablespoon tomato paste

1 teaspoon thyme

2 bay leaves

½ teaspoon coarse salt

½ teaspoon freshly ground black pepper

2 peeled carrots, sliced into ½-inch pieces

1 cup sliced white mushrooms

Cooked wide noodles or spaetzle

Cut the beef into 1-inch cubes and set aside. Heat oil in a Dutch oven over medium heat; add half the beef. Brown 2 minutes without stirring; then turn the beef and brown it on all sides. Remove from the pot and brown the remaining meat. Return the first half of the cooked beef to the Dutch oven. Add onion and garlic; cook 2 minutes, stirring often until onion and garlic soften. Sprinkle meat with the flour; cook 2 minutes, stirring, until the mixture is thick.

Pour in consommé, water, and wine. Stir in tomato paste, herbs, and seasonings. Bring the mixture to a boil, cover, and reduce heat to low. Simmer, stirring occasionally, until beef is tender, about 1½ hours. Add carrots and cook 10 to 15 minutes until they begin to soften. Stir in mushrooms and correct the seasonings. Cook 5 minutes until mushrooms soften. Serve over noodles or spaetzle.

Recipe serves 6.

We find the layered flavors of Pacific Rim cuisine thoroughly delightful. Taken separately, each ingredient has a simple purity; when combined in a carnival of color, contrasting textures, and layered flavors that enhance each other, without obscuring any individual's essence, we call it greatness. Moreover, it's good for you!

We can either go a bit sweet (peppers just can't resist sweetness) or with a tall, graceful, dryness. Think Alsace! Washington State Rieslings! Rhine wine! Australian sweeties! Texas Muscat Canelli! Just balance the sugars to match the piquant.

Chinese Almond Chicken Stir-Fry

This is one of our family's most-loved meals. The array of vegetables, still crisp and fresh-tasting from a relatively brief time in the wok, and the tender pieces of marinated chicken provide a healthy but savory meal our sports-minded sons thrive on. From the time they were young, stir-frying was one way to guarantee they would eat their vegetables. And supplying everyone with chopsticks, individual rice bowls, and a fortune cookie at each place setting ensures the meal is fun.

This recipe feeds a crowd, but all of the ingredients may be cut in half to feed a family or group of four. To tailor this dish to everyday meals, purchase ingredients already chopped or sliced to save time.

INGREDIENTS:

8 to 10 chicken breast halves

⅓ cup light soy sauce (divided)

2 tablespoons sherry

2 tablespoons cornstarch

1 14.5-ounce can lowfat chicken broth

3 tablespoons peanut oil, divided

3 cups coarsely chopped celery

1 cup coarsely chopped onion

1 bunch bok choy, coarsely chopped

1 bunch bok choy, coarsely chopped

1 8-ounce package sliced mushrooms

2 green bell peppers

1 red bell pepper, coarsely chopped

½ pound snow peas, stems trimmed

½ cup whole almonds

Cooked rice

Entrées

Wash, skin, and bone chicken breasts. Slice the meat into bite-size pieces and place them in a large bowl; add 3 tablespoons of soy sauce and the sherry. Toss to mix, cover with plastic wrap, and chill.

Spoon cornstarch into a liquid measure and whisk in a small amount of chicken broth until mixture is smooth. Add additional chicken broth to measure ½ cup; set aside.

Heat a wok or large skillet over medium-high heat. Add 1 tablespoon of oil and swirl to coat the bottom of the wok. Add 1/3 of the marinated chicken to wok, and allow it to sear; then stir-fry quickly until tender. Transfer chicken to a large bowl and stir-fry remaining chicken with additional oil as needed; set aside.

Add remaining oil to wok. Stir-fry celery, onion, and bok choy until crisp-tender. Add mushrooms, peppers, snow peas, and almonds; stir-fry 1 minute. Return the reserved chicken to the wok, and stir in the cornstarch mixture and enough of the remaining chicken broth to make a thick sauce.

Heat through and spoon almond chicken onto a large platter or into a large bowl. Serve over cooked rice.

Recipe makes 8 to 10 servings.

The second wine suggestion, Eroica, is a historical joint effort by Dr. Loosen of Germany's finest and the quiet genius of Chateau S. Michelle. The last, Jeffrey Grosset "Polish Hill," is a world-class dry Riesling with enormous presence.

$+ Hugel et fils
Pinot Gris Reserve
(Alsace, France)

$$ Chateau St.
Michelle/Dr. Loosen/"Eroica"
(Columbia Valley, Washington)

$$ Jeffrey Grosset
"Polish Hill" Riesling
(Clare Valley, Australia)

This savory pastry is extremely satisfying at the end of a long day. Traditionally, an Alsace Riesling or Pinot Blanc is served. We enjoy these wines, but there are times when the caramel richness of a dark beer seems perfect, or perhaps a simple, good quality Chardonnay. Both work very well here.

$ Kostriker Black Beer
(Germany)

$+ La Crème Chardonnay
(Sonoma, California)

$+ Domaine Weinbach Gewürztraminer
(Alsace, France)

Chicken Pot Pie

This American favorite takes a bit of time to prepare, but it's worth every minute. Creamy, satisfying, and full of old-fashioned goodness, this recipe for chicken pot pie, topped with fluffy baking powder biscuits, tastes just like grandmother made it.

INGREDIENTS:

1 3-pound chicken, rinsed

2 carrots, peeled and coarsely chopped

3 bunches celery leaves

1 medium onion, coarsely chopped

1 large potato

1 bouquet garni (2 bay leaves, ½ teaspoon whole peppercorns, ½ teaspoon dried thyme, 3 cloves, and several sprigs fresh parsley, tied in a square of cheesecloth)

Water to cover

Place chicken in a large stockpot. Add carrots, celery leaves, onion, and bouquet garni. Pour in enough water to cover chicken; cover the stockpot. Cook over high heat just until the water comes to a low boil, then reduce the heat to low and simmer the chicken 1 hour. When the chicken is cooked, transfer to a large platter; cool until it's easy to handle. Remove the meat from the bones, cutting the chicken into bite-size pieces. Save the chicken broth for later use.

Meanwhile, peel and dice the potato and cook it in a medium saucepan just until tender. Do not overcook. Drain; set aside.

Entrées

Assembly:

¼ cup flour

1 cup plus 2 tablespoons
half-and-half

1¾ cups reserved chicken
broth, strained

1¼ teaspoons salt

Generous grinding of
black pepper

Reserved chicken pieces

Reserved diced potato

3 carrots, peeled and sliced

2 celery stalks, sliced

½ medium onion, peeled
and diced

1 cup frozen mixed vegetables,
if desired

1 recipe biscuits

Heat oven to 425 degrees.

In a large saucepan, gradually whisk half-and-half into flour until
smooth; pour in chicken broth. Cook over medium heat until the
sauce thickens, adding a little extra broth if the mixture is too thick.
Season with salt and pepper. Stir in chicken pieces, diced potato,
carrots, celery, onion, and mixed vegetables. Spoon into a large
casserole dish. Top with biscuits and bake in a preheated 425 degree
oven 40 to 45 minutes, until casserole is hot and bubbly and biscuits
are golden brown.

Biscuits:

2 cups flour

3 teaspoons baking powder

½ teaspoon salt

¼ cup solid shortening,
such as Crisco®

¾ cup milk

Stir together flour, baking powder, and salt, then cut in shortening
until the mixture is in pea-size pieces. Stir in milk all at once. Turn
the mixture out onto a floured surface and knead it several times.
Pat into a round disk, about ¾ inch thick. Cut biscuits with a biscuit
cutter and place them on top of the casserole. Bake as directed.

Recipe serves 6.

We love preparing pizza at home, with just the right toppings and, of course, a glass of wine while the oven does its thing. Now, depending on your preferences, the wine changes. Lots of spicy pepperoni? A soft, low-acid red such as Beaujolais, or Valpolicella. A kitchen-sink masterwork? Try a Zinfandel or a hillside Shiraz. Vegetarian? Why, Pinot Grigio, of course. Just cheese? Believe it or not, a Chardonnay works wonders.

$ Bogle "Old Vine" Zinfandel (Amador, California)
$+ Allegrini "Palazzo della Torre" Valpolicella (Veneto, Italy)
$$ Gallo Estate Chardonnay (Sonoma, California)

Homemade Pizza

One taste of this homemade pizza and you'll never order delivery again! Let your family and friends help sprinkle on the toppings for extra fun.

INGREDIENTS:

Pizza Dough:

1 envelope active dry yeast

1½ cups warm water

Pinch of sugar

1½ tablespoons olive oil

2 teaspoon salt

3 to 3½ cups bread flour

1 tablespoon cornmeal

1 recipe Pizza Sauce

3 cups shredded mozzarella cheese

Assorted toppings

Place yeast in a large bowl. Add warm water and sugar, stir, and place the bowl in a warm oven that has been heated at the "warm" setting for 2 to 3 minutes. Turn the oven off before placing bowl in oven. Allow the yeast to soften approximately 10 minutes.

Remove the yeast mixture from the oven. Stir in olive oil, salt, and enough bread flour to make a soft dough. Sprinkle the countertop liberally with flour. Turn the dough out onto floured surface and knead it 5 minutes, incorporating most of remaining flour, until it is soft and shiny. The dough should spring back when touched with fingers.

Grease a large bowl with olive oil. Transfer the dough to the bowl, turning once to oil the whole surface. Cover with a towel and set aside in a warm place until the dough has doubled in volume, approximately 45 minutes.

Entrées

Preheat the oven to 425 degrees.

Punch the dough down, cut in half, and form each half into a ball. On a floured surface, roll out the dough into a 10-inch round and place it on a baking sheet sprinkled with half of the cornmeal. Repeat with the remaining pizza dough. If a thick-crusted pizza is preferred, cover pizzas with a lightweight towel and allow dough to rise 15 to 20 minutes. Top with pizza sauce, cheese, and desired toppings. Bake pizzas at 425 degrees approximately 15 minutes until cheese has melted and pizza is hot. Slice and serve immediately.

Pizza Sauce:

1 tablespoon olive oil	2 teaspoons dried oregano
½ cup chopped onion	1 teaspoon dried sweet basil
3 Roma tomatoes, chopped	½ teaspoon crushed anise seed
3 to 4 cloves garlic, minced	1 tablespoon grated Parmesan cheese
1 15-ounce can tomato sauce	
Pinch of sugar	Ground black pepper, to taste

Heat a medium saucepan over medium-low heat; add oil. Sauté onion until translucent, about 3 minutes. Add tomatoes and cook 5 minutes until soft; stir in garlic and cook 1 more minute.

Stir in tomato sauce, sugar, herbs, Parmesan cheese, and black pepper. Reduce the heat to low and simmer it until you're ready to assemble the pizzas. Sauce may be made ahead and refrigerated. Makes enough sauce for 2 pizzas.

Recipe makes 2 large pizzas.

Bolognese Sauce (Lauren Groveman's Way) for Any Pasta, but Preferably Pappardelle

I am honored that my good friend Lauren Groveman, noted author, cooking teacher, award-winning radio host, and host of PBS television's Home Cooking with Lauren Groveman *has shared this recipe from her cookbook* Lauren Groveman's Kitchen: Nurturing Food for Family and Friends *(Chronicle Books). This delightful dish is ideal for cozy family meals and warm, friendly gatherings.*

Lauren Groveman writes,

This famous meat sauce, which originated in the northern Italian city of Bologna, is a hearty topping for any pasta. But I prefer it with pappardella noodles, which look like thin lasagna noodles or long ribbons with curly edges—the perfect strand to stand up to such a substantial sauce. Since this sauce freezes perfectly, I purposely wrote a large recipe to provide you with an extra batch or two tucked away in your freezer for easy and perhaps unexpected entertaining. Although it's traditional to use white wine in this sauce, I prefer the taste of red. But feel free to substitute. If desired, fold cooked green peas into the lightly buttered pasta before ladling the sauce on top. Or plant tiny fresh mozzarella balls on top of each serving and garnish with fresh basil. And be sure to pass a bowl of freshly grated Reggiano at the table.

This dish has it all—sweet, pungent, tart, earthy, tangy, acidic, salty, and fat. There are some serious flavors intermingling here. Luckily, tradition serves us well, suggesting the rounded elegance of Dolcetto or a Brunello. These are muscular wines with plenty of tannin that provide a guideline to follow. The new-school Barberas are also quite well-suited.

$$ Michel Chiarlo Barbera d'Asti
(Piamonte, Italy)

$$$ Bruno Rocca Dolcetto d'Alba
(Piamonte, Italy)

$$$ Banfi Brunello
(Toscano, Italy)

Entrées

INGREDIENTS:

Sauce:

4 cups cleaned, thinly sliced leeks, trimmed whites and 1 inch of the tender green

10 cloves garlic, chopped

2 stalks celery, trimmed and sliced

2 carrots, peeled and sliced

1 stick butter (1/4 pound)

2 pounds ground veal

4 thin slices prosciutto (preferably imported from Parma), chopped

1 cup Rich Beef Stock or canned beef broth, diluted with water if too salty

¼ cup extra-virgin olive oil

1½ pounds sweet Italian sausage (casing removed)

Freshly ground black pepper to taste

1 cup dry red or white wine

3 pounds ripe plum (Roma) tomatoes, peeled, seeded, and coarsely chopped or 2 28-ounce cans whole tomatoes, drained and coarsely chopped (approximately 5 cups)

1 29-ounce can tomato purée

1 cup chopped fresh basil leaves (chopped as needed to prevent basil from turning black)

1 6-ounce can tomato paste

1 pound fresh button mushrooms, wiped clean and sliced

½ cup heavy cream (preferably not ultrapasteurized)

½ cup freshly grated Reggiano Parmesan cheese

Salt to taste

To serve:

Homemade egg noodles, cut with the pappardelle or fettuccine attachment, or dried pappardelle, freshly cooked, drained, and lightly buttered (allow 2 to 3 ounces per person)

Sprigs of basil, for garnish

Fresh mozzarella balls (called bocconcini), for garnish (optional)

continued on next page

1. To process the vegetables and sweat them: Combine leeks, garlic, celery, and carrots (in batches if necessary) in the bowl of a food processor fitted with the steel blade. Process using on-off turns until chopped very small but not puréed. The vegetables should remain distinguishable. If you don't have a food processor, mince vegetables individually using a chef's knife, and then combine them. Melt butter in a nonreactive, heavy-bottomed 8-quart Dutch oven over medium heat. While it melts, tear off a sheet of waxed paper large enough to cover the bottom interior of the pot. Brush 1 side of the paper with some of the butter. When the butter is hot and bubbling, stir in the vegetable mixture and lay the greased side of the waxed paper directly on top of the vegetables. Reduce heat to very low and let the vegetables sweat 15 to 20 minutes, lifting the paper occasionally to stir and redistribute them.

2. To brown the veal with prosciutto: Heat a 10- to 12-inch non-reactive skillet over medium-high heat. When hot, add ground veal and break it up with a fork or wooden spoon. Stir in chopped prosciutto and cook until veal is no longer pink, 3 to 4 minutes. Using a slotted spoon, remove veal and prosciutto to a bowl. Pour out any liquid that remains in the skillet, but don't wipe out the interior. Return the skillet to high heat and add beef stock or broth. Bring to a brisk simmer and deglaze the pan by scraping up any browned bits of caramelized veal. Reduce stock to about ½ its original volume and pour into the bowl with the browned veal.

3. To brown the sausage: Wipe out the pan and return it to medium-high heat. Add 2 tablespoons olive oil and, when hot, add the sausage and break it up with a fork. Season the sausage with black pepper and cook until no longer pink, 3 to 4 minutes. Remove with a slotted spoon and add to the veal. Pour out any fat from the skillet and deglaze once more, but this time with wine. When the wine is reduced by ½, add it to the meat mixture and set aside.

4. To combine the sauce: Remove waxed paper from vegetables and stir in 2 cups of the chopped tomatoes, the tomato purée, and ½ cup freshly chopped basil. Add the meat mixture, along with the deglazing liquids, and stir in tomato paste and a good amount of black pepper. Bring the mixture to a simmer, reduce the heat to low, and cook with the cover ajar 30 minutes.

5. To cook mushrooms and finish the sauce: Heat a 10-inch skillet over medium-high heat and, when hot, add remaining 2 tablespoons olive oil. When oil is hot, add sliced mushrooms and cook, stirring constantly, until they are golden and tender, about 3 minutes. Remove from heat. To simmered sauce, add cooked mushrooms, the remaining 3 cups chopped tomatoes, and cream; simmer another 10 minutes. Stir in another ½ cup chopped basil and remove from heat. Stir in grated Reggiano Parmesan cheese; season with salt and some additional pepper if necessary. Serve immediately, store in the refrigerator, or freeze.

6. To serve: Ladle hot sauce over freshly cooked pasta, garnish each plate with a sprig of fresh basil, and if desired, gently press 2 tiny mozzarella balls on top of each serving so the bottom of each ball melts, while the top keeps its shape.

Recipe makes about 16 cups of sauce; for each main-course serving, use 1 scant cup sauce and 2 to 3 ounces dried pasta.

This beloved, but rich, cream sauce is loaded with tasty butterfat, so in a wine, we need good acidity to keep from being overpowered by the sheer richness of it. Something crisp and refreshing, such as a Pinot Grigio, is ideal.

$ Cavit Pinot Grigio
(Fruili, Italy)

$ Duckpond Pinot Gris
(Willamette, Oregon)

**$$ Livio Felluga
Pinot Grigio**
(Fruili, Italy)

Fettuccine Alfredo

There is something very reassuring about a dish of Fettuccine Alfredo. Perhaps it's the rich flavors of butter and cream, presented in utter simplicity, or the resemblance to a dish from many of our childhoods, macaroni and cheese, only in grown-up form. Whatever the reason, it's one of my favorite comfort foods.

INGREDIENTS:

2 tablespoons olive oil

2 tablespoons butter

3 tablespoons white wine

1 cup heavy cream

Salt and freshly ground black pepper, to taste

2 tablespoons chopped flat leaf parsley

10 ounces prepared fettuccine

Freshly grated Parmesan cheese

In a large saucepan over medium-low heat, heat olive oil and butter until the butter melts. Stir in wine and heavy cream. Raise the heat to medium-high and bring the mixture to a boil; cook 1 minute. Season with salt and ground black pepper.

Remove saucepan from the heat. Stir in parsley and prepared fettuccine until well mixed.

Serve the fettuccine with grated Parmesan cheese.

Recipe makes 2 servings.

Entrées

Penne with Crimini Mushrooms, Pancetta, and Cream

There is only one phrase to describe this dish – love at first bite! From first taste to last, the flavors and textures of this Italian-inspired pasta combine for a sublime experience.

INGREDIENTS:

2 tablespoons olive oil

2 tablespoons butter

3 ounces diced pancetta

1 large minced shallot

2 cloves minced garlic

½ pound sliced crimini or white mushrooms

¾ cup dry white wine

1¾ cups heavy cream

Coarse salt and freshly ground black pepper, to taste

16 ounces prepared penne pasta

1 tablespoon olive oil

¼ cup pasta cooking water, or more, if necessary

3 tablespoons chopped fresh parsley

Freshly grated Parmesan cheese

Heat a large saucepan over medium-low heat; add oil and butter, swirling pan to mix. Stir in pancetta, cooking just until fat is rendered; do not brown. Add shallot, sauté until soft, then stir in garlic. Cook mixture 1 minute, stirring constantly. Add mushrooms and sauté 2 minutes, stirring often, until they are lightly browned.

Raise heat to medium; deglaze the pan with white wine, stirring up any brown bits from the mushrooms and pancetta. Add heavy cream and bring the mixture to a boil; cook 10 minutes, stirring occasionally until the sauce has thickened slightly. Season with salt and pepper.

Meanwhile, cook penne pasta according to package directions. Drain, reserving ¼ cup cooking water in the bottom of the pan. Add 1 table-spoon olive oil, swirling the pot to mix. Return penne to the pot; toss to coat. Remove the saucepan from the heat, stir in parsley and prepared pasta, and mix well to coat. Pour pasta into a large serving bowl, or serve in wide, shallow bowls with grated Parmesan cheese.

Recipe serves 4.

This sensuous dish brings the palate alive with the near-forbidden (these days), heady textures and flavors of heavy cream and salty pancetta, casually draped across a back-ground of silky pasta. With all these yummy fats and richness, we require a wine of good acidity. The salty, dry-cured ham, already tamed by the cream and but-terfat, would be enhanced by a restrained fruitiness. Salt tends to make tannic wines taste bitter, so a white with little barrel exposure is our choice. The classic pairing is a Pinot Grigio. We also enjoy the pear, honey, nut, and orange peel nuances of a Lugana.

$ Tiefenbrunner Pinot Grigio
(Friuli, Italy)

$$ Terlano Pinot Grigio
(Alto Adige, Italy)

$$+ Zenato Lugana RSV "Sergio"
(Piamonte, Italy)

The main components in this recipe are creamy ricotta, acidic tomatoes, pungent garlic, basil, and sweet tomato sauce. The low fat content suggests a low-acid wine, but the acidic tomatoes nudge that acid level back up to medium.

We're looking for a medium to light body that won't over-whelm the dish, with just enough fruit to work with the basil. Dolcetto is the classic pairing, but Rhône and California's field-blends have much to offer, as well.

$ **Laurel Glen's "Reds"** (Sonoma Mountain, California)

$$ **Augusto Dolcetto d'Alba** (Piamonte, Italy)

$$$ **Patric LeSec Chateauneuf-du-Pape "Les Gallets Blonds"** (Rhône, France)

Stuffed Pasta Shells

This is one of those great all-around recipes—perfect for family meals, potluck suppers, casual buffets, and those times when a heartfelt, get-well meal makes all the difference for a neighbor or friend. You can make this dish ahead of time, and leftovers keep well in the refrigerator.

INGREDIENTS:

Sauce:

3 tablespoons olive oil

1 medium chopped onion

4 to 5 cloves garlic, minced

6 medium Roma tomatoes, chopped

½ teaspoon sugar

Freshly ground black pepper to taste

1 15-ounce can tomato sauce

1 tablespoon dried oregano

1 tablespoon chopped fresh basil

Heat a large saucepan over medium-low heat; add olive oil and chopped onion. Sauté onion several minutes until translucent, stir in garlic, and cook 1 more minute. Add tomatoes; raise the heat to medium and cook several minutes until tomatoes soften, stirring often. Season with sugar and pepper. Stir in prepared tomato sauce.

Reduce the heat to low. Add herbs, rubbing dried oregano between your hands to release flavor. Simmer sauce 15 to 20 minutes, stirring occasionally. If desired, purée sauce with a handheld blender for desired smoothness. While the sauce simmers, prepare shells.

Entrées

Pasta Shells:

½ package large pasta shells (approximately 25 to 30 shells)

1 16-ounce lowfat or nonfat ricotta cheese

¼ teaspoon salt

1 tablespoon snipped fresh chives

2 tablespoons chopped fresh basil

Grated Parmesan or Romano cheese, for garnish

Preheat the oven to 375 degrees.

Cook pasta shells according to package directions; drain. Do not overcook the pasta. Spoon a small amount of sauce into the bottom of a casserole dish.

In a small bowl, stir together cheese, salt, chives, and basil. Fill each shell with 1 tablespoon ricotta mixture and place shells in casserole dish, with the opening facing down. Spoon enough sauce over the stuffed shells to cover.

Cover the dish with foil and bake in a preheated 375-degree oven for 45 to 55 minutes, or until sauce is bubbly and shells are soft. Sprinkle with grated Parmesan or Romano cheese and serve.

Recipe serves 4.

Some of the most satisfying dishes are simple. This is such a dish. Acidic tomatoes and creamy cheese... piled on a foundation of neutral pasta.

We find the traditional Dolcetto delicious, but the old field-blends of California definitely rock our world. Instead of blending different batches of wine from separate vineyards before bottling, as we do today, the Italian immigrants of the 1860s left their mark in the vineyard by planting it with their favorite mixture of varietals, all combined in one place. At harvest, they simply picked everything and crushed it. Done!

$ **Larel Glen "Reds"**
(Sonoma Mountain, California)

$ **Marietta "Old Vine Red"**
(Sonoma, California)

$$$ **Ridge Mateo**
(Paso Robles, California)

Vegetarian Eggplant Lasagna

After weeks of indulging in sumptuous holiday meals, this simple, uncomplicated, lowfat entreé is fresh and particularly satisfying. While this lasagna is the ultimate comfort food, add soft candlelight, a bottle of good red wine, and soft music, and it becomes a feast for the senses any time of the year.

INGREDIENTS:

1 large eggplant

2 to 3 tablespoons olive oil

2 teaspoons salt

2 teaspoons olive oil

15 lasagna noodles

1 recipe Tomato Sauce

1 15-ounce container lowfat or nonfat ricotta

¾ pound mozzarella, thinly sliced

5 large basil leaves, torn into ½-inch pieces

Tomato Sauce:

2 28-ounce cans peeled Italian-style plum tomatoes

2 tablespoons olive oil

3 large cloves garlic, minced

1½ teaspoons salt

1½ teaspoons dried oregano

½ teaspoon freshly ground black pepper

¼ teaspoon sugar

Entrées

To make the sauce, process tomatoes through a food mill to remove seeds and set aside. Preheat a large saucepan over low heat; add olive oil and garlic. Cook garlic 1 minute until light brown. Stir in reserved tomatoes, salt, oregano, pepper, and sugar.

Raise heat to medium-high. Bring the sauce to a boil, stirring occasionally. Reduce heat to medium low and simmer 30 to 35 minutes, uncovered, until it thickens and is reduced by ¼, stirring occasionally. Remove from the heat and keep warm.

Peel eggplant, slice it in quarters lengthwise, and slice the quarters into ¼-inch-thick slices. Heat a large skillet over medium-low heat; add 1 tablespoon of the olive oil and swirl pan to coat. Arrange slices of eggplant to cover bottom of skillet. Sauté 2 minutes until eggplant is lightly browned, turn over, and sauté 1 more minute. Transfer slices to paper towel to drain. Repeat the process until all eggplant slices are cooked; set aside.

Bring a large, covered Dutch oven of water to a boil. Add salt, 2 teaspoons olive oil, and lasagna noodles. Boil lasagna approximately 10 minutes, until it's al dente. Drain in a large colander.

Preheat the oven to 375 degrees.

To assemble the lasagna, coat bottom of a 9- by 13-inch baking pan with a scant amount of tomato sauce. Top with a layer of prepared pasta, a scant layer of tomato sauce, eggplant slices, dollops of ricotta cheese, torn basil, and mozzarella. Repeat process for a total of 4 layers. Top with a fifth layer of pasta and dress liberally with the remaining tomato sauce and mozzarella. Cover the pan tightly with foil.

Bake lasagna in preheated oven 35 to 40 minutes, or until hot and bubbly. Remove from the oven, set aside 10 minutes to set, and serve.

Recipe makes 8 servings.

Cape Cod Rice Pilaf

The summers my sisters and I spent on Cape Cod while we were growing up provided some of our happiest memories. Each summer, my mother and the four of us spent carefree mornings on the beach, followed by lunch back at the house and several more hours by the water's edge. Unfortunately for my father, life at the office went on as usual, and he could join us only at the beginning and end of our summer vacations.

Together with our good friends, the Mahoneys, who had three kids and owned the summer house next door to ours, we swam, learned to embroider and knit, built sand castles, and strolled down Old Silver Beach to the refreshment stand on the public beach. At night, all the kids played hide-and-seek in the Mahoneys' front yard, or sat around playing poker or a card game called Spoons, placing bets with wooden matches.

When my sister Lynn and I were a little older, we spent part of our summer days learning to cook. The kitchen in our weathered, gray-shingle house was old and basic. It had a big, old, free-standing range and oven against one wall, and this is where Lynn and I learned to make Mrs. Ruth Mahoney's rice pilaf.

Lynn and I cooked rice pilaf a lot—a whole lot. In those days, we tended to focus on two or three recipes for weeks and cook them to death. It's no wonder that once we had moved on to other recipes, I forgot all about rice pilaf until I had been married for several years. One day, the memory came out of nowhere, and I could picture myself as a young girl, standing next to Lynn, stirring rice pilaf at that massive stove in our Cape Cod summer house. I had no recipe, but after a summer of nonstop rice pilaf, it wasn't hard to figure it out.

Side Dishes & Salads

So, here is my recipe for Cape Cod Rice Pilaf. It may have changed a bit since Mrs. Mahoney first taught us how to make it, but she taught us well. I have served this rice dish during many family meals and for numerous dinner parties. I even served it one evening when my dear friend, Martin Yan, came to dinner. It is colorful, has great flavor, and pairs well with everything from chicken to fish and from beef to pork.

INGREDIENTS:

2 tablespoons olive oil

1 tablespoon butter

½ cup fideo mediano or fideo angel hair pasta

⅓ cup diced onion

¼ cup diced carrot

1 cup long grain rice

2¾ cups chicken broth

Salt and freshly ground pepper, to taste

1 tablespoon chopped fresh parsley

Heat a large saucepan over medium-low heat; add olive oil and butter, swirling the pan to mix. Stir in fideo and cook, stirring occasionally, until fideo lightly browns, about 2 to 3 minutes.

Add onion and carrot, sautéing 1 or 2 minutes until vegetables begin to soften. Stir in rice. Sauté rice 1 minute, stirring constantly; pour in chicken broth. Season the mixture with salt and pepper.

Increase heat to high and bring rice mixture to a boil. Reduce heat to low, cover, and cook 25 to 30 minutes, or until all of broth is absorbed. When rice has finished cooking, add parsley and stir gently with a fork to separate the individual grains.

Serve the pilaf immediately; any leftover pilaf may be covered and refrigerated several days, or placed in an airtight container and frozen for up to 1 month.

Recipe serves 8.

Mexican Rice with Fideo and Roasted Corn

This south-of-the-border side dish packs plenty of flavor, and is a wonderful accompaniment to grilled meats and Tex-Mex favorites.

INGREDIENTS:

1 ear of corn

1 poblano pepper, peeled

2 tablespoons olive oil

2 tablespoons butter

1 cup uncooked long-grain rice

¼ cup fideo (vermicelli) or fideo angel hair pasta

½ cup chopped onion

½ teaspoon ground cumin

2½ cups chicken broth

¼ teaspoon kosher salt

Soak corn in husk in cold water 20 minutes; drain, and remove enough husk to expose one side of corn. Grill corn and poblano pepper over hot coals until the corn is roasted and skin on the pepper is blistered and dark, about 10 minutes.

Set corn aside to cool; place pepper in a plastic zipper bag to steam. When the pepper is cool, peel off the skin, remove the seeds, and chop the pepper. Set aside. Slice kernels from corn with a sharp knife. Set aside.

Heat a medium saucepan over medium-low heat; add oil and butter. Stir in rice and fideo; cook 5 minutes, stirring occasionally, until fideo turns light brown. Add onion and corn kernels; cook 2 minutes until onion becomes translucent. Stir in ground cumin.

Add chicken broth, salt, and chopped poblano pepper. Bring mixture to a boil over high heat, cover, and reduce heat to low. Cook until liquid is absorbed.

Fluff rice with a fork and serve.

Recipe serves 6.

Roasted Glazed
Winter Vegetables

While there may be a chill in the air outdoors, the sweet aroma of caramelized winter vegetables roasting in the oven will make you feel warm and comfy inside. My neighbor, Susan Geyer, proclaimed this vegetable side dish "one of the tastiest things to ever pass my lips."

Oven roasting brings out the flavor and natural sweetness of these winter root vegetables, further enhanced by brown sugar and a drizzle of maple syrup. Arrange the vegetables artistically on a serving platter and serve with roasted meats or poultry.

INGREDIENTS:

8 carrots with stems

3 turnips

1 large sweet potato

1 medium red onion

1 head garlic

3 tablespoons olive oil

3 tablespoons maple syrup

2 tablespoons brown sugar

Preheat oven to 450 degrees.

Peel carrots, taking care to retain root end and 3 inches of stem. Peel turnips and sweet potato; slice into 1-inch cubes. Transfer carrots, turnips and sweet potato to a large roasting pan. Peel and slice onion into wedges; add to roasting pan.

Separate the garlic cloves, but do not peel them. Scatter the garlic in roasting pan. Drizzle vegetables with olive oil and toss to coat.

Roast vegetables in a preheated oven 30 minutes, or until tender, stirring occasionally. When vegetables are just tender, drizzle with maple syrup and sprinkle with brown sugar. Stir; roast an additional 5 minutes.

Transfer vegetables to a serving platter and serve immediately.

Recipe serves 6.

Caesar Salad

For those concerned about consuming raw eggs, this delicious, classic salad uses coddled eggs. However, pregnant women, very young children, and those with compromised immune systems should not eat raw or coddled eggs at all.

INGREDIENTS:

2 large cloves garlic

2 anchovy fillets (optional)

2 egg yolks, coddled

2 tablespoons freshly squeezed lemon juice

1 teaspoon Dijon mustard

3 drops Worcestershire sauce

Freshly ground black pepper

¼ cup freshly grated Parmesan cheese

⅔ cup virgin olive oil

1 head romaine lettuce

2 to 3 tablespoons grated Parmesan cheese for garnish

1 cup Garlic Croutons, for garnish

In a large serving bowl, smash garlic and anchovy fillets with a fork. Mix in coddled egg yolks (directions follow), lemon juice, mustard, Worcestershire sauce, pepper, and Parmesan cheese.

To coddle egg yolks, separate whites from yolks, reserving whites for another use. Bring a small saucepan of water to a boil. Carefully place egg yolks in a strainer; lower into the boiling water. Cook egg yolks 30 seconds; remove and drain. Add yolks to dressing ingredients.

Slowly add olive oil to the salad dressing while whisking with a fork. Add lettuce and toss well with dressing. Garnish with additional Parmesan cheese and croutons.

Recipe serves 4 to 6.

Garlic Croutons

Homemade croutons are the perfect finishing touch on a salad and can turn ordinary greens into something extraordinary. They keep well for several days in a plastic zipper bag, so when entertaining, make them well ahead to save time on the day of the event.

INGREDIENTS:

2 tablespoons olive oil

2 cups bread cubes cut from a baguette or other firm-textured bread

1 clove garlic, peeled

Pinch of coarse salt

Preheat a skillet over medium-low heat. Add olive oil and swirl to coat the bottom of the pan. Smash garlic lightly with the flat side of a large knife and add garlic to the pan.

Add bread cubes and toss to coat with oil. Sprinkle with coarse salt.

Cook bread cubes slowly until golden brown on all sides. Remove the garlic clove and discard.

Transfer croutons to a large shallow bowl or tray to cool. When thoroughly cool and dry, store in a large plastic zipper bag. Serve over salads or in cream soups.

Recipe makes 2 cups.

Tomato and Asadero Salad with Basil

Mexican Asadero cheese, sometimes referred to as Oaxaca, is a semisoft cow's milk cheese. Its mild flavor pairs beautifully with fresh garden tomatoes and basil.

INGREDIENTS:

1 bunch red leaf lettuce

1 12-ounce package Asadero cheese

3 large garden tomatoes, sliced

Fresh basil leaves

Freshly ground black pepper

1 recipe Lime-Cilantro Dressing

Rinse lettuce and spin dry. Tear into large pieces and arrange on a serving platter or salad plates. Slice cheese into ¼-inch-thick slices.

Arrange tomato and cheese slices on lettuce, overlapping and alternating slices. Tear basil leaves and scatter them over the tomatoes and cheese. Season with ground black pepper and drizzle with Lime-Cilantro Dressing.

Recipe serves 4 to 6.

Lime-Cilantro Dressing

2½ tablespoons freshly squeezed lime juice

1¼ teaspoons Dijon mustard (preferably Maille)

⅛ teaspoon sugar

Coarse salt, to taste

Freshly ground black pepper, to taste

½ cup vegetable oil

2 tablespoons chopped fresh cilantro

Whisk all ingredients together in a small bowl until mixture is emulsified. Spoon over salads.

Recipe makes 2/3 cups.

Side Dishes & Salads

Mango Mesclun Salad with Blackberry Vinaigrette

The sweetness of the mango, blackberries, and Crème de Mure, combined with the acidity of the raspberry vinegar and field greens, results in this delightful salad, quite refreshing on a summer day.

I have also found it travels wonderfully. When our older son, Timothy, graduated from engineering school at The University of Texas at Austin, I packed several festive meals for family celebrations. I wrapped the washed greens in paper towels and transported them in large plastic zipper bags, and combined the vinaigrette ingredients in a small jar.

Just before serving, I tossed the chilled greens, mangos, and blackberries in a large serving bowl. A quick shake of the pre-mixed dressing, and the salad was ready!

INGREDIENTS:

- 1 bunch green or red leaf lettuce, rinsed and dried
- ½ pound mesclun or spring mix, rinsed and dried
- 1 ripe mango, sliced
- 1 cup fresh blackberries, for garnish
- ¼ cup extra-virgin olive oil
- 2 tablespoons raspberry vinegar
- 2 tablespoons seedless blackberry jelly
- 1½ tablespoons Crème de Mure (blackberry liqueur)
- Salt and freshly ground black pepper, to taste

Arrange leaf lettuce and mesclun mix on individual salad plates or in a large serving bowl. Garnish with sliced mango and fresh blackberries.

In a small jar, combine oil, vinegar, jelly, liqueur, and seasonings. Tighten lid on the jar and shake until thoroughly combined. Pour vinaigrette over the salad.

Recipe serves 8 to 10.

Variegated Salad
with New Potatoes and Ham

I love salads that look pretty and use leftover ingredients from other meals. Substitute potatoes from last night's dinner for a delicious approach to using leftovers. The spicy mustard dressing pairs wonderfully with the potatoes and ham.

INGREDIENTS:

4 medium red new potatoes

1 small bunch leaf lettuce

1 small bunch fresh spinach

4 ¼-inch-thick ham slices

2 tablespoons mayonnaise

¼ teaspoon dry mustard

1 tablespoon minced onion

Coarse salt and freshly ground
   black pepper, to taste

Dash of paprika

¼ cup milk

Early in the day, gently scrub new potatoes. Place in a medium saucepan with enough water to cover, cover the saucepan, and bring to a boil over high heat. Reduce heat to medium-low and cook potatoes until a sharp knife easily pierces them, about 8 to 10 minutes, depending on size. Drain, transfer to a bowl, cover, and refrigerate until cold.

Wash and spin-dry lettuce and spinach. To remove tough stems from spinach, grasp leaf on both sides of stem and pull stem downward. Discard.

Arrange lettuce and spinach on a large platter or on individual salad plates. Slice chilled potatoes into ¼-inch-thick slices and arrange them across the greens, overlapping edges. Slice ham into thin strips and arrange over the center of the salad.

In a small bowl, stir together the mayonnaise, dry mustard, onion, salt and ground pepper, and paprika. Whisk in milk until the mixture is smooth and thick. Spoon dressing over the salad and serve.

Recipe serves 4 to 6.

Composed Green Salad with Vinaigrette D'Agnes

This salad is arranged artistically with ingredients on hand in the refrigerator. Asparagus to garnish the top of this salad is quickly blanched, then chilled in ice water, but if I have leftover asparagus, I'll make this salad simply as a creative and delicious way to use it up.

INGREDIENTS:

1 bunch asparagus	2 Roma tomatoes
1 small bunch green leaf lettuce	Sliced black olives
1 small bunch red leaf lettuce	Freshly grated Parmesan cheese
1 Belgian endive	1 recipe Vinaigrette d'Agnes

Trim asparagus, place in a skillet filled with ½ inch of water, cover, and bring to a boil. Reduce heat to medium-low, and cook asparagus 1 to 2 minutes, depending on thickness, until crisp-tender. Drain and immediately plunge asparagus in a large bowl of ice water to stop the cooking process.

Rinse and spin-dry leaf lettuces and arrange on 4 salad plates. Rinse endive and slice it horizontally into thin slices; arrange in the center of the salads. Drain the asparagus and group 4 to 5 spears over the endive.

Slice tomatoes thinly and arrange slices around the perimeter of the salad. Scatter black olives on top of the salad and garnish with grated Parmesan cheese.

Drizzle salads with Vinaigrette d'Agnes (page 65).

Recipe makes 4 salads.

Southwestern Black Bean Salad

This is a terrific hot-weather salad when everyone wants to eat light, fresh meals. It's also an ideal side dish for grilled meats or Tex-Mex enchiladas.

INGREDIENTS:

2 ears fresh corn

4 Roma tomatoes, seeded and diced

¾ cup diced red onion

2 15-ounce cans black beans, drained and rinsed

1 15-ounce can Great Northern beans, drained and rinsed

¼ cup freshly squeezed lime juice

2 tablespoons olive oil

1 tablespoon red wine vinegar

¾ teaspoon kosher salt

Freshly ground black pepper, to taste

Remove husk and silk from corn; place in a pot with enough water to cover. Cover the pot and bring to a boil. Reduce heat to medium-low and cook 5 minutes. Drain and cool. Slice the corn from the cob.

In a large bowl, combine corn, diced tomatoes, onion, and all beans; toss gently.

In a small bowl, whisk together lime juice, olive oil, vinegar, salt, and pepper. Pour the mixture over the salad; toss gently.

Sprinkle cilantro over the salad and toss to mix. Transfer salad to a large serving bowl. Cover and refrigerate several hours until cold; serve chilled.

Recipe serves 8.

Soups & Sandwiches

Homemade Beef Stock

The secret to the richest soups and sauces is homemade stock. Here, I've demystified the process for you, so you can enjoy chef-quality, beef-based soups and sauces at home.

INGREDIENTS:

- 4 to 5 pounds beef back ribs and marrow bones
- 3 stalks celery, chopped
- 2 large carrots, peeled and chopped
- 1 medium onion, peeled and chopped
- 1 large turnip, peeled and diced
- 1 bouquet garni (2 bay leaves, ½ teaspoon whole peppercorns, ½ teaspoon dried thyme, 3 cloves, and several sprigs fresh parsley, tied in a square of cheesecloth)

Preheat oven to 400 degrees. Place beef ribs and bones in a large roasting pan, and surround with vegetables. Roast, uncovered, for 1½ hours, stirring occasionally during the final 30 minutes. Drain fat and transfer meat and vegetables to a large stockpot.

Deglaze the pan with 2 cups boiling water, scraping up the dark bits of meat and vegetables. Pour deglazed liquid into the stockpot, and add 10 cups of water and the bouquet garni.

Bring mixture almost to a boil, skimming all the scum from surface with a large spoon. Reduce heat to low, partially cover the stockpot, and simmer the mixture 3 to 4 hours until a dark, rich broth has formed. Cool, then place the stockpot in the refrigerator overnight.

The next day, remove congealed fat from beef stock's surface with a large spoon. Wipe remaining fat from inside the stockpot with a paper towel. Remove the bouquet garni and bones and strain the vegetables from the stock with fine cheesecloth. The remaining stock should be clear and dark in color. Refrigerate up to several days or transfer the stock to freezer containers and freeze up to 5 months.

Recipe makes approximately 2 quarts of beef stock.

Homemade Chicken Stock

With this recipe, you can vary the amount of water according to the size of your stockpot and your needs. You can even make a pretty fair chicken broth for a small pot of last-minute noodle soup by simmering cooked chicken bones with bits of meat clinging to them. Add the vegetables and seasonings, and home-made chicken noodle soup is but a simmer away! Precook the noodles to keep the chicken broth clear.

INGREDIENTS:

3 pounds chicken pieces with bones

10 cups water (2½ quarts)

3 stalks celery with leaves

2 large carrots, peeled and chopped

1 medium onion, peeled and quartered

3 whole cloves

1 bouquet garni (2 bay leaves, 5 sprigs fresh thyme, 4 sprigs fresh parsley, cracked peppercorns)

2 chicken bouillon cubes

Place chicken pieces in a large stockpot and add water. Add celery stalks with leaves and carrots. Insert whole cloves into onion quarters and add them to the pot.

To create the bouquet garni, place bay leaves, thyme, parsley, and peppercorns in a square of cheesecloth. Gather the ends of cheese-cloth together and tie securely with string. Drop the bouquet garni into the pot.

Cover and bring the mixture to a low boil over high heat. Reduce heat to low and skim off any scum that forms on top of the stock. Add bouillon cubes and simmer 2 to 3 hours.

Remove chicken pieces and bouquet garni. Strain soup stock through a fine sieve or cheesecloth.

Cool and refrigerate the stock up to 3 days, or pour into containers and freeze up to 3 months.

Recipe makes approximately 2½ quarts of chicken stock.

Randy's World-Famous Bean Soup

My husband starts his bean soup in the morning and allows it to simmer all afternoon. By evening, its fragrance permeates our home and makes me feel that all is right with the world.

INGREDIENTS:

2 pounds mixed dry beans, such as Great Northern, black, black-eyed peas, cranberry, kidney, pinto, or small white

1 very meaty ham bone

3 carrots, peeled and sliced into ½-inch pieces

2 potatoes, peeled and sliced into 1-inch pieces

2 small onions, coarsely chopped

16 cups cold water (4 quarts)

1 tablespoon dried oregano

2 teaspoons dried basil

½ teaspoon Spice Islands fines herbes

2 bay leaves

Salt and freshly ground black pepper

Tabasco (optional)

Rinse beans in a large bowl of water, sorting to remove the damaged ones. Drain.

Place ham bone, beans, carrots, potatoes, and onions in a large stockpot. Add water, oregano, basil, and fines herbes, rubbing the herbs between your hands to release their flavor before adding them to the stockpot. Add bay leaves.

Cover and bring the mixture to a boil over high heat; reduce heat to low and simmer 5 to 6 hours, stirring occasionally.

During the final 30 minutes of cooking, remove the ham bone and cut off the meat. Discard the bone and return the meat to the soup. Season with salt and pepper and Tabasco, if desired.

Recipe serves 8 to 10.

Leftover bean soup may be cooled and stored in covered containers in the refrigerator for several days, or it may be frozen. When reheating soup, add ½ pound sliced, precooked link sausage, if desired.

Old Chicago Minestrone

When it's cold and blustery outdoors, and even a sweater fails to keep you warm inside, it's time to cook a big pot of hearty, fragrant soup. I love soups that are a meal in themselves, and this version of minestrone is thick with cannellini and dark red kidney beans, chickpeas, and shell pasta in a rich tomato broth.

If you prefer to eat vegetarian meals, substitute 2 tablespoons of olive oil for the pancetta and replace chicken broth with vegetable.

INGREDIENTS:

4 ounces pancetta, or 4 strips bacon

1 cup chopped celery, about 2 stalks

1 medium onion, chopped

3 large carrots, peeled and sliced

4 to 5 cloves garlic, minced

1 28-ounce can chopped tomatoes

5 cups chicken broth or chicken stock

1 cup water

Salt and freshly ground pepper, to taste

2 cups small pasta shells, uncooked

1 cup canned chickpeas, drained and rinsed

1 15-ounce can red kidney beans, drained and rinsed

1 15-ounce can cannellini or Great Northern beans, drained and rinsed

5 mustard leaves, rinsed and chopped

2 teaspoons dried oregano

Soups & Sandwiches

Slice pancetta or bacon into 1-inch pieces. Cook in a large Dutch oven over medium heat until the fat begins to melt; stir in celery, onion, and carrots. Cook vegetables 4 to 5 minutes until tender. Add garlic and cook 1 more minute.

Pour in tomatoes, broth or stock, and water. Season the soup with salt and freshly ground pepper. Cover and bring to a gentle boil, reduce heat to low, and simmer 30 minutes until the vegetables are soft.

Cook pasta in boiling salted water until it's almost al dente. Drain and set aside.

Add chickpeas, kidney beans, and cannellini or Great Northern beans to the soup. Cover and simmer 30 minutes. Stir in cooked pasta, mustard leaves, and oregano. Cover and heat 10 more minutes; serve.

Recipe serves 8 to10.

Vegetable Beef Barley Soup

This fragrant soup, so thick with tender beef and vegetables and al dente barley, is the ultimate comfort food. For extra richness, it starts with homemade beef stock, but feel free to substitute canned beef broth if you're out of the stock. Start this soup early in the day or, better yet, make it a day ahead to allow flavors to develop.

INGREDIENTS:

1 cup dry lima beans

2½ pounds chuck roast

4 tablespoons olive oil (divided)

2 cups sliced carrots

2 cups sliced celery

1 medium onion, chopped

3 quarts homemade beef stock or canned beef broth

2 cups peeled and cubed Yukon Gold potatoes

¾ cup barley

1½ cups fresh or frozen cut green beans

1 cup fresh or frozen kernel corn

Salt and freshly ground black pepper, to taste

Sort through lima beans and remove any stones and broken beans. Place the beans in a medium bowl filled with cold water; soak 1 hour.

Slice beef into 1-inch cubes. Heat a large stockpot over medium high heat; add 2 tablespoons of the olive oil and swirl to coat the bottom of the pot. Add half the beef and cook, without stirring, 4 to 5 minutes until it is very brown. Briefly stir the beef and cook it until brown on all sides; transfer to a clean bowl. Add 1 tablespoon oil to the pot and cook the remaining beef, allowing it to cook undisturbed during the initial browning. When the beef is brown on all sides, transfer to the bowl with the other cooked meat.

Soups & Sandwiches

Reduce heat to medium. Add remaining 1 tablespoon olive oil to the stockpot and swirl it to coat the bottom of the pot. Add carrots, celery, and onion and sauté several minutes until vegetables have softened. Return the beef to the stockpot and add beef stock or broth. Drain lima beans and add them to the pot.

Cover and bring soup to a low boil; then reduce heat to low. Spoon off any brown scum that forms along the edges of the stockpot. Simmer 1 hour.

Meanwhile, in a medium saucepan, parboil cubed potatoes in enough water to cover, just until tender, about 5 minutes. Drain and set aside.

After soup has cooked 1 hour, add barley and simmer 1 hour. During the final 15 minutes of cooking, stir in green beans, corn, and parboiled potatoes. Add salt and pepper and serve when vegetables are tender.

Recipe serves 10.

New England Clam Chowder

When I was growing up, our family moved frequently to accommodate my father's profession, but during those years, we had a summer house on Cape Cod, Massachusetts, overlooking the ocean. That quaint, two-story house, with its gray shingles, white trim, and green shutters provided a kind of stability and constancy in our lives.

Every summer, our next door neighbor, Ruth Mahoney, would prepare at least one large pot of New England Clam Chowder. No restaurant could match her creamy, rich concoction, thick with clams, potatoes, and cream, and just a touch of melted butter swimming on the surface. Oh, how I loved Mrs. Mahoney's chowder, especially on a cold and rainy, early-summer day, when the beach was deserted except for a few hearty souls who strolled along the water's edge in search of shells, pieces of driftwood, and smooth-edged sea glass.

I have developed my own version of New England Clam Chowder that captures the same creamy richness and flavor I remember from my childhood. This version uses readily available canned baby clams, so you can prepare clam chowder whenever you crave this New England classic.

Soups & Sandwiches

4 slices bacon, diced

1 cup onion, diced

1 cup diced celery (about 2 stalks)

3 tablespoons flour

2 10-ounce cans whole baby
clams, drained, juice reserved

1 cup bottled clam juice

2 cups half-and-half

1 cup heavy cream

2 to 3 tablespoons
Martini & Rossi
Dry Vermouth

4 cups peeled and diced
Yukon Gold potatoes

¼ teaspoon white pepper,
or to taste

½ teaspoon kosher salt,
or to taste

Oyster crackers, for garnish

Cook bacon in a Dutch oven over medium heat, just until the fat is rendered. Stir in onion and celery; cook until soft. Sprinkle with 3 tablespoons flour; cook 2 minutes until onion and celery begin to release their juices.

Gradually stir in reserved clam juice and bottled clam juice until the mixture is smooth. Cook 10 minutes, stirring frequently; the mixture will be somewhat thick.

Pour in half-and-half, cream, and vermouth. Stir in potatoes and reserved clams; season with salt and pepper. Reduce heat to medium-low, partially cover the Dutch oven, and cook 20 minutes, stirring frequently. Do not allow the chowder to boil.

Adjust seasonings and serve with oyster crackers.

Recipe serves 8 to 10.

Cream of Mushroom Soup

A simple meal featuring this fragrant, creamy soup is delicious when accompanied by a green salad and rolls or muffins, but I love serving Cream of Mushroom Soup as a first course on more elegant occasions.

INGREDIENTS:

1 pound mushrooms

6 tablespoons unsalted butter

1 medium onion, chopped

¾ cup diced celery

¼ cup flour

4 cups chicken or vegetable broth

3 tablespoons Martini & Rossi Dry Vermouth

1 cup heavy cream

⅛ teaspoon white pepper

Salt, to taste

2 tablespoons chopped fresh parsley, for garnish

Place mushrooms in a colander; rinse them quickly with cold water and dry with paper towels; slice. Reserve 3 cups mushroom slices; coarsely chop the remaining mushrooms and set aside.

Melt butter in a Dutch oven over medium heat. Add onion and celery; cook 5 minutes, stirring occasionally, until onion is soft and translucent. Stir in chopped mushrooms; cook 2 minutes until mushrooms are soft. Sprinkle with ¼ cup flour; cook 1 minute, stirring constantly.

Gradually add broth, stirring until the mixture is smooth. Cook until the soup is hot. Add vermouth, cream, and reserved sliced mushrooms. Heat the soup until it's hot, but do not boil. Season with salt and white pepper. Sprinkle the soup with chopped parsley and serve in cups or bowls.

Recipe serves 6 to 8.

Soups & Sandwiches

Creamy Wild Rice and Mushroom Soup

This satisfying, fragrant soup, with a layering of hearty flavors softened by the addition of cream, is perfect on a cold winter day after everyone comes in from outdoor activities with flushed faces and cold hands.

INGREDIENTS:

2 tablespoons olive oil

2 cups peeled and diced carrots

1½ cups diced celery

1 medium onion, chopped

1 pound mushrooms, sliced

3 tablespoons flour

2½ quarts homemade chicken stock or lowfat canned chicken broth

¾ cup uncooked wild rice

1 cup heavy cream or half-and-half

Salt and freshly ground black pepper, to taste

1 tablespoon chopped fresh parsley

Preheat a large stockpot over medium heat, add olive oil and swirl to coat the bottom of the pot. Add carrots, celery, and onion and sauté 5 minutes until the vegetables are softened. Gently stir in mushrooms and sauté 2 minutes.

Reduce heat to medium-low. Sprinkle flour over the vegetables and cook, stirring constantly, 2 minutes. Gradually pour in a small amount of chicken stock, stirring gently to loosen flour from the bottom of the stockpot. As the mixture thickens, add additional stock, stirring well. When mixture is smooth and thick, pour in remaining chicken stock.

Raise heat to medium-high, cover, and bring soup to a low boil. Reduce heat to low, stir in wild rice, and simmer 1 hour. Stir in cream or half-and-half and check the soup for seasonings. Cover and cook 10 minutes. Correct seasonings and stir in chopped parsley; cook 5 more minutes.

Recipe serves 8.

The combination of crisp and creamy textures, savory and piquant flavors, and red to yellow to white colors, requires a wine as exuberant and multi-faceted as the dish. The shy beauty, Pinot Blanc, comes to mind. Delicate pear and lemon flavors predominate, but its high, though balanced, acidity and attractive willowy body have the backbone to stand up to this challenging soup. The same grape as Italy's Pinot Grigio, it changes a bit when grown in Alsace or Oregon.

$ Tiefenbrunner Pinot Grigio
(Alto Aldige Italy)

$+ Willakenzie Pinot Blanc
(Oregon)

$+ Pierre Sparr Pinot Blanc RSV
(Alsace, France)

Thick and Creamy Tortilla Soup

This soup reminds me of one I enjoyed years ago at the Remington Hotel in Houston, Texas. Roasted and dried chiles give it a nice spicy flavor, while tomatoes keep it from being too hot. For a gourmet touch, thin sour cream with a little milk, spoon onto the soup, and swirl with a knife just before serving.

INGREDIENTS:

2 poblano peppers

2 tablespoons vegetable oil

1 medium onion, peeled and chopped

4 cloves garlic, minced

2 large tomatoes, seeded and chopped

1 28-ounce can crushed tomatoes

2 14½-ounce cans lowfat chicken broth

1 bay leaf

1 medium-heat dried chile (Guajillo or Arbo)

1½ teaspoons cumin

Salt and pepper, to taste

6 stale corn tortillas

1 tablespoon vegetable oil

4 chicken breast halves, skinned, poached, and shredded

Sour cream thinned with milk, for garnish

Chopped avocado (optional)

Soups & Sandwiches

Grill or broil poblano peppers until skin blackens. Place hot peppers in a plastic zipper bag and seal to steam until soft; peel away skin and discard. Slice peppers open, remove stem, and reserve seeds. Slice peppers into 1-inch pieces; set aside.

Heat Dutch oven over medium-low heat; add oil. Sauté onion until soft; stir in garlic and cook 1 minute. Raise heat to medium. Add chopped tomatoes; cook 5 minutes until soft, stirring often. Stir in canned tomatoes, chicken broth, and bay leaf. Add chopped poblano peppers and reserved seeds. Cover and bring soup to a boil, reduce heat to low and simmer 10 minutes.

Grind dried Guajillo or Arbo chile and seeds in a small electric food mill or coffee grinder until the mixture forms a powder. Add to the soup; stir in cumin, salt, and pepper. Slice tortillas in half; then into thin strips with kitchen shears. Sauté in the remaining oil until strips are crisp, about 1 minute. Remove and drain on paper towels; set aside.

Remove bay leaf. In small batches, pureé the soup in a blender, taking care not to overfill it. Transfer pureéd soup to a large saucepan and reheat it over low heat, stirring often. Adjust seasonings.

To serve, place shredded chicken and crisp tortilla strips in soup bowls and ladle the hot soup into the bowls. Top with sour cream and chopped avocado or additional tortilla strips.

Recipe serves 8.

Grilled Smothered Flank Steak Sandwiches

Originally developed as a Super Bowl treat, these hearty main-dish sandwiches have a Southwestern slow-burn-in-the-back-of-the-throat flavor and are ideal for quick meals. For ease of preparation, caramelize the onions while heating the grill and seasoning the flank steak, because they take time to reach optimum golden sweetness.

INGREDIENTS:

2 to 3 large onions, peeled and sliced

2 tablespoons olive or vegetable oil

2 teaspoons salt

1½ teaspoons cumin

¾ teaspoon garlic powder

¾ teaspoon onion powder

½ teaspoon cayenne pepper

½ teaspoon coriander seed, crushed

¼ teaspoon freshly ground black pepper

2 pounds beef flank steak

Juice of 1 lime

1 package hoagie rolls (6 to 8 rolls)

Preheat the outdoor grill. In a large skillet, sauté onions in oil over medium heat until caramel colored, stirring occasionally. Remove them from heat and keep warm.

In a small bowl, stir together the seasonings. Rub the mixture on both sides of the flank steak and grill the steak to desired degree of doneness. Transfer to a cutting board and squeeze the juice of 1 lime over steak. Slice thinly at an angle.

To serve, split the rolls in half lengthwise. Top with slices of flank steak and caramelized onions. If desired, drizzle the rolls with Lime-Cilantro Dressing (page 134) before adding the meat.

Recipe makes 6 to 8 sandwiches.

Mozzarella and Tomato on Focaccia

Like a salad in a sandwich, the classic combo of tomato and mozzarella team up with fresh basil, red onion, feta cheese, and a drizzle of olive oil to form a hearty meal.

On a sunny day, pack up a basket of these sandwiches and take them for a picnic in the park, or wrap them in parchment and serve them at your next tailgate party. To serve, slice sandwiches on the diagonal right through the parchment paper, and pile them into a lined basket.

INGREDIENTS:

2 slices focaccia or other country-style bread

3 teaspoons olive oil (divided)

3 slices mozzarella

3 slices ripe tomato

Salt and freshly ground black pepper, to taste

3 large fresh basil leaves

1 slice red onion

1 large piece leaf lettuce

¼ cup alfalfa sprouts

2 tablespoons feta cheese, crumbled

Brush cut sides of bread with 1 teaspoon of the olive oil. Layer mozzarella and tomato on the bread, and season with salt and freshly ground pepper. Drizzle with remaining olive oil and top with fresh basil.

Separate red onion into rings; place on top of the basil, along with the lettuce and sprouts. Sprinkle with crumbled feta.

Serve immediately or wrap the sandwich in parchment paper.

Recipe makes one sandwich.

Southern-Style Baking Powder Biscuits

With bacon and eggs or as a quick bread for dinner, old-fashioned baking powder biscuits are an American tradition. It takes just a few minutes to whip up a batch of these tall, melt-in-your-mouth biscuits and even less time for them to disappear!

INGREDIENTS:

2 cups flour

1 tablespoon baking powder

¾ teaspoon salt

⅓ cup solid shortening, such as Crisco®

¾ cup milk

Preheat oven to 400 degrees. In a large bowl, stir together flour, baking powder, and salt. Cut in shortening until the mixture resembles crumbs. Pour in milk all at once and stir quickly just until moistened.

Turn dough out onto a lightly floured surface and knead 5 or 6 times. Roll the dough ½ inch thick and cut with a 2-inch biscuit cutter.

Transfer the biscuits to an ungreased cookie sheet and bake in a preheated oven 13 to 15 minutes until the tops of the biscuits are golden brown.

Remove from the oven, place hot biscuits in a cloth-lined basket, and serve with butter, jam, or honey.

Recipe makes approximately 14 biscuits.

Breads

Popovers

Years ago, while visiting Chicago's Water Tower, my good friend from nursing school, Meredith Cowan, and I indulged in a restaurant's signature popovers during lunch. I was immediately smitten by these tall, individual breads that promise so much but are deceptively airy and light. Popovers are easy to make at home and taste divine for breakfast or dinner. They begin to deflate almost immediately once out of the oven, so serve them right away.

INGREDIENTS:

1 cup flour

½ teaspoon salt

3 eggs

1 cup milk

2 tablespoons unsalted butter, melted

Preheat oven to 400 degrees.

In a small bowl, stir together the flour and salt; set aside.

In a large bowl, whip eggs with an electric mixer on low speed until foamy and slightly thick. Stir in milk and melted butter.

Gently whisk flour mixture into egg mixture to form a smooth batter. Spoon the batter into a well-greased popover tin, filling each cup ⅔ full.

Bake on the middle rack of the oven 10 minutes, then lower the heat to 350 degrees. Bake 30 to 35 minutes more until the popovers are very high, firm, and golden brown. Slit each popover with the point of a sharp knife to allow steam to escape. Bake 3 to 5 more minutes.

Carefully remove the popovers from the pan and serve them hot with butter or honey.

Recipe makes 6 to 7 popovers.

Pumpkin 'n' Spice Bread

When the first cool winds of autumn arrive, I always bake something spicy to fill our home with the aromas of cinnamon and spice. This quick bread recipe yields two loaves, so you can enjoy one and share the other with a friend.

INGREDIENTS:

3 cups flour

1¾ cups sugar

1 teaspoon baking soda

1 teaspoon salt

¾ teaspoon baking powder

1½ teaspoons cinnamon

1 teaspoon ground cloves

1 teaspoon freshly grated nutmeg

4 eggs

1 15-ounce can puréed pumpkin

⅓ cup vegetable oil

1 cup milk

Preheat oven to 350 degrees. In a medium bowl, stir together the flour, sugar, baking soda, salt, baking powder, cinnamon, cloves, and nutmeg until well blended.

In a large bowl, whisk eggs lightly, then whisk in canned pumpkin and vegetable oil until the mixture is smooth. Stir in milk, mixing well.

Add the dry ingredients to the pumpkin mixture, stirring well to form a thick batter. Pour batter into 2 greased and floured 9- by 5-inch loaf pans. Bake in a preheated oven 55 to 60 minutes, or until a cake tester comes out clean when inserted into the center of each loaf.

Remove the breads from the oven and cool 15 minutes. Loosen them from the pans and cool on wire racks. Serve warm or cool completely, wrap in plastic wrap, place in freezer bags, and freeze up to 2 months.

Recipe makes 2 loaves.

Country Oatmeal Wheat Bread

Serve this hearty bread with soups and casseroles.

INGREDIENTS:

2 cups warm water

2 envelopes active dry yeast

¼ cup brown sugar, packed

1½ tablespoons olive oil

2¾ cups all-purpose flour

1½ cups whole wheat flour

½ cup regular oatmeal
  (not quick-cooking)

1¼ teaspoons salt

1 tablespoon melted butter

1 tablespoon oatmeal,
  for garnish

In a large bowl, stir together water and yeast. Set aside in a warm place 5 minutes, until yeast has softened and is creamy in appearance. Stir in brown sugar and olive oil.

In a medium bowl, mix 2¼ cups all-purpose flour, and the wheat flour, oatmeal, and salt, stirring well with a wooden spoon. Add enough of the remaining all-purpose flour to make a soft dough.

Turn the dough out onto a floured surface and knead it 4 to 6 minutes, adding additional all-purpose flour as needed, until the dough is shiny and the surface springs back when pressed lightly with a fingertip. Place the dough in a large greased bowl, turning once. Cover with a towel, and set aside in a warm place until the dough has doubled in size, about 1 hour.

Punch down the dough, gather in the edges, and transfer to a lightly floured surface. Knead 4 to 5 times and shape it into a round loaf. Place the loaf on a greased cookie sheet, cover with a towel, and set aside to rise until doubled in size, about 30 minutes.

Preheat the oven to 350 degrees. Gently brush the loaf with melted butter, sprinkle with remaining oatmeal, and bake 30 to 40 minutes until the bread is golden brown and sounds hollow when tapped. Transfer the bread to a wire rack to cool.

Recipe makes one large round loaf.

Apple Streusel Muffins

Nothing starts the day like the aroma of cinnamon wafting from the oven, but don't reserve these light and tender muffins just for breakfast. These cakelike apple and cinnamon muffins are equally delicious with dinnertime casseroles and roasts.

INGREDIENTS:

Muffins:

2 cups flour

¾ cup sugar

1 tablespoon baking powder

1 teaspoon cinnamon

½ teaspoon freshly grated nutmeg

4 teaspoon ground allspice

½ teaspoon salt

6 tablespoons unsalted butter, melted

1 cup milk

2 eggs

1 cup peeled chopped apple

⅓ cup dried cranberries or cherries

Streusel Topping:

¾ cup packed brown sugar

2 tablespoons flour

3 tablespoons slivered almonds

1 teaspoon cinnamon

2 tablespoons butter, melted

Breads

Preheat oven to 400 degrees. In a large mixing bowl, stir together flour, sugar, baking powder, cinnamon, nutmeg, allspice, and salt; set aside.

In a small bowl, whisk together melted butter, milk, and eggs. Pour this egg mixture all at once into the dry ingredients, stirring just until dry ingredients are incorporated. Add chopped apple and dried cranberries or cherries; stir to mix.

Spoon the batter into lined muffin cups, filling each cup ¾ full; set aside.

In a small bowl, stir together brown sugar, flour, almonds, and cinnamon. Add melted butter and stir with a fork until the mixture is crumbly. Spoon streusel mixture on top of muffins.

Bake 18 to 20 minutes until a tester inserted into the center of a muffin comes out clean. Serve muffins hot from the oven or allow them to cool to room temperature. Leftover muffins may be placed in a plastic zipper bag for later use or frozen up to 1 month.

Recipe makes approximately 14 muffins.

Focaccia con Rosmarino

I still remember the first time a waiter served me focaccia. The bread was warm from the oven, and its fragrance of yeast and fresh herbs was intoxicating.

Focaccia is easy to make, so I love serving it when we entertain guests. It's a great recipe to round out an Italian meal, particularly as an accompaniment to the salad course. Served with bowls of olive oil dipping sauce and glasses of wine, freshly baked focaccia adds zest to a gathering of friends around the table.

INGREDIENTS:

1 envelope active dry yeast
  (1 scant tablespoon)

1½ cups warm water

¼ teaspoon sugar

1 teaspoon salt

2 tablespoons olive oil

3 to 4 cups bread flour

¼ cup olive oil

2 teaspoons sea salt or
  kosher salt

2 tablespoons chopped
  fresh rosemary

In a large bowl, sprinkle yeast and sugar over warm water, stir, and set aside in a warm place 10 to 15 minutes until the mixture begins to foam. With a large wooden spoon, stir in salt, 2 tablespoons olive oil, and 2 cups flour. Mix well.

Breads

Add enough of the remaining flour to form a soft dough. Turn the dough out onto a floured surface and knead until dough is smooth and springs back when pressed lightly with a fingertip. Shape the dough into a ball and place in an oiled bowl, turning once to coat all surfaces with oil. Cover with a towel and set aside in a warm place to rise, approximately 40 minutes. After the dough has doubled, punch it down with your fist, turn in the edges of the dough, and transfer it to a lightly floured surface. Knead several times until the dough is smooth.

Cut the dough in half and shape each half into an 8-inch round, approximately 1 inch thick. Place each round on a greased baking sheet and cover with a towel. Set aside to rise, about 30 minutes. Dimple the risen rounds at 1-inch intervals with a fingertip, brush them with remaining oil, and sprinkle them with salt and chopped rosemary.

Preheat oven to 425 degrees. Bake 12 to 15 minutes, or until breads are golden brown. To serve, slice focaccia and dip in Olive Oil and Balsamic Dipping Sauce (page 162).

Recipe makes 2 large loaves.

For faster bread, eliminate the first rise. After kneading dough, divide in half and shape each half into an 8-inch round. Proceed with remaining instructions.

Olive Oil and Balsamic Dipping Sauce

My good friend, Eric Little, who collaborated with me on the wine notes for this cookbook, taught me the finer points of creating a truly flavorful dipping sauce for focaccia and other Italian breads. One taste of this sauce, and you'll never be satisfied with plain olive oil again!

INGREDIENTS:

½ cup virgin olive oil

2 teaspoons balsamic vinegar

2 tablespoons freshly grated Parmesan cheese

¼ teaspoon coarse salt

Freshly ground black pepper

Pour olive oil into a shallow plate. Sprinkle on vinegar, Parmesan cheese, salt, and pepper. Swirl the mixture with a knife to mix.

Place the dipping sauce in the center of the table, or for larger groups, place several plates of dipping sauce around the table.

Dip focaccia or other Italian bread into the sauce and enjoy!

Recipe makes approximately ⅓ cup.

Old-Fashioned Strawberry Ice Cream Soda

Across the country, old-fashioned ice cream soda shops still delight children of all ages. While the shops are not as numerous as they once were, patrons of the Highland Park Pharmacy in Dallas, Texas; the Union Dairy in Freeport, Illinois; and countless other establishments still enjoy sodas made the time-honored way.

Now you can enjoy this old-fashioned treat at home. This strawberry ice cream soda recipe tastes just like you remember. The secret is in the mixing—a technique I learned while sitting on a swivel stool across the counter from a "soda jerk."

INGREDIENTS:

⅓ cup frozen sliced sweetened strawberries, thawed

2 tablespoons milk

2 generous scoops vanilla ice cream (divided)

Chilled seltzer water

Whipped cream, maraschino cherries, and sprinkles, for garnish

In a tall glass or mug, combine strawberries, milk, and 1 scoop of ice cream. Using a spoon, mash the strawberries into the ice cream and milk, until mixture is very smooth. Add ¼ cup seltzer water and stir well to mix.

Add the remaining scoop of ice cream and fill the glass with seltzer water, stirring gently to mix. Top with a swirl of whipped cream, a cherry, and sprinkles. Add a straw and serve.

Recipe makes one soda.

Old-Fashioned Chocolate Ice Cream Soda:

If you crave chocolate ice cream sodas in the summertime, substitute ⅓ cup Hershey's chocolate syrup for the sweetened strawberries. It's a chocoholic's dream come true!

All-American Apple Pie

How often have we heard the phrase, "As American as Mom and apple pie"? With a buttery, flaky crust that almost melts in the mouth and a natural-juice apple filling with just the right amount of cinnamon and spice, my classic apple pie recipe is just the thing for your next Fourth of July picnic, or anytime you want to celebrate the good ol' USA.

INGREDIENTS:

Pastry:

2 cups all-purpose flour

½ cup sifted cake flour0

1 teaspoon salt

2 tablespoons sugar

½ cup cold unsalted butter, cut into 8 pieces

¼ cup shortening

6 tablespoons ice water

Place flours, salt, and sugar in bowl of a food processor; pulse several times to mix. Add cold butter and shortening; pulse until butter is pea-size.

Add 5 tablespoons ice water. Process at low speed until pastry forms crumbs; add the remaining ice water if the mixture appears dry. Process on low until the pastry forms a ball.

Remove the pastry, divide it in half, and wrap each half in plastic wrap. Refrigerate at least 30 minutes.

Desserts

Filling:

7 large Granny Smith or other tart, firm apples

Juice of ½ lemon

1 cup sugar

2 tablespoons flour

1¾ teaspoons cinnamon

¼ teaspoon freshly grated nutmeg

3 tablespoons unsalted butter, melted

1 egg

1 tablespoon water

2 teaspoons sparkling or granulated sugar

Peel and core apples. Slice them into a large bowl; sprinkle with lemon juice, and toss well, to keep them from browning. In a small bowl, stir together the sugar, flour, cinnamon, and nutmeg; pour over the apples. Toss to coat the apples thoroughly, then pour in melted butter and toss to mix.

Preheat the oven to 375 degrees. Roll out the bottom pastry on a floured pastry cloth, fold it in half, and transfer it to a 10-inch pie plate. Unfold the pastry and adjust it to fit the bottom of the pie plate. Pour the apple mixture into the pie shell, spooning extra juices over apples.

Roll out the top crust, fold it in half to lift, and unfold it over apples. Trim the pastry and crimp to seal the edges. Cut several slits in the top crust so steam can escape.

In a small bowl, whisk egg and water together with a fork to form an egg wash. Brush this over the pastry and sprinkle with sparkling or granulated sugar.

Bake in a preheated oven 40 to 50 minutes, or until pastry is golden brown and filling is bubbly. Transfer the pie to a wire rack to cool. Serve warm or at room temperature with a scoop of vanilla ice cream, if desired. Cover leftover pie and refrigerate up to several days.

Recipe makes one 10-inch double-crust pie.

Old Glory Cherry Pie

When fresh, orchard cherries are at their peak, it's time to make homemade cherry pie. Several styles of cherry pitters make the job of removing the cherry pits quick and easy. And the extra time involved is well worth the trouble, because there is no substitute for the flavor of a fresh-from-the-orchard cherry pie.

This delicious pie proudly displays the red, white, and blue. Red and blue food coloring are mixed into an egg wash, which is carefully brushed over the free-form pastry flag with a clean, narrow paintbrush before baking. It's a pie you can be proud of at your next summertime celebration.

INGREDIENTS:

Pastry:

2½ cups flour

¼ cup sugar

1 teaspoon salt

1¼ cups cold unsalted butter

2 eggs

2 egg yolks

1 tablespoon ice water

1 egg (for egg wash)

1 tablespoon water

Red and blue food coloring for garnish

2 teaspoons sparkling or granulated sugar (Sparkling sugar is a large-grain, coarse sugar that does not melt while baking.)

Place flour, sugar, and salt in the bowl of a food processor; pulse several times to mix. Slice butter into tablespoon-size pieces, add to processor, and pulse until butter is pea-size. Add 2 eggs, yolks and ice water; pulse until the pastry comes together into a ball. Remove it from the processor, divide in half, and wrap both halves in plastic wrap. Chill at least 30 minutes.

Desserts

Roll one chilled pastry out on a floured pastry cloth or counter and place in a 10-inch pie plate. Spoon cherry pie filling into the pastry, dot with butter, and top with the remaining pastry. Save any scraps, reroll them, and, using a sharp knife, cut out a flag. Lightly score the pastry with knife to create stars and stripes; set aside.

In a small bowl, whisk together remaining egg and water to form an egg wash. Brush the entire surface of the crust with egg wash. Position the flag in the center of the top crust and brush it lightly with egg wash. Cut several slits around the perimeter of the top crust to allow steam to escape.

Spoon 2 tablespoons egg wash into each of 2 small cups. Stir red food coloring into one cup and blue into other cup. Using a small paintbrush, paint red stripes and a blue background for stars onto the flag. Sprinkle top of pastry with sparkling or granulated sugar.

Bake at 375 degrees 30 to 35 minutes until the pastry is golden brown and the filling is bubbly. Remove from the oven and cool on a wire rack. Serve pie warm or chill it in refrigerator.

Cherry Filling:

5 cups fresh cherries, pitted (about 2¼ pounds)

1 cup sugar

3 tablespoons flour

1½ tablespoons fresh lemon juice

1 tablespoon butter

Use a cherry pitter to remove pits, and place the cherries in a large mixing bowl. In a medium bowl, stir sugar and flour together until well mixed. Add lemon juice and toss to mix. Spoon into the pie shell and dot with the butter.

Recipe makes one 10-inch pie.

Lemon Meringue Pie

I always think of my grandfather, Sebastian Schnoes, when I think of lemon meringue pie. It was his favorite dessert, and as a teenager and young adult, I made it for him whenever he and my grandmother came to visit. Ultimately, I created this made-from-scratch version, using freshly squeezed lemon juice. The flavor and texture of this classic pie are sublime; Granddad would have loved it.

INGREDIENTS:

Pastry:

1 cup all-purpose flour

¼ cup sifted cake flour

1 tablespoon sugar

½ teaspoon salt

5 tablespoons cold unsalted butter

2 tablespoons Crisco® shortening

2 to 3 tablespoons ice water

Place flours, sugar, and salt in the bowl of a food processor; pulse several times to mix. Slice cold butter into 5 pieces. Add cold butter and shortening; pulse until butter is pea-size. Pour in ice water; pulse until the pastry comes together into a ball. Remove the pastry, wrap it in plastic wrap, and chill it at least 30 minutes.

Preheat oven to 425 degrees. Roll out the pastry on a floured pastry cloth or surface. Transfer it to a 10-inch pie plate, flute the edges, and prick the crust with a fork. Bake the pie shell 10 to 12 minutes until pastry is lightly browned. Remove from the oven and cool completely.

Desserts

Filling:

1¼ cups sugar

1 package unflavored gelatin

⅓ cup cornstarch

¼ teaspoon salt

3 egg yolks

1½ cups water

½ cup freshly squeezed lemon juice

1 teaspoon lemon zest

In a large saucepan, stir together the sugar, gelatin, cornstarch, and salt. Whisk in egg yolks, water, lemon juice, and zest. Cook over medium heat, stirring constantly, until the mixture thickens and just comes to a boil. Remove the saucepan from the heat; set aside 15 minutes to cool, stirring every 5 minutes. Pour into cooled pie shell.

Meringue:

4 egg whites, room temperature

¼ teaspoon cream of tartar

½ cup sugar

Preheat oven to 400 degrees.

With a mixer on high speed, whip egg whites and cream of tartar until the whites are foamy. Gradually add sugar, beating until the meringue forms stiff peaks.

With an offset spatula or knife, spread the meringue over the lemon filling, sealing it well at the edges of pastry. Bake in a preheated 400-degree oven 5 to 10 minutes until meringue is pale brown. Cool 40 minutes, then refrigerate until ready to serve.

Recipe makes 8 servings (one 10-inch pie).

Black Plum Galette

A few summers ago, when the black plums were especially plump and beautiful, I created this glorious tart while on vacation in the Rocky Mountains. To save time, I left the skin on the plums, which gave the tart a lovely pink color.

INGREDIENTS:

Pastry:

1¼ cups flour	1 egg
2 tablespoons sugar	1 egg yolk
½ teaspoon salt	1 tablespoon ice water
6 tablespoons cold unsalted butter	

Place flour, sugar, and salt in the bowl of a food processor; pulse several times to mix. Slice butter into 6 pieces, add it to the processor, and pulse until it is pea-size. Add whole egg, yolk and ice water; pulse until the pastry forms a ball. Remove from the processor, wrap in plastic wrap, and chill at least 30 minutes.

Filling:

2¾ pounds large black plums (about 9)	¾ teaspoon cinnamon
¾ cup sugar	¼ teaspoon nutmeg
3 tablespoons flour	⅓ cup melted red currant or apple jelly

Desserts

Preheat oven to 400 degrees. Wash and slice plums, with skins on, into a large bowl, discarding the pits. In a small bowl, stir together the sugar, flour, cinnamon, and nutmeg until well blended. Pour this mixture over the plums and stir well to mix thoroughly.

Roll out the pastry on a floured pastry cloth or surface and fit it into a 10-inch tart pan. Arrange the plums in two layers in the pastry, and spoon half the sugared plum juice over the plums. Place the galette on a baking sheet and bake 30 to 35 minutes until the edges of the pastry are golden brown and the fruit is soft.

Cool galette 30 minutes, then brush fruit with melted currant jelly. Serve warm or chilled.

Recipe makes 8 servings (one 10-inch galette).

Strawberries 'n' Cream Shortcakes

Heart-shaped biscuits, tender and sweet, are paired with ripe, juicy strawberries and a cloud of sweetened cream for this delightful variation of an American favorite.

INGREDIENTS:

2 cups flour

⅓ cup sugar

2½ teaspoons baking powder

½ teaspoon salt

6 tablespoons cold unsalted butter

¾ cup heavy cream

3 tablespoons milk

1 teaspoon vanilla

1 egg

1 tablespoon water

2 tablespoons sparkling or granulated sugar

1 quart strawberries, washed, hulled, and sliced

Sugar to sweeten strawberries, to taste

1 cup heavy cream

1 tablespoon confectioners' sugar

Preheat oven to 375 degrees. In a large bowl, stir together flour, sugar, baking powder, and salt; set aside. Slice cold butter into 6 pieces; cut into flour mixture with a pastry blender until butter is pea-size.

In a glass measuring cup, stir together cream, milk, and vanilla. Pour all at once into the flour mixture and stir until the pastry is moistened. Do not overmix.

Desserts

Shape the dough into a large round and place it on a floured pastry cloth. Roll pastry ½-inch thick and cut it with a floured 3-inch heart-shaped biscuit cutter. Place the biscuits on a lightly greased cookie sheet.

In a small bowl, whisk egg and water together with a fork. Brush the tops of the biscuits with the egg wash and sprinkle with sparkling or granulated sugar. Bake 12 to 14 minutes, or until the tops of the biscuits are golden brown. Transfer the hot biscuits to a wire rack to cool.

Meanwhile, sprinkle sliced strawberries with sugar and stir to mix. Cover and chill until ready to serve. Whip heavy cream and confectioners' sugar until soft peaks form. Cover and chill up to 1 hour.

To serve, split the biscuits in half. Place the bottom halves on dessert plates and top with sweetened strawberries and a dollop of whipped cream. Position top halves of biscuits at an angle and serve.

Recipe makes approximately 12 shortcakes.

Strawberry Cream Tart

Luscious, sweet strawberries, glistening with a blush of red plum jelly, top this light and refreshing tart. Inside, a layer of vanilla bean pastry cream awaits discovery, cradled in flaky, buttery pastry.

INGREDIENTS:

Pastry:

1 cup all-purpose flour

¼ cup sifted cake flour

½ teaspoon salt

1 tablespoon sugar

¼ cup cold unsalted butter

2 tablespoons shortening

2 to 3 tablespoons ice water

Place flours, salt, and sugar in a food processor; pulse several times to mix. Slice the butter into 4 pieces; add it to the processor, along with the shortening. Pulse until butter is pea-size. Add water and process until the pastry forms a ball. Wrap the pastry in plastic wrap and refrigerate at least 30 minutes.

Preheat oven to 400 degrees. Roll out the pastry on a floured pastry cloth to fit an 8- by 12-inch rectangular tart pan. Transfer the pastry to the pan, trimming it to overhang the tart pan by ½ inch. Fold the excess pastry over, forming double-thick sides. Prick the bottom of the pastry with a fork.

Place the tart pan on a baking sheet and bake 10 to 12 minutes until pastry is golden brown. Cool and set aside while preparing filling.

Desserts

Filling:

1 vanilla bean

1 cup milk

3 egg yolks

½ cup sugar

2 tablespoons flour

1 tablespoon unsalted butter

2 quarts fresh strawberries, hulled

½ cup plum jelly

Using a sharp knife, slit vanilla bean lengthwise. Scrape out the seeds, and place them and bean in a medium saucepan; add milk. Scald the milk and vanilla bean, remove from heat, and set aside.

In a medium bowl, beat egg yolks with sugar and flour until thick and pale in color. Remove the vanilla bean from the milk. Whisk a small amount of hot milk into the egg mixture to temper the eggs; then pour the tempered egg mixture into the remaining hot milk in the saucepan. Cook over medium heat, stirring constantly until the mixture thickens. Do not boil.

Pour the pastry cream into a medium bowl, gently rub top of the pastry cream with butter, and cover with a small cloth and plastic wrap. Refrigerate the pastry cream until cold.

To assemble tart, remove the tart shell from pan and transfer it to a serving tray. Spoon chilled pastry cream into the shell and top with strawberries.

Melt plum jelly in a small saucepan over low heat and brush it over berries. Refrigerate the tart until ready to serve.

Tart may be assembled two hours before serving.

Recipe makes 8 to 10 servings (one 8- by 12-inch tart).

Angel Food Cake

This tall, light-as-angels'-wings cake is always popular. Serve it alone or with sliced, fresh fruit or a scoop of ice cream. If you've never tasted homemade Angel Food Cake, you're in for a real treat. One bite, and you'll think you've gone to heaven.

INGREDIENTS:

1 cup sifted cake flour

½ cup sugar

12 egg whites

1½ teaspoons cream of tartar

2 teaspoons vanilla

½ teaspoon salt

1 cup sugar

Preheat oven to 350 degrees. Place oven rack in the second position from the bottom.

In a small bowl, stir together cake flour and ½ cup sugar; set aside.

Whip egg whites until foamy, add cream of tartar, and continue whipping until a very soft meringue is formed. Add vanilla and salt.

Whip the meringue at high speed and gradually sprinkle in the remaining sugar. Continue whipping until the meringue is glossy and forms stiff peaks, but is not dry.

Sprinkle ½ the flour mixture over the meringue. Using a large rubber spatula, gently fold in flour mixture. Sprinkle remaining flour over the meringue and gently fold it into the meringue until well blended, taking care not to deflate the meringue.

Gently spoon the mixture into a 10-inch ungreased tube pan. Smooth the top of the batter with a spatula. Bake in preheated oven 40 to 45 minutes until top crust is light brown and dry to the touch. Remove from oven and turn tube pan upside down over a bottle to cool completely.

Recipe makes 10 to 12 servings (one cake).

Desserts

Apfelküchen

This moist German apple cake has a lovely, light texture. Serve it for dessert at night and breakfast the next morning.

INGREDIENTS:

1 cup unsalted butter, softened

1¾ cups sugar

3 eggs

2 teaspoons vanilla

2½ cups flour

1 teaspoon salt

1 teaspoon baking soda

¼ teaspoon baking powder

½ cup milk

2 medium apples, peeled, cored, and chopped

1 medium apple, peeled, cored, and thinly sliced

2 tablespoons sugar (divided)

¼ teaspoon cinnamon

Preheat oven to 350 degrees. In the large bowl of an electric mixer, cream butter and sugar until light and fluffy, about 8 minutes. Add eggs, one at a time, mixing well after each addition. Stir in vanilla.

In a medium bowl, stir together flour, baking soda, salt, and baking powder until well mixed. Gradually add dry ingredients to the creamed mixture, alternately with the milk, starting and ending with the flour mixture. Stir in chopped apples.

Grease a 10-inch tube pan and sprinkle the sides with 1 tablespoon of sugar. In a small bowl, mix remaining sugar with cinnamon and sprinkle the mixture on the bottom of the tube pan. Lay the apple slices in a spiral on top of cinnamon sugar.

Spoon the batter on top of the apples. Bake in a preheated oven 50 to 60 minutes, or until a cake tester inserted into the center of the cake comes out clean. Cool the cake 30 minutes. Remove the cake from the pan by inverting it on a large plate, then transfer it to a wire rack to finish cooling. The cinnamon apple spiral will be on top of the cake.

Recipe makes one 10-inch cake.

Carrot Cake with Cream Cheese Frosting

For birthdays or any day, everyone loves this traditional layer cake. Starting as a dense batter, with finely shredded carrot and just the right amount of spice, this moist cake is surprisingly light and tender. For variety, add raisins and chopped nuts.

INGREDIENTS:

Cake:

2 cups flour	¼ teaspoon ground cloves
2 teaspoons baking powder	½ cup unsalted butter, softened
1 teaspoon salt	1 cup sugar
1¼ teaspoons cinnamon	2 eggs
½ teaspoon freshly grated nutmeg	⅔ cup milk
¼ teaspoon ginger	1½ cups grated carrot

Preheat oven to 350 degrees. In a medium bowl, stir together flour, baking powder, salt, and spices; set aside.

In the large bowl of an electric mixer, cream butter and sugar until light and fluffy, about 8 minutes. Add eggs, one at a time, beating well after each addition.

Gradually beat flour mixture into creamed mixture, alternately with the milk, to form a very thick, creamy batter. Stir in grated carrot.

Grease and flour two 9-inch round cake pans; spoon the batter into the pans. Bake 30 to 35 minutes, or until a cake tester inserted into the center of the cakes comes out clean. Remove the cakes from the oven and cool them 20 minutes. Remove them from the pans and cool completely on a wire rack.

Desserts

Cream Cheese Frosting:

6 ounces cream cheese, softened

6 tablespoons unsalted butter, softened

4 cups sifted confectioners' sugar

1 tablespoon milk

½ teaspoon vanilla

In the bowl of an electric mixer, beat cream cheese and butter until smooth. Gradually add confectioners' sugar, beating well after each addition. Stir in milk and vanilla.

Place the bottom cake layer on a serving plate. Spread frosting on top of the layer with an offset spatula or knife, then place the second layer on top of the first. Frost the sides of cake. Spread the remaining frosting on top of the cake and refrigerate until ready to serve.

Recipe makes one 9-inch 2-layer cake.

Springtime Orange Cake

I created this lovely light cake with its essence of fresh orange for a garden birthday celebration for my dear friend, Dyan Anderson. It was a glorious spring-like day, despite the late-February date, and I invited a small group of Dyan's friends to join us for lunch in the garden.

I set a table near my English garden, which was already alive with pink tulips, white alyssum, and pansies in hues of blue, pink, and purple. The table was draped in several layers of white, lacy linens, and I arranged large wicker chairs around the table with a soft, oversized, embroidered white linen pillow tucked into each chair.

Lunch was followed with gaily wrapped gifts and this scrumptious cake, frosted with fluffy white frosting and decorated with a shell border, flowers, and inscription. I will always love this cake for the memories it recalls of a special day of love and friendship.

INGREDIENTS:

¾ cup unsalted butter, softened	2¾ cups flour
1¾ cups sugar	2½ teaspoons baking powder
2 teaspoons grated orange zest	1 teaspoon salt
2 eggs	¼ teaspoon baking soda
1 teaspoon vanilla	1⅓ cups milk

Preheat oven to 350 degrees. In the large bowl of an electric mixer, cream butter, sugar, and orange zest until light and fluffy, about 8 minutes. Add eggs and vanilla, beating until thoroughly combined.

In a medium bowl, stir together the flour, baking powder, salt, and baking soda until well blended. Gradually beat dry ingredients into the creamed mixture, alternately with milk, scraping the bowl often, until the batter is thick and smooth.

Desserts

Pour the batter into 2 greased and floured 9-inch round pans. Bake in a preheated oven 30 to 35 minutes, or until a tester inserted into the center of the cakes comes out clean.

Remove from the oven and cool on a wire rack 20 minutes. Remove the cakes from the pans and cool completely.

Frost the layers with Fluffy White Frosting.

Fluffy White Frosting:

2 egg whites, at room temperature

⅓ cup water

¼ teaspoon cream of tartar

1¼ cups sugar

½ teaspoon vanilla

Place the egg whites and water in a large heatproof bowl. Beat with an electric mixer until the mixture begins to foam. Add the cream of tartar.

Place the bowl over a pan of simmering water, but do not allow the bowl to touch the water. Continue beating the egg white mixture until it is doubled in volume. Gradually add the sugar, beating until the frosting is thick and glossy. Remove it from the heat and stir in the vanilla.

Place the bottom cake layer on a serving plate. Spread frosting on top of the layer with an offset spatula or knife, then place the second layer on top of the first. Frost the sides of the cake. Spoon the frosting onto the top of the cake and spread to seal the edges.

Spoon remaining frosting into a decorator bag fitted with a shell tip and pipe a decorative edge around cake.

Recipe makes one 9-inch cake.

Apple Fritters

These little gems taste like apple doughnuts and are a whole lot easier to make. Dusted with cinnamon powdered sugar, they are a tasty impromptu treat on an unexpected snow day or rainy weekend.

INGREDIENTS:

1 cup all-purpose flour

½ cup sifted cake flour

2 teaspoons baking powder

½ teaspoon salt

2 eggs

1 cup milk

2 tablespoons unsalted butter, melted

1 teaspoon vanilla

1 cup shredded apple

Vegetable oil for deep-frying

¾ cup confectioners' sugar, for garnish

1 teaspoon cinnamon, for garnish

In a small bowl, stir together the flours, baking powder, and salt; set aside.

In a large bowl, whisk the eggs until light. Stir in milk, melted butter, and vanilla. Gradually whisk in the flour mixture until smooth. Stir in shredded apple.

Add oil to a large skillet or electric skillet to a depth of 1 inch. Heat over medium heat, or 350 degrees on the electric skillet.

When the oil is hot, fry 2-tablespoon portions of batter. Cook the fritters 1 minute; then turn them over with a large slotted spoon and cook on other side 1 to 1½ minutes until the fritters are puffy and golden brown. Drain on paper towels.

Mix confectioners' sugar and cinnamon together in a small bowl and dust the warm fritters with this mixture. Serve warm.

Recipe makes 18 3-inch fritters.

Desserts

Pound Cake Supreme

This versatile, buttery-tasting pound cake has a tender crumb and light texture. Enjoy it all by itself or dress it up with a serving of berry or custard sauce, ice cream, fresh strawberries and whipped cream, or a generous helping of chocolate fudge sauce. Bake this cake in loaf pans, and it becomes the foundation for Baked Alaska, or slice it into small squares to make an English trifle or to serve with Chocolate Fondue.

INGREDIENTS:

1 cup unsalted butter, softened	1 teaspoon baking powder
2¼ cups sugar	½ teaspoon salt
4 eggs	1 cup milk
2¾ cups flour	2 teaspoons vanilla

Preheat oven to 325 degrees. In the large bowl of an electric mixer, cream butter and sugar until the mixture is light and fluffy, about 8 minutes. Add eggs, one at a time, beating well after each addition.

In a medium bowl, stir together flour, baking powder, and salt until well blended. Gradually add the flour mixture to the creamed mixture alternately with milk, until the batter is thick and smooth, scraping the bowl often. Stir in vanilla.

Spoon batter into a greased and floured 12-cup Bundt or tube pan. Bake in a preheated oven 1 hour, 10 minutes, or until a cake tester inserted into center of cake comes out clean. Remove from the oven and cool 15 minutes in the pan on a wire rack. Remove from the pan and cool completely.

Recipe makes 1 cake.

To bake pound cake in 9- by 5-inch loaf pans, raise the oven temperature to 350 degrees and bake cakes 50 to 55 minutes. Use loaf pound cakes as the foundation for Baked Alaska; recipe makes 2 loaf cakes.

Chocolate Pound Cake

This easy-does-it cake is tender, with a light chocolate flavor. I take this cake to block parties and committee meetings, and it's always popular. Baked in a tube pan, it looks pretty with a confectioner's sugar glaze drizzled along the top and down the sides and a sprinkling of multicolored nonpareils.

INGREDIENTS:

3 squares unsweetened chocolate

2¾ cups flour

1 teaspoon baking powder

1 teaspoon salt

½ teaspoon baking soda

1 cup unsalted butter, softened

2¾ cups sugar

4 eggs

2 teaspoons vanilla

1 cup plus 2 tablespoons milk

1 recipe Sugar Glaze

Multicolored nonpareils, for garnish

Preheat oven to 325 degrees. Melt chocolate in a double boiler over hot, not boiling water, or melt it in the microwave at 50 percent power, until it is very soft, but has retained much of its shape, about 2 minutes. Stir until smooth; set aside.

In a medium bowl, stir together flour, baking powder, salt, and baking soda until well mixed.

In the large bowl of an electric mixer, cream butter with sugar until light and fluffy, about 8 minutes. Add eggs, beating well after each addition. Stir in vanilla and melted chocolate.

Desserts

Gradually add dry ingredients to the creamed mixture alternately with the milk, until the batter is thick and smooth. Grease and flour a tube pan. Spoon the batter into the pan and bake in a preheated oven 1 hour, 15 minutes, or until a cake tester inserted into center of cake comes out clean.

Remove cake from the oven; cool 30 minutes. Insert a sharp knife between the inside of the pan and the cake and run it around the whole cake. Remove the cake from the pan, and cool it completely on a wire rack. To garnish, drizzle the cake with Sugar Glaze and sprinkle with nonpareils.

Sugar Glaze:

1½ cups sifted confectioners' sugar

2 to 3 tablespoons milk

¼ teaspoon vanilla extract

In a medium bowl, whisk together confectioners' sugar, milk, and vanilla until the mixture is smooth. Drizzle the glaze from a spoon in a lacy pattern, allowing some of the glaze to dribble down the sides of the cake. Sprinkle the top of the cake with nonpareils while the glaze is still moist.

Recipe makes one cake.

Chocolate Chip Brownies

For anyone who can never get enough chocolate, these brownies have double the amount, thanks to a generous helping of choco-late chips added to the batter. For last-minute gatherings, or casual events that would be incomplete without a chocolate dessert, these cakelike brownies are just the ticket.

INGREDIENTS:

3 squares unsweetened chocolate

½ cup butter

1½ cups sugar

3 eggs

1⅓ cups flour

1 teaspoon baking powder

½ teaspoon salt

1 cup chocolate chips

Preheat oven to 350 degrees. In top of a double boiler set over simmering water, melt chocolate and butter, stirring occasionally, until the mixture is smooth.

Pour the chocolate mixture into a large bowl. Add sugar and eggs, beating well with a large spoon.

In a small bowl, stir together flour, baking powder, and salt; add to the chocolate mixture, stirring well. Stir in chocolate chips.

Pour mixture into a greased 13- by 9-inch baking pan. Bake 20 to 25 minutes, or until a tester inserted into center comes out clean. Cool brownies in the pan, then cut into bars.

Recipe makes 24 2¼-inch brownies.

Desserts

Old-Fashioned Sugar Cookies

I have been making these soft, thick sugar cookies since I first started baking. I used to mail them to my grandmothers because they loved their soft texture and classic vanilla flavor, not to mention the extra dusting of sugar on the top of each one.

For holidays, sprinkle the cookies with tinted sugar—pink, pale green, or yellow in the springtime, red or green for Christmas, and blue for Hanukkah.

INGREDIENTS:

⅔ cup unsalted butter, softened

⅔ cup granulated sugar

2 eggs

2 teaspoons vanilla

2 cups flour

2 teaspoons baking powder

½ teaspoon salt

Sparkling or granulated sugar, for garnish

Preheat oven to 375 degrees. In the large bowl of an electric mixer, cream the butter and sugar until light and fluffy, about 4 minutes. Add eggs, beating well after each egg; stir in vanilla.

In a medium bowl, stir together flour, baking powder, and salt until well mixed. With a large spoon, gradually stir the flour mixture into the creamed mixture to form a soft dough.

Lightly grease cookie sheets. Using floured hands, roll teaspoons of cookie dough into small balls, place them on cookie sheets, and flatten them with the bottom of a glass dipped in flour. Sprinkle cookies with sparkling or granulated sugar and bake in a preheated oven 8 to 11 minutes until they are puffed and barely brown around edges.

Transfer the cookies to wire racks to cool. They will keep well in an airtight container 1 to 2 weeks.

Recipe makes 4 dozen (48) cookies.

Chicken Scaloppine, pages 28–29

Belgian Endive and Pear Salad with Roquefort, page 66

Grilled Lemon Chicken, page 99

Caesar Salad, pages 132–133

Tomato and Asadero Salad, page 134

Cream of Mushroom Soup, page 148

Thick and Creamy Tortilla Soup, pages 150–151

Grilled Smothered Flank Steak Sandwich, page 152

Strawberries 'n' Cream Shortcakes, pages 172–173

Creamy Chilled Cantaloupe Soup, page 230

Roasted Duck Breasts with Port Wine Cherry Sauce, pages 240–241

Louisiana Chicken Andouille Gumbo, pages 250–251

Panna Cotta, page 262

Pears in Light Custard Sauce, page 264

Red Plum Buttermilk Tarts, pages 280–281

Meringue Ghosts, page 337

Entrées
Sandwiches
Side Dishes
Desserts

Entertaining at Home

I love entertaining. I love setting an extra place or two around our table and welcoming friends to join us. I love sharing a precious hour or two with a dear friend over a pot of hot tea and fresh-from-the-oven, buttery scones. And I adore filling our home with a collection of friends, neighbors, and colleagues, surrounded by good food, good wine, and the flicker of candle-light in every corner.

I am uncertain whether I live to entertain or entertain to live, but the two are unquestionably intertwined. By the time I was seven years old, I was already entertaining by preparing breakfast for my sisters every Saturday morning. Granted, my kitchen skills were rather limited then, but that did not hinder me from a ritual I thoroughly enjoyed.

What amazes me about that weekly tradition is, even then, I served the breakfast in courses. Now, tell me, how many seven-year-olds serve any meal in courses? Surely, this was an indication of where my path eventually would lead.

While my sisters watched Saturday morning cartoons and my parents gratefully slept an extra hour, I prepared and served a fruit cocktail as the first course. Influenced by my love of "Shirley Temple" cocktails, I prepared my signature fruit cocktail by slicing fresh fruit into bite-size pieces that were mixed and presented in small cups. A maraschino cherry with stem garnished the top of each cocktail, but the pièce de résistance was several tablespoons of lemon-lime soda or ginger ale, poured slowly over the top of the fruit, and a teaspoonful of cherry juice for flavor and color.

While Lynn, Nancy, and Judy devoured their fruit cocktails, I poured cereal and prepared toast. All of this was eaten on the living room floor or on TV trays in front of the television; in those days, I was concerned only with the presentation of the food, not the ambience of the surroundings. This Saturday morning ritual lasted many years, and, I am happy to say, my youngest sister, Judy, continued the tradition for her own children when they were young.

My mother and father entertained frequently, so I had many opportunities to learn the art of entertaining and become acquainted with the aspects of hosting guests in one's home. The most important lessons I learned from my mother were organizational skills, table settings, and arranging a buffet to facilitate easy access and prevent awkward moments, and that the focus of the gathering is all about pampering one's guests to make them feel special.

With four daughters, my parents had a built-in staff to assist with table arrangements, food preparation, serving, and cleanup. They also pressed us into service for occasional entertainment. During the years we lived in Connecticut, many social gatherings ended with Lynn playing piano; Dad's friend and colleague, Duncan Sutphen, playing the saw or gutbucket; his wife, Barbara, playing the spoons; and "the girls" leading everyone in song. These were special moments we all treasure.

In my years of writing and teaching about entertaining, as well as everyday conversations with friends and acquaintances, I have encountered two main groups of people—those who love to entertain and do so effortlessly and those who never entertain. Generally, the reason people give for not entertaining is a lack of time, but on gentle questioning, they admit the true reason is they don't think they know how to do it.

To me, entertaining is a fancy word for opening my heart to another and setting a place for that person at our family table. We may be having meat loaf or a pot of soup, or Randy may be grilling steaks outside, but I know what is being served is less important than simply sharing it with another.

All entertaining is a variation of this fundamental sharing of food and friendship in one's home. Whether the gathering is a cocktail party, seated formal dinner, bowls of chili around a blazing hearth on a cold winter's day, backyard barbecue, or last-minute invitation to a dinner of chicken noodle casserole, it all boils down to sharing time, a bit of food and wine, and part of oneself to stay connected with those around us. It is this connectedness that adds richness to our lives and the lives of others, keeping us close in heart, mind, and spirit.

This section is filled with recipes and recollections we hope will inspire you to open your heart and home to those around you. If entertaining comes naturally, it is my hope these recipes will make it all the more fun and delicious. But if you have never entertained and are not quite sure where to start, this section is filled with easy-to-manage recipes for hors d'oeuvres, cocktails, entrées, side dishes, and desserts to get you started. Select one or two recipes, invite a friend or two to join you, and ask guests to bring one of their favorite dishes to share. Then light some candles and enjoy the blessings of being together. There is no greater gift.

The acidity of the tomatoes, the pungent garlic, basil, and coarse salt are a beautiful combination with a lighter-bodied red. We have many delicious choices. We can pair this appetizer with the silky, ripe cherry, plum, and cedar of a Rioja from Spain; the petite, but muscular dried cherry and smoke of a Dolcetto from Italy; or the crushed berry and mocha of Malbec from Argentina. Each of these delightful wines has a subtle elegance that will pair with this dish successfully and pleasurably.

$ Trapiche Malbec
(Argentina)

$$ Murrieta Rioja RSV
(Rioja, Spain)

$$$ Prunotto Dolcetto d'Alba
(Piamonte, Italy)

Crostini with Garden Tomatoes and Basil

When the summer garden yields a bumper crop of sweet, juicy tomatoes, invite some friends to come sip wine and nibble on these crostini, topped with fresh-from-the-garden tomatoes.

INGREDIENTS:

½ French baguette

⅓ cup olive oil

1 large clove garlic, peeled

1 large clove garlic, peeled and minced

1 large tomato, seeded and diced

¼ cup chopped fresh basil

Pinch of coarse salt

2 teaspoons olive oil

Slice baguette at an angle into ½-inch-thick slices; transfer to a cookie sheet. Brush the top of the bread with olive oil and rub it with the whole garlic clove.

Preheat the broiler. Place baguette slices under broiler 1 to 2 minutes until bread is golden brown, taking care not to burn it. Remove from the oven, turn the slices over, and brush with olive oil. Return the pan to the oven and broil 1 more minute.

Remove the crostini from cookie sheet and cool them on a wire rack. Crostini may be made 1 day ahead and stored in an airtight container.

Dice seeded tomato into small pieces and mix with chopped basil, minced garlic, and salt. Drizzle the mixture with olive oil, cover, and chill up to 2 hours until ready to assemble.

To serve, spoon the tomato mixture on top of the crostini. Serve immediately so the crostini do not become soggy.

Recipe makes approximately 18 hors d'oeuvres.

Appetizers

Portabella Havarti Turnovers

Light as a feather, these filled puff pastry triangles are absolutely sublime. My guests always go wild over them, so I keep plenty in the freezer for last-minute entertaining.

INGREDIENTS:

1 sheet frozen puff pastry, thawed

1 large Portabella mushroom

½ cup shredded Havarti cheese

1 egg

1 tablespoon water

Open the thawed puff pastry sheet and place it on a lightly floured pastry cloth. Roll the pastry to ⅛ inch thick and slice into 3½- by 3½-inch squares.

Remove the woody stem from the Portabella mushroom. Clean the mushroom with a damp paper towel and slice it in half. Turn the mushroom on its side and, with a sharp knife, trim off the black gills; discard. Trim the remaining portabella half, discarding the gills. Dice the mushroom.

Spoon a scant amount of diced mushroom and cheese into the center of a pastry square. Fold the pastry over to form a triangle and seal the edges with the tines of a fork. Place the turnovers on an un-greased cookie sheet and chill in the refrigerator up to 2 hours.

Alternatively, place the turnovers on a cookie sheet and freeze them. Transfer frozen turnovers to a plastic zipper bag and freeze up to 2 months.

To serve, preheat the oven to 400 degrees. Whip egg and water with a fork and brush the egg wash over the turnovers. Bake in a hot oven 7 to 9 minutes, or until pastry is puffed and golden brown; serve immediately.

Recipe makes approximately 15 turnovers.

We find butter-rich pastry, savory mushrooms, and Havarti cheese call for a crisp, high-acid Chardonnay—we're talking white Burgundy, here. Because the Chardonnay grapes in Burgundy, France, do not have time to ripen soft and golden as they do in California, at harvest, these green, hard grapes are very acidic. Luckily, over the centuries, the French have developed a secondary fermentation called malolactic. This converts the harsh malic acids into soft lactic (yes—milk!) acids.

During the process, a by-product is produced—the same "butter" used in movie popcorn. The result is a very food-friendly, delicate Granny Smith–apple structure, with buttery pear flavors, and a flinty, crisp finish. This can be a very special wine of great depth and complexity.

$+ Chateau Greffiere Macon La Roche-Vineuse "VV"
(Burgundy, France)

$$ Verget Chablis
(Burgundy, France)

$$$ Testarossa Chardonnay "Michaud Vineyard"
(Chalone, California)

New Potatoes with Sautéed Mushrooms and Crème Fraîche

These perfectly divine hors d'oeuvres may be made entirely ahead, except for a quick heating in the oven and the last-minute tiny dollop of crème fraîche. Placing the potatoes in a bed of rock salt prevents them from rolling around on the serving tray and adds a bit of salty flavor.

INGREDIENTS:

15 new or small red potatoes

1 tablespoon olive oil

1 tablespoon unsalted butter

2 cups finely chopped white mushrooms

3 green onions, white and pale green sections only, finely chopped

2 tablespoons chopped parsley

2 teaspoons Marsala or dry sherry

½ teaspoon coarse salt

⅛ teaspoon freshly ground black pepper

1 teaspoon bread crumbs

2 tablespoons crème fraîche or sour cream, for garnish

Fresh parsley, for garnish

Place potatoes in a large saucepan filled with enough water to cover them. Cover the saucepan and bring the water to a boil over high heat. Reduce the heat to medium and cook the potatoes just until tender, about 5 to 8 minutes. Drain, transfer the potatoes to a bowl or platter, and set aside to cool.

Appetizers

Preheat a large skillet over medium-low heat. When the skillet is hot, add oil and butter, swirling the pan to coat. Add mushrooms and green onions; sauté until mushrooms are soft.

Stir in parsley, Marsala, salt, and ground black pepper. Cook the mixture 1 to 2 minutes, stirring constantly. Sprinkle it with bread crumbs and stir to mix; remove from heat.

Slice the potatoes in half and scoop out a small amount of potato from the center of each one. Fill the centers with the mushroom mixture, mounding it slightly. If desired, cover and refrigerate until just before serving.

To serve, preheat the oven to 400 degrees. Transfer the potatoes to a baking sheet and bake in a preheated oven 5 minutes. Remove from the oven and garnish each potato with a tiny dollop of crème fraîche or sour cream and a leaf of parsley.

Recipe makes 30 hors d'oeuvres.

Goat Cheese and Hazelnut Delight

This recipe is an adaptation of one shared with me by my sweet and generous friend, Nathalie Dupree. Nathalie is a PBS television chef known for her expertise in gracious, but realistic, Southern entertaining. My version fits that description perfectly.

INGREDIENTS:

1 pound fresh goat cheese (about 2 cups)

¾ cup unsalted butter, softened

3 tablespoons finely ground hazelnuts

2 tablespoons sherry

¼ teaspoon salt

¾ cup chopped dried apricots, for garnish

¼ cup dried cranberries or dried cherries, for garnish

Raisin bread toast points

In the large bowl of an electric mixer, beat goat cheese and butter just until smooth. Add hazelnuts, sherry, and salt and blend until the mixture is smooth.

Line a quiche pan with plastic wrap, allowing the edges to overhang the pan. Fill the bottom of pan with chopped apricots and cranberries. Drop dollops of the cheese mixture on top of dried fruits and gently spread to the edges of the pan with a knife or offset spatula.

Cover the cheese mixture tightly with plastic wrap and chill several hours or overnight until firm. To unmold, remove the top layer of plastic wrap, place a large platter upside down on top of the quiche pan, and invert. Remove the quiche pan, using the plastic wrap lining to loosen the cheese from the pan. Gently peel the plastic wrap from the cheese spread. The dried fruit layer will now be on top.

Garnish the platter with whole dried apricots and serve with raisin bread toast points.

Recipe serves 16.

When a recipe calls for chopped dried apricots, use kitchen shears to snip them into small pieces. It's so much easier than chopping!

Appetizers

Medjool Dates with Mascarpone

These simple but elegant hors d'oeuvres combine the natural sweetness of large Medjool dates with the creamy, sweet flavor of mascarpone cheese. Piping the soft cheese into the center of each date with a cake decorator bag fitted with a star tip produces an exquisite-looking, bite-size cocktail snack.

INGREDIENTS:

1 pound Medjool dates (about 24 large)

4 ounces mascarpone cheese

Split the centers of dates open lengthwise with a paring knife, taking care not to slice all the way through the date. Remove the pit and discard.

Squeeze dates at the ends to open the pocket, in the same way that you would open a baked potato. Using a cake decorator piping bag fitted with a large star tip, or a small spoon, fill the centers of the dates with mascarpone cheese.

To serve, place filled dates on a silver tray lined with a doily, in a candy compote, or on an attractive platter.

Recipe makes approximately 24 hors d'oeuvres.

Shrimp with Maple Bacon

Every host knows the popularity of boiled shrimp as an hors d'oeuvre. Now, guests can savor one of their favorites in a whole new way. Here, raw shrimp are wrapped in maple bacon, then oven-baked until the shrimp is tender and the bacon lightly crisp. For a beautiful presentation, serve these pretty hors d'oeuvres on a tray garnished with tropical flowers.

INGREDIENTS:

24 large raw shrimp

6 slices maple bacon

Clean and devein shrimp, leaving tails intact, if desired. Slice bacon into quarters, so each slice yields four 1- by 3-inch pieces.

Wrap the middle of each shrimp with a slice of bacon, securing the bacon with a toothpick. Cover and refrigerate the bacon-wrapped shrimp until shortly before serving.

Just before serving, preheat the oven to 400 degrees. Bake the shrimp 8 minutes; then turn them over and bake 2 more minutes to crisp the underside of the bacon. Turn the shrimp over again and bake 5 to 8 more minutes until shrimp are tender and bacon is lightly crisped.

Recipe makes 24 hors d'oeuvres.

Appetizers

Sweetheart Cream with Strawberries

Serve this creamy dip on hors d'oeuvres buffets, or with flutes of dry Champagne on a warm summer evening. Sweetened Neufchâtel cream cheese, garnished with a swirl of strawberry sauce, is presented with ripe, fresh strawberries for dipping.

INGREDIENTS:

3 quarts ripe strawberries

2 8-ounce packages Neufchâtel cream cheese, softened

½ cup sour cream

5 tablespoons sugar

1¼ teaspoons vanilla

1 recipe Strawberry Sauce

Wash strawberries, leaving stems intact. Drain and set aside.

In the large bowl of an electric mixer, whip Neufchâtel cheese with sour cream, sugar, and vanilla until smooth.

Spoon the mixture into a large serving bowl and surround with fresh strawberries. Garnish with a swirl of Strawberry Sauce.

Strawberry Sauce:

2 large ripe strawberries

¾ teaspoon sugar

½ teaspoon fresh lemon juice

¼ teaspoon Triple Sec

Purée strawberries, sugar, lemon juice, and Triple Sec in a mini food processor until smooth and strain into a small bowl.

To garnish Sweetheart Cream, spoon the sauce onto the cream in a thin line and swirl gently with a knife to create a marbled appearance.

When making Strawberry Cream ahead of time, do not spoon mixture into serving bowl. Cover it and chill until 30 minutes before serving. To serve, remove from the refrigerator and allow the mixture to soften 30 minutes. Stir well and spoon into a serving bowl; garnish with Strawberry Sauce.

Smoked Turkey on Cranberry Brioche

Turkey and cranberries just naturally go together. Here's a new twist on this classic pairing for your next cocktail party. Bake the cocktail-size brioche one day ahead, or up to 1 month before your event, wrap well, and freeze. Since this recipe makes three tea-size brioche, it's designed to feed a crowd; for smaller gatherings, use one bread and freeze the remaining ones for use later.

INGREDIENTS:

½ cup warm water

1 package active dry yeast

¼ teaspoon sugar

2½ cups bread flour

¼ cup sugar

¼ cup unsalted butter, softened

½ teaspoon salt

2 eggs

⅔ cup dried cranberries

1 8-ounce container soft cream cheese

Thinly sliced smoked turkey breast

3 9-inch-long metal tea bread cylinders, with end caps

In a small bowl, sprinkle yeast and ¼ teaspoon sugar over warm water; stir. Set aside in a warm place until the yeast begins to foam, about 15 minutes.

In the bowl of an electric mixer, combine 2 cups of the flour and the sugar, butter, salt, and eggs. Beat until the mixture is crumbly. Pour in the yeast mixture and beat until smooth.

Stir in cranberries and just enough of the remaining flour to form a soft dough. Turn the dough out onto a lightly floured surface and knead it several minutes, until the dough is smooth and springs back when touched with a fingertip. Transfer to a large greased bowl, turning once to grease the dough's surface. Cover with a towel and set aside in a warm place until the dough doubles in size, about 45 minutes.

Punch the dough down and knead it several times until smooth. Divide the dough into 3 equal portions and roll each with your hands into a short, fat snakelike form. Spray tea bread cylinders with nonstick cooking spray, insert the bread dough and replace the caps on each end of the cylinders. Set aside in a warm place until the dough rises, about 20 minutes.

Preheat the oven to 375 degrees and bake the breads 18 to 20 minutes. Place cylinders on a wire rack, remove the ends, and cool 10 to 15 minutes. Remove the breads from the cylinders; cool completely.

To serve, slice the breads into ½-inch-thick slices. Spread with softened cream cheese and top with thinly sliced smoked turkey breast. Pipe additional cream cheese in a small rosette shape, if desired.

Recipe makes three 9-inch tea breads.

Jalapeño Salsa

This is my version of Southwestern salsa. Those who like it really spicy may wish to add an extra jalapeño or splash of hot pepper sauce, while those just getting the hang of Mexican foods may wish to include only one jalapeño pepper. Just remember, all you Northern neophytes, keep your hands away from your face when working with jalapeños; their oil can make the eyes burn.

INGREDIENTS:

2¼ pounds ripe tomatoes (about 7 medium)

2 cloves garlic, peeled

1 small onion, quartered and coarsely chopped

2 large jalapeños

2 tablespoons freshly squeezed lime juice

¾ teaspoon coarse salt

Freshly ground black pepper, to taste

2 tablespoons chopped fresh cilantro

Bring a saucepan of water to boil, lower the tomatoes into the water, and boil 30 seconds to loosen their skin. Peel, quarter, and seed the tomatoes. Place them in bowl of a food processor; add garlic and onion.

Slice the stem ends from jalapeños; discard. Slice the chiles in half and, with the tip of a knife, trim out the membrane and seeds; discard. Chop chiles into several pieces and add them to the processor, along with lime juice, salt, and pepper.

Pulse the mixture until the vegetables are finely chopped; do not overprocess. Transfer salsa to a small mixing bowl; stir in chopped cilantro. Cover tightly with plastic wrap and chill several hours or overnight. The flavors will meld while chilling.

Recipe makes approximately 3¾ cups salsa.

Tapenade on Pain Grillé

During a cruise along the East Coast, Randy and I enjoyed lunch in a wonderful restaurant in Bar Harbor, Maine, where the house specialty was steamed lobster. While we waited for our lunches, a basket of hot, homemade yeast rolls and a small crock of tapenade were delivered to every table. The tapenade had just the right balance of salty olives, fresh lemon juice, and olive oil.

For hors d'oeuvres, I serve tapenade on toast points or Pain Grillé, French grilled mini toasts available in some specialty supermarkets.

INGREDIENTS:

½ cup chopped pitted kalamata olives

½ cup chopped pitted green Spanish olives

¼ cup roasted sweet red peppers, packed in oil, drained

½ cup extra-virgin olive oil

2 tablespoons chopped fresh Italian parsley

1½ tablespoons freshly squeezed lemon juice

¾ teaspoon dried oregano

¼ teaspoon freshly ground black pepper

Place kalamata and Spanish olives and roasted red peppers in a food processor; pulse until olives and peppers are finely chopped. Add olive oil, parsley, lemon juice, oregano, and black pepper. Pulse several times to mix.

Transfer tapenade to a bowl, cover, and chill at least 1 hour to allow flavors to meld.

To serve, spoon tapenade onto Pain Grillé or toast points and arrange on a serving tray.

Recipe makes approximately 1¾ cups tapenade.

Simple Syrup

Simple syrup is the foundation of many cocktails, so I keep a jar of it in the refrigerator for impromptu celebrations.

INGREDIENTS:

1 cup water

1 cup sugar

Combine water and sugar in a small saucepan. Cook over medium heat 3 to 5 minutes, stirring occasionally, until the sugar melts. Cool and store in a covered jar in the refrigerator. The mixture keeps several weeks.

Recipe makes 1⅔ cups.

Raspberry Cosmopolitan

This sophisticated drink is smooth, with the right balance of sweet and tart. It looks gorgeous in a martini glass.

INGREDIENTS:

1 lime wedge

2 tablespoons granulated sugar for glass rim

3 fresh raspberries, for garnish

2 ounces vodka

2 ounces cran-raspberry juice

2 ounces freshly squeezed lime juice

1 ounce Cointreau

1 ounce simple syrup

Moisten the rim of glass with a lime wedge. Pour sugar into a saucer and dip the rim of the glass into sugar to coat. Place fresh raspberries in the bottom of the glass, and set aside.

Fill a cocktail shaker ½ full with ice cubes. Pour in vodka, cran-raspberry juice, lime juice, Cointreau, and simple syrup. Cover and shake until cocktail is chilled and well blended. Strain into a glass and serve.

Recipe makes 1 cocktail.

Cocktails

Sidecar

A good friend and colleague, Carla Nichols, introduced me to this very festive cocktail. In fact, I later built an entire cocktail party around the Sidecar, making it the signature drink of the evening, and it was one of the most successful parties I have ever given.

For the party, I hired a bartender to make Sidecars one at a time, so guests could watch their cocktails being prepared. Blending the ingredients, the action of the cocktail shaker, and garnishing the martini glass with multicolored sparkling sugar to produce a jeweled effect was a recipe for built-in party entertainment. Several years later, people still comment to me about that party!

INGREDIENTS:

2 ounces Remy Martin Fine Champagne Cognac VSOP

1 ounce Cointreau

1 ounce freshly squeezed lemon juice

1 lemon wedge

½ ounce simple syrup (p. 204) (optional)

Multicolored sparkling sugar or granulated sugar, for garnish

Fill a cocktail shaker ½ full with ice. Pour in Cognac, Cointreau, and lemon juice. Shake until chilled and well blended.

Rub a lemon wedge around the rim of the martini glass. Pour sparkling sugar onto a medium plate and shake to distribute it around the plate. Dip the rim of the glass into sugar.

Strain the cocktail into the glass and serve. If it's too tart, add ½ ounce simple syrup to the cocktail shaker, along with the other ingredients.

Recipe makes 1 cocktail.

Classic Margarita

Living in Texas, I am surrounded by some of the best places to enjoy a really great Margarita. In fact, the birthplace of the Frozen Margarita is less than two miles from my home. I have several recipes for Margaritas that I really love. Depending on my mood, I may opt for the Classic Margarita, made with tequila and Cointreau; the Frozen Margarita, blended with tequila, triple sec, and ice until thick and frothy; or a quick and easy version— Barb Mullen's Margarita, a recipe given to me by my dear friend, Barb, and made with frozen limeade. It's no wonder my sons call me "Margarita Mama"!

INGREDIENTS:

2 ounces good-quality tequila

1 ounce Cointreau

1 ounce freshly squeezed
  lime juice

½ teaspoon confectioners'
  sugar (optional)

1 lime wedge

Coarse salt, for garnish

Fill a cocktail shaker ½ full with ice. Pour in tequila, Cointreau, lime juice, and confectioners' sugar, if desired. Shake until chilled and well blended.

Rub a lime wedge around the rim of a Margarita glass. Pour coarse salt onto a medium plate and shake to distribute the salt around the plate. Dip the rim of the glass into the salt.

Strain the cocktail into the glass and serve.

Recipe makes 1 cocktail.

Cocktails

Barb Mullen's Frozen Margarita

My sweet friend and former neighbor, Barb Mullen, is a registered dietitian and terrific cook. Her recipe for Margaritas is delicious and convenient, because it uses frozen limeade instead of fresh limes. I always keep a can or two of limeade in my freezer during our warm Texas weather so I can whip up a batch of Margaritas at the drop of a sombrero.

INGREDIENTS:

1 6-ounce can frozen limeade

6 ounces tequila

3 ounces triple sec

2 teaspoons confectioners' sugar

3 cups ice cubes

1 lime, sliced into wedges, for garnish

Coarse salt, for garnish

Place frozen limeade in a blender. Using the empty can as a liquid measure, measure tequila and triple sec and pour them into blender. Add confectioners' sugar and pulse just to mix.

Add ice cubes and purée until mixture is thick and smooth.

Rub a lime wedge around the rims of the glasses. Pour coarse salt onto a medium plate and dip the glass rims in the salt.

Pour the Margarita mixture into glasses and garnish with a wedge of lime. Pour any unused Margarita mixture into a freezer-proof container and freeze up to 2 weeks.

Recipe makes 4 to 6 cocktails.

Frozen Rum-Rita

Enjoy all the tropical fun and flavor of a frozen Margarita without the tequila. My journeys to the Caribbean have inspired me to pair rum with Cointreau for a deliciously refreshing island cocktail.

INGREDIENTS:

4 ounces amber rum

2 ounces Cointreau

2 ounces freshly squeezed
lime juice

1 teaspoon confectioners' sugar

2 cups ice cubes

2 tablespoons lime juice,
for rims of glasses

3 tablespoons kosher salt

2 slices lime, for garnish

Measure rum, Cointreau, lime juice, and confectioners' sugar into a blender. Add ice cubes, cover the blender tightly, and blend until the mixture is smooth and creamy in appearance.

Pour additional lime juice into a saucer and salt into another saucer. Turn Rum-rita glasses upside down; dip the rims of glasses in the lime juice, then in the salt.

Pour the Rum-rita into glasses and garnish with a slice of lime.

Recipe makes 2 cocktails.

Cocktails

Bob Schnoes's Manhattan

Whenever I visit, Dad fixes me a Manhattan on the rocks, with two cherries. This new-again cocktail is smooth, slightly sweet, and a worthy addition to sophisticated cocktail parties.

INGREDIENTS:

3 to 4 large ice cubes

2 ounces good-quality bourbon whiskey

1 ounce Martini & Rossi Rosso Vermouth

1 teaspoon maraschino cherry juice

2 maraschino cherries

Fill a glass with ice, and add bourbon, vermouth, and cherry juice. Stir gently; garnish with cherries and serve.

Recipe make 1 cocktail.

Bob Schnoes's Classic Manhattan

Classic cocktails from the 1940s and '50s have made a big comeback in recent years, and are a surefire way to bring excitement to today's entertaining.

INGREDIENTS:

1 cup ice cubes

2 ounces good-quality bourbon

1 ounce Martini & Rossi Rosso Vermouth

1 teaspoon maraschino cherry juice

2 maraschino cherries

Fill a cocktail shaker ½ full with ice and add bourbon, vermouth, and cherry juice. Cover the shaker and shake gently to mix; strain into a martini glass. Garnish with two cherries threaded onto a cocktail pick.

Recipe makes 1 cocktail.

My Mother's Brandy Manhattan

This is my mother's favorite Manhattan. She prefers the depth and flavor of brandy. Try a fine Champagne Cognac for a truly refined cocktail.

INGREDIENTS:

3 to 4 large ice cubes

2 ounces Remy Martin Fine Champagne Cognac VSOP or other brandy

1 ounce Martini & Rossi Rosso Vermouth

1 teaspoon maraschino cherry juice

2 maraschino cherries

Fill a glass with ice and add brandy, vermouth, and cherry juice. Stir gently.

Garnish with cherries and serve.

Recipe makes 1 cocktail.

Kir Royale

Burgundy, and Dijon in particular, is famous for crème de cassis, a liqueur distilled from black currants, and mixed with Champagne to create Kir Royale. Serve it in tall, narrow flutes, so the crème de cassis does not overmix with the Champagne.

INGREDIENTS:

2 to 3 ounces crème de cassis

Chilled dry Champagne or sparkling wine

Pour liqueur into a Champagne flute, fill with chilled Champagne, and serve.

Recipe makes 1 cocktail.

Cocktails

Pink Rum Desire

When I visited the Mount Gay Rum distillery in Barbados, I was introduced to a smooth, creamy cocktail very similar to this one. Upon returning home, I added a few touches of my own to come up with this pretty-in-pink summer cocktail. For an extra festive touch, dip the rim of each glass in rum, and then in multicolored sparkling sugar. Your glasses will glitter like semi-precious jewels, adding a personal touch to your entertaining.

INGREDIENTS:

2 ounces Mount Gay Rum Extra Old

2 ounces Remy Red liqueur

4 ounces cream of coconut (not coconut milk)

2 ounces evaporated milk

2 cups ice cubes

Dash of freshly grated nutmeg

2 tablespoons rum, for garnish

3 tablespoons multicolored sparkling sugar, for garnish

2 straws

2 paper parasols

Pour rum, Remy Red, cream of coconut, and evaporated milk into a blender. Add ice cubes and nutmeg and blend until smooth.

Pour the remaining rum into one small saucer, and the sparkling sugar into another. Dip rims of 2 tall glasses into the rum, then into the sugar.

Pour the cocktails into the glasses; add straws and paper parasols and serve immediately.

Recipe makes 2 cocktails.

Berry Spritzer

Several years ago, one of my dearest friends, Dyan Anderson, hosted a ladies' birthday luncheon for me. It was very elegant, and since my birthday is just after Valentine's Day, much of the menu was accented with hearts.

Before lunch, as guests were still arriving, Dyan served a refreshing, Valentine-hued spritzer in crystal tumblers. Heart-shaped ice cubes made of frozen spritzer floated in each glass. Here is my version of Dyan's birthday cocktail. Serve it in delicate sherry glasses or Champagne flutes.

INGREDIENTS:

2 cups fresh or frozen strawberries

½ cup fresh or frozen raspberries

1 tablespoon sugar

2 cups orange juice

1 1-liter bottle ginger ale or lemon-lime soda, chilled

Purée strawberries, raspberries, sugar, and orange juice in a blender until smooth; refrigerate up to several hours.

Just before serving, pour the fruit base into a large pitcher and gently stir in chilled ginger ale. Pour the spritzer into sherry glasses or Champagne flutes.

Recipe serves 10 to 12.

Cocktails

Black Currant Spritzer

This nonalcoholic cocktail is so beautiful and tasty, you'll never miss the alcohol. Serve it in a martini or saucer Champagne glass.

INGREDIENTS:

½ cup lemonade

3 ounces Looza or other brand black currant nectar

1½ ounces simple syrup, chilled (page 204)

Splash of fresh lime juice

3 ounces lemon-lime soda, chilled

1 lime wedge

Granulated sugar for glass rim

Fill a cocktail shaker ½ full with ice. Pour in lemonade, black currant nectar, simple syrup, lime juice, and lemon-lime soda. Shake until chilled and well blended.

Rub a lime wedge around the rim of a martini or saucer Champagne glass. Pour sugar onto a medium plate and shake to distribute it around the plate. Dip the rim of the glass into sugar.

Strain the cocktail into the glass and serve.

Recipe makes 3 cocktails.

Virgin Black Currant Cosmopolitan

Like its sophisticated cousin, this nonalcoholic version of the ever-popular Cosmopolitan is sleek and elegant.

INGREDIENTS:

½ cup lemonade

2 ounces Looza or other brand black currant nectar

1 ounce simple syrup, chilled (page 204)

Splash of fresh lime juice

1 lime wedge

Sparkling or granulated sugar, for glass rim

Fill cocktail shaker ½ full with ice. Pour in lemonade, black currant nectar, simple syrup, and lime juice. Shake until chilled and well blended.

Rub a lime wedge around the rim of a martini glass. Pour sugar onto a medium plate and shake to distribute it around plate. Dip the rim of glass into the sugar.

Strain the cocktail into the glass and serve.

Recipe makes 1 cocktail.

Cocktails

Mock Frozen Mango Daiquiri

Intriguing and festive, this tropical frozen daiquiri is thick and rich, but contains no alcohol. Serve it on hot summer evenings with a wedge of fresh mango, or garnish this colorful cocktail with a tiny paper parasol and infuse your next dinner party with an air of celebration.

INGREDIENTS:

1 large ripe mango, peeled and sliced

¾ cup white cranberry juice, chilled

1 ounce freshly squeezed lime juice

2 tablespoons superfine sugar

½ ounce simple syrup (page 204)

2 cups ice cubes

Wedges of mango, for garnish

In a blender, combine sliced mango, white cranberry juice, lime juice, sugar, and simple syrup. Blend until smooth.

Add ice cubes and blend until the mixture is smooth and thick.

Serve in goblets or tapered flutes with a wedge of fresh mango.

Recipe makes 3 cocktails.

A Proper Pot of Tea

The key to the success of afternoon tea is the tea itself. This is the time to splurge on a good-quality loose tea and a proper teapot. Loose tea may be spooned directly into the pot. Once brewed, a tea strainer is placed over each tea cup to catch the leaves as the hot liquid is poured.

Although at first glance this may seem a bit of a bother, graceful rituals are an inherent part of afternoon tea. Gracefully moving a silver tea strainer from cup to cup, as each guest's tea is poured, becomes as much a part of the ceremony as the ritualistic three turns of the tea bowl as it is placed before the guest is part of the Japanese tea ceremony.

You may use a tea ball instead. This is an enclosed ball with multiple holes, usually attached to a small chain. The tea ball is opened, loose tea is spooned in, and the tea ball lid is replaced. The ball is then lowered into a teapot and boiling water is added. The tea ball's many holes allow the flavor of the loose tea into the pot, without tea leaves escaping into the tea.

Because tea's brisk flavor depends on having enough oxygen in the water, it is important to use cold tap water when filling the tea kettle. Water that has stood for any length of time does not contain the same amount of oxygen as fresh, cold tap water. Flavor also depends on bringing the teakettle to a full boil, but not allowing it to boil for an extended time, as oxygen is lost and the tea will taste flat.

The Family Table: Where Great Food, Friends, and Family Gather Together (Capital Lifestyles)

Rost, Christy

E2-S020-I6

No CD

Used - Good

UM-617-019

9781931868471

40481055

Afternoon Tea

Many Americans mistakenly refer to a gracious tea given in the afternoon as "high tea," probably because they translate the word "high" to mean very elegant. Actually, the term, "high tea," refers to the British custom of a hearty, late-afternoon supper served with cups of tea. Afternoon tea refers to a late-afternoon repast of light savories, such as finger sandwiches and scones, and dainty cakes and sweet tarts.

INGREDIENTS:

1 teapot

1 teaspoon loose tea for each cup, plus one for the pot

Milk, lemon slices, and sugar

Fill a teakettle ½ full with fresh, cold tap water. Heat over high heat until the water is hot; slowly pour into teapot to warm the pot. Discard any water still in the kettle.

Refill teakettle with fresh, cold tap water. Heat over high heat until it comes to a full boil. Empty hot water out of the teapot, spoon loose tea into pot, and add boiling water.

Allow tea to steep 5 minutes. While tea is steeping, cover the teapot with a tea cozy or terry towel to keep it warm.

Pour tea through a tea strainer into cups. Serve with milk, lemon, and sugar.

Cucumber Tea Sandwiches

During afternoon tea, one of my favorite savories is the cucumber tea sandwich. These dainty, miniature sandwiches echo the atmosphere of quiet elegance of this much-loved ritual. When hosting tea, I always prepare more cucumber tea sandwiches than I think I'll need, because my guests love the simplicity of these cool, thinly sliced dainties as much as I.

INGREDIENTS:

1 English cucumber

1 loaf soft white sandwich bread

½ cup unsalted butter, softened

Peel cucumber and slice it paper-thin. Remove crusts from the bread with a long serrated knife.

Arrange 8 slices of bread on a cutting board and spread each thinly with butter. Arrange cucumber slices on top of butter, overlapping slices slightly. Top with 8 slices of unbuttered bread.

Slice sandwiches diagonally, then slice them diagonally in the other direction to transform each sandwich into 4 small triangles.

Repeat with additional bread and cucumber slices as needed. Arrange tea sandwiches on a platter and cover with a piece of barely damp paper towel and plastic wrap. Chill until ready to serve.

Recipe serves 12.

Afternoon Tea

Orange Blossom Tea Sandwiches

Dainty sandwiches with an orange-flavored cream cheese filling pair wonderfully with hot tea.

INGREDIENTS:

1 8-ounce package cream cheese, softened

Finely grated zest of one orange

2½ teaspoons freshly squeezed orange juice

2 teaspoons sugar

¼ teaspoon vanilla

2 to 3 drops orange food coloring (optional)

5 canned mandarin orange segments, drained

16 slices white or wheat sandwich bread

In the medium bowl of an electric mixer, beat cream cheese with orange zest 2 minutes to allow the zest's flavor to infuse the cream cheese.

Add orange juice, sugar, and vanilla, and food coloring, if desired. Beat until smooth.

Chop mandarin orange segments until fine, drain on paper towels, and gently fold into the cream cheese mixture.

Slice crusts from the bread; spread cream cheese mixture on 8 slices and top each with a plain bread slice.

Using a long serrated knife, slice sandwiches into thirds, each measuring approximately 1 inch by 3½ inches.

Recipe makes 24 finger sandwiches.

Cream Scones

Since afternoon tea is one of my favorite occasions, I have been making scones for years, constantly adjusting my recipes to produce a buttery, lighter-textured scone similar to ones I have loved in England.

Well, by jove, I think I've got it! These scones are positively decadent, with a rich, buttery flavor and melt-in-your-mouth texture that makes them hard to resist. My family and friends love them, but the best compliment I ever received was from a student in one of my cooking classes. He was born and raised in Scotland, and after tasting one of my Cream Scones, he told me they were just like the ones his Scottish grandmother made.

INGREDIENTS:

2½ cups flour

3 tablespoons sugar

2½ teaspoons baking powder

1 teaspoon salt

½ cup cold unsalted butter

⅓ cup dried currants

1 egg

1 cup heavy whipping cream

2 teaspoon vanilla

1 egg

1 tablespoon water

Seedless raspberry jam, for garnish

Devon cream or 1 cup heavy cream sweetened with 1 tablespoon confectioners' sugar, for garnish

Preheat oven to 375 degrees. In a large bowl, combine flour, sugar, baking powder, and salt, mixing well.

Slice cold butter into 8 pieces. Cut into flour mixture with a pastry blender or 2 knives until butter is pea-size. Stir in currants.

Afternoon Tea

In a small bowl, beat egg slightly with a fork; stir in cream and vanilla. Pour the cream mixture all at once into the flour mixture, stirring to form a soft dough. Do not overmix.

Turn the dough out onto a lightly floured pastry cloth or counter and knead a few times until smooth. Flecks of butter should still be visible. Roll the dough ¾ inch thick. Cut with a 2¼-inch biscuit cutter (I prefer a heart-shaped one), and place scones on a lightly greased cookie sheet.

Beat egg and water in a small bowl to form an egg wash. Brush the mixture on top of scones. Bake in a preheated oven 15 to 17 minutes until scones are puffed and golden brown.

Serve scones warm or at room temperature with jam and Devon cream. If Devon cream is unavailable, whip 1 cup heavy cream with 1 tablespoon confectioners' sugar (the confectioners' sugar will stabilize the cream so it does not separate).

Recipe makes 15 scones.

Serving scones can be quite an art in itself. When "taking tea" in the elegant and historic Hotel Adolphus in Dallas, Texas, the tea captain splits each scone horizontally once the plate of savories has been served to each guest. With great fanfare, he deftly places a quenelle of seedless raspberry jam on the lower half of each scone, followed by a quenelle of rich Devon cream on the upper half. Guests then divide the jam and cream onto each half as desired.

At home, I provide a bowl of jam and a bowl of cream for my guests to help themselves. Since many people are unsure how best to enjoy scones, a gently delivered suggestion or demonstration assists guests without making them feel awkward.

French Cream Tarts

Dainty cream cheese pastries, filled with crème pâtissière and garnished with berries or sliced fruit, are reminiscent of Victorian teas of yesteryear. Although they are a bit labor intensive to make, the silky French pastry cream, cradled in flaky pastry and garnished with glistening fresh fruit, provides deliciously divine elegance to birthday and bridesmaids' teas and other auspicious occasions.

INGREDIENTS:

Cream Cheese Pastry:

2 cups flour	6 ounces cream cheese, softened
¼ teaspoon salt	1 cup unsalted butter, softened

In a food processor, pulse flour and salt to mix. Add cream cheese and butter; process until a soft dough is formed. Remove from the processor, form the pastry into a large disc, and wrap it in plastic wrap. Chill 1 hour.

Preheat oven to 400 degrees. Roll pastry out on a floured pastry cloth or surface to a thickness of ⅛ inch. Cut pastry ½ inch wider than miniature tart pans. Carefully pat pastry into the tart pans, cutting off excess by rolling a rolling pin across the top of the tart pan, or by pinching off the excess with your fingers.

Prick the surface of the pastry well with a fork. Place an empty tart pan or a piece of foil filled with dried beans or metal pie weights inside to prevent the pastry from puffing during baking. Place the tart pans on a cookie sheet and bake in a preheated oven 7 to 8 minutes until the edges of the pastry are light brown. Remove inner tart pans or beans or pie weights and bake 2 more minutes until inner pastry is dry.

Remove from the oven and cool the tart shells 2 minutes; then remove from the tart pans and finish cooling. Tart shells may be stored in an airtight container several days or frozen until needed.

Fill tart shells with pastry cream up to 1 hour before serving.

Afternoon Tea

French Pastry Cream:

1 vanilla bean

1¼ cups milk

2 egg yolks

¼ cup sugar

3 tablespoons flour

¼ cup red plum or apple jam (optional)

Split vanilla bean down the center with a sharp knife. Scrape out seeds and transfer them and the bean to a medium saucepan; add milk. Scald the milk with the vanilla bean over medium heat. Remove the saucepan from the heat when small bubbles begin to form around the edges of the pan.

In a medium bowl, beat egg yolks and sugar with an electric mixer until the mixture is pale in color. Add flour and beat until mixture thickens.

Remove the vanilla bean from the milk. Beat half of the hot milk into the egg mixture; then pour the egg mixture into the saucepan of remaining milk. Heat the mixture over medium heat, whisking constantly, until it comes to a boil and thickens, taking care that it doesn't burn.

Remove from the heat and pour the pastry cream into a bowl. Rub the top of the pastry cream with butter and cover with plastic wrap placed directly on top of the mixture to prevent a skin from forming. Chill until mixture is cold, several hours or overnight.

One hour before serving, whip the pastry cream with a whisk or electric mixer until it's smooth and spoon it into the tart shells.

Garnish the tarts with small berries or sliced strawberries or kiwi. If desired, melt jam in a small saucepan or in the microwave and brush it over the fruit.

Recipe makes 20 to 24 miniature tarts.

Ginger Tea Cake

Afternoon tea refreshments should be light and delicate, and this spicy tea cake fits that description to a "tea." What's more, it takes only minutes to make and perfumes the house with a delightful "homey" fragrance. Dusted with confectioners' sugar and served from a pretty cake platter, Ginger Tea Cake looks every bit as elegant as more elaborate desserts, and tastes divine!

INGREDIENTS:

½ cup unsalted butter, softened

¾ cup packed light brown sugar

¼ cup granulated sugar

1 egg

1¼ cups flour

1 teaspoon baking powder

¾ teaspoon salt

¾ teaspoon ginger

¼ teaspoon cinnamon

¼ teaspoon allspice

½ cup milk

1 tablespoon confectioners' sugar, for garnish

Preheat oven to 350 degrees. In the large bowl of an electric mixer, cream butter and sugars at medium speed until the mixture is light and fluffy. Add egg and beat 1 minute.

In a medium bowl, stir together flour, baking powder, salt, ginger, cinnamon, and allspice. Gradually add flour mixture to the creamed mixture, alternating with the milk. The batter will be thick.

Line a 9-inch round cake pan with parchment paper, then grease and flour the pan and the paper. Spoon the cake batter into pan and bake in preheated oven 30 to 35 minutes, or until a cake tester inserted into the center of the cake comes out clean.

Cool the cake on a wire rack 25 minutes; remove cake from pan and cool completely. Just before serving, sift confectioners' sugar over top.

Recipe makes one 9-inch tea cake.

Afternoon Tea

Jewel Tea Cookies

When I host an afternoon tea or dessert party, I always include these delicate cookies. They are so light and buttery, they almost melt in your mouth, and the dusting of confectioners' sugar around the perimeter is a beautiful counterpoint to the glistening, melted jam in the center.

INGREDIENTS:

2 cups flour

½ teaspoon baking powder

¼ teaspoon salt

1 cup unsalted butter, softened

⅔ cup sugar

1 egg yolk

1¼ teaspoons vanilla

5 ounces apricot, raspberry, or blackberry preserves, preferably seedless

Confectioners' sugar, for garnish

Preheat the oven to 350 degrees. In a small bowl, stir together flour, baking powder, and salt; set aside. In the large bowl of an electric mixer, cream the butter and sugar until light and fluffy, about 8 minutes. Add the egg yolk and vanilla; beat well.

Add the flour mixture to the butter mixture and, using a large spoon, mix until the ingredients are thoroughly combined. Using floured hands, form teaspoons of dough into small balls and place them on ungreased cookie sheets. Dip a finger into the flour, then press on the center of each cookie to form an indentation. Fill each center with ¼ teaspoon of preserves.

Bake the cookies in a preheated oven 10 to 12 minutes, or until the bottom edges are barely brown. Cool the cookies 1 minute, then remove from cookie sheets to a wire rack. When thoroughly cool, sift confectioners' sugar over cookies through a fine mesh sieve. Sugar will gradually melt over preserves, leaving only the edges dusted with sugar.

Recipe makes 3½ dozen (42) 2-inch cookies.

Lemon Tea Cake with Roses

This lovely, one-layer cake has a delicate essence of fresh lemon, beautifully complemented by a simple vanilla glaze. Tiny, pink frosting rosebuds grace the perimeter of this cake, which is well suited to an afternoon tea, lady's birthday, or Easter celebration.

INGREDIENTS:

Cake:

⅓ cup unsalted butter, softened	1¼ cups sifted cake flour
¾ cup sugar	¾ teaspoon baking powder
1 tablespoon lemon zest	½ teaspoon salt
1½ tablespoons lemon juice	¼ teaspoon baking soda
1 egg	½ cup milk

Preheat oven to 350 degrees. In the large bowl of an electric mixer, cream butter, sugar, and lemon zest until very light, about 8 minutes. Add lemon juice and egg, beating until well blended.

In a medium bowl, stir together flour, baking powder, salt, and baking soda. Gradually beat the flour mixture, alternately with milk, into the creamed mixture. The batter will be thick and fluffy.

Line a 9-inch round cake pan with parchment paper, then grease and flour the pan and the paper. Pour the cake batter into the pan and bake in a preheated oven 25 minutes, or until the top is golden and a tester inserted into the center of the cake comes out clean.

Cool the cake on a wire rack 30 minutes, remove it from the pan, and cool it completely.

Afternoon Tea

Glaze:

2 cups sifted confectioners' sugar

1 tablespoon unsalted butter, melted

2½ tablespoons milk

½ teaspoon vanilla

Whisk together sugar, melted butter, milk, and vanilla until smooth. Pour over the cake, spreading the glaze with an offset spatula or knife. Cover the cake completely; set aside until the glaze hardens. When the glaze is dry, decorate the cake with real or buttercream roses.

Recipe serves 12.

Buttercream Roses:

2 tablespoons unsalted butter, softened

1 cup confectioners' sugar, sifted

2 teaspoons milk

¼ teaspoon vanilla

Food coloring to tint frosting

In the medium bowl of an electric mixer, cream butter, confectioners' sugar, and milk until the mixture is smooth and creamy; stir in the vanilla.

Divide the frosting between two small bowls. Stir pink or yellow food coloring into half of the frosting for the rosebuds and green food coloring into the remaining frosting for the leaves. Transfer frostings into decorator piping bags fitted with Wilton tip #426 for the rosebuds and Wilton tip #67 for the leaves.

Frosted Tea Cookies

These are a variation of Jewel Tea Cookies, embellished with a swirl of frosting instead of jam. For ladies' teas, I tint the frosting in pastel colors, but for Christmas holiday celebrations, I use red or green frosting.

INGREDIENTS:

1 recipe Jewel Tea Cookies, omitting jam (page 225)

2½ tablespoons unsalted butter, softened

2½ cups sifted confectioners' sugar

2 tablespoons milk

Dash of salt

½ teaspoon vanilla

2 drops food coloring

Using the same basic recipe as Jewel Tea Cookies, omit the jam after indenting each cookie and bake as before. Cool the cookies completely.

In a medium bowl, beat butter with ¾ cup of the confectioners' sugar and 1 tablespoon of the milk until smooth. Add salt and vanilla. Beat in remaining confectioners' sugar and milk. If the frosting is too stiff, add additional milk, a few drops at a time. Tint with food coloring, mixing well.

Fill a pastry bag fitted with a star tip ½ full of frosting. Twist the top of the bag closed and pipe a generous swirl of frosting into the center of each cookie.

Allow the frosting to harden several hours. Store cookies up to 1 week in an airtight container with parchment paper between each layer.

Recipe makes 3½ dozen (42) 2-inch cookies.

Chilled Strawberry Soup

When the weather is warm and strawberries are plentiful and sweet, I enjoy serving this pastel-pink fruit soup as a first course or even as a dessert. Just before serving, I swirl a few drops of cream or strawberry purée through the soup. It's as pretty as a picture.

INGREDIENTS:

2 tablespoons unsalted butter

2 quarts strawberries, hulled and sliced (about 6 cups)

½ cup sugar

½ teaspoon lemon zest

2 cups milk

1 cup heavy cream

¼ teaspoon vanilla

Cream or strawberry purée, for garnish

Melt butter in a large heavy saucepan over medium-low heat. Stir in strawberries, sugar, and lemon zest. Sauté strawberries 5 to 10 minutes until soft, stirring often.

Pour in milk, cream, and vanilla. Adjust the heat to medium and bring the mixture to a boil, stirring frequently. Boil mixture 2 minutes, stirring constantly. Remove from heat; set aside 20 minutes to cool.

Purée half the mixture in a blender and strain it through a fine sieve into a large bowl. Repeat with the remaining mixture. Alternatively, purée the mixture in the saucepan with a portable hand blender until smooth; strain into a bowl.

Cover the bowl with plastic wrap and chill several hours or overnight. To serve, ladle soup into bowls or cream soup cups. Garnish with a few drops of cream or strawberry purée and swirl with a knife.

Recipe makes 5 bowls or 10 cups of soup.

Creamy Chilled Cantaloupe Soup

This is a creamy, pastel-colored fruit soup to start summer meals on a cooler note. The natural sweetness of ripe cantaloupe is tempered by the tartness of orange juice and vanilla yogurt, which prevents the soup from being too sweet. How lovely and refreshing this soup would be as a first course when dining alfresco under a canopy of leafy trees and summer stars.

INGREDIENTS:

1 medium ripe cantaloupe

¼ cup orange juice

½ cup lowfat vanilla yogurt

1 cup whipping cream

1 tablespoon honey

Sour cream, for garnish

Mint leaves, for garnish

Peel, seed, and slice cantaloupe into 1-inch pieces. In a blender, place half the cantaloupe pieces and the orange juice. Purée until smooth. Add the remaining cantaloupe and purée.

Add yogurt, whipping cream, and honey to the cantaloupe mixture, puréeing after each addition. Chill soup in the refrigerator at least 1 hour, or until cold.

To serve, whirl soup in the blender just to mix. Pour into chilled soup bowls and top each serving with a dollop of sour cream. Garnish with a sprig of fresh mint.

Recipe makes 6 to 8 servings.

Soups

French Onion Soup

Because this soup is loved by so many, I think it is a very appropriate choice when entertaining, especially because it's so easy to make. You may even make the soup one day ahead, reheat it, and then garnish it with just-toasted baguette slices and cheese.

INGREDIENTS:

- 3 tablespoons olive oil
- 3 tablespoons unsalted butter
- 3 pounds onions, sliced (3 to 4 very large onions)
- 6 cups homemade beef stock or canned beef broth
- 1¼ teaspoons kosher salt (adjust if using canned broth)
- Freshly ground black pepper
- 5 tablespoons sherry
- ⅛ teaspoon Worcestershire sauce
- 1 French baguette, sliced and toasted
- Gruyère or Parmesan cheese, for garnish

Heat a Dutch oven over medium heat; add oil and butter. When the butter has melted, stir in onions. Cook onions 10 to 15 minutes, without stirring, until the bottom layer begins to brown and caramelize.

Quickly stir the onions, then reduce the heat to low. Cook the onions 10 to 15 minutes more, stirring occasionally, until they are thoroughly caramelized and dark brown in color. Do not allow them to burn.

Stir in beef stock, seasonings, sherry, and Worcestershire sauce. Cover and cook 20 to 30 minutes to allow flavors to meld.

To serve, preheat the oven to 350 degrees. Ladle soup into ovenproof bowls or soup mugs and top with a slice of toasted baguette. Sprinkle generously with grated Gruyère or Parmesan cheese. Place soup bowls in a roasting pan filled with 2 inches of boiling water and bake until the cheese melts.

Recipe makes 6 servings.

Cream of Cauliflower Soup

The year Randy and I celebrated our twenty-fifth anniversary, I purchased a set of twelve cream soup cups. When I first spotted these miniature treasures in a cluttered old shop, I fell in love with them. Imagine my amazement when the owner informed me the pattern is called "25th Anniversary," by Limoges. They are pure white with gold handles and a gold swirl along the rim. I cherished them from that first moment, knowing they would be elegant vessels for this Cream of Cauliflower Soup.

INGREDIENTS:

1 tablespoon olive oil	4 cups chicken broth
½ medium onion, chopped	½ head of cauliflower
½ cup chopped celery	1 cup half-and-half or milk
1 tablespoon flour	Salt and white pepper to taste

Heat a large saucepan over medium-low heat until hot; add olive oil. Sauté onion and celery in hot oil 5 minutes until soft. Sprinkle with flour; stir well. Add a small amount of chicken broth to the vegetables, stirring until thickened. Pour in remaining chicken broth and stir to mix. Bring the mixture to a boil, reduce the heat, and simmer, uncovered, 5 to 10 minutes.

While the soup base simmers, chop ½ of the cauliflower head into small pieces, add to soup. Bring to a boil; cover and simmer over low heat 15 to 20 minutes until cauliflower is very soft.

In several batches, purée the soup in a blender, being very careful not to overfill the blender with hot liquid, as this may cause the mixture to explode from the top when the blender is turned on. As the soup is processed, transfer the purée to another saucepan. Add half-and-half or milk to puréed soup; stir to blend. Season to taste. Heat the soup over medium heat until hot; do not boil.

Recipe serves 4.

Potato Leek Chowder with Sherry

This elegant cream soup makes an exquisite first course. A touch of sherry provides extra richness. Serve the chowder in cream soup cups, small bowls, or demitasse cups, garnished nutmeg and a sprinkling of chives. Avoid last-minute stress by preparing the chowder one day ahead. Omit the sherry until the chowder is reheated for serving.

INGREDIENTS:

5 medium Yukon Gold potatoes

¾ cup chopped onion

2 leeks, white part only, chopped

5 slices bacon

4 cups chicken broth

1½ cups half-and-half

2 to 3 tablespoons dry sherry

1 teaspoon coarse salt

Dash white pepper

Freshly grated nutmeg,
   for garnish

Chopped fresh chives,
   for garnish

Peel and slice potatoes into 1-inch cubes. Place in a large saucepan with just enough water to cover them. Cover and cook just until potatoes are tender, about 5 to 7 minutes. Drain and set aside.

Slice root ends and green part off leeks; discard. Wash the leeks well to remove sandy soil from between layers. Chop and set aside.

Slice bacon into 1-inch pieces and sauté in a Dutch oven over medium-low heat until the fat is rendered, about 3 minutes. Stir in onion and leeks; sauté several minutes until soft. Pour in chicken broth, cover, and bring to a low boil. Simmer 5 minutes.

Stir in half-and-half and season with salt and white pepper. Gently stir in the potatoes, and add sherry, if desired. Cook until the chowder is hot; do not boil. To serve, ladle chowder into soup bowls or cups and garnish with a dash of freshly grated nutmeg and chopped chives.

Recipe serves 10.

Grilled Rib Eye Steaks with Ginger Rum Sauce

My romantic husband, Randy, and I have fallen in love with cruising. Once aboard the magnificent cruise ship, our cares float away and we are instantly transported to a magical space in time, where the biggest decisions of the day are which sites to see and what to select from the menu.

One of our favorite destinations is the Caribbean, with its crystal-clear, turquoise waters, tropical islands, festive music, and colorful cultures. While in the Islands, we often visit farmers' markets, spice shops, or small grocery stores in search of spices and condiments we can take home to enhance our daily meals.

This recipe is a result of our fondness for cruising the Caribbean. Mellow amber rum, aged in oak casks for eight to ten years, is combined with fresh ginger, Demerara sugar, shallots, and a bit of balsamic vinegar to create a flavorful marinade with just a hint of sweetness for tender rib eye steaks. While the steaks are grilling, sautéed garlic and beef broth are stirred into the marinade, and the entire mixture is reduced, then finished with butter, to create a thick, rich sauce.

Bringing a bit of the tropics to your entertaining is deliciously easy with this positively divine, Caribbean-inspired recipe. Create a seaside centerpiece for your table with pillar candles in sherbet colors and a collection of seashells, anchored in a tray of play sand. Add tropical cocktails with paper parasols, and you and your guests have the makings of a private island paradise.

Entrées

INGREDIENTS:

....

¾ cup amber rum, aged
   8 to 10 years

1 tablespoon Billington's or
   other Demerara sugar

2 teaspoons balsamic vinegar

2 slices fresh ginger, peeled

1 large shallot, minced

6 rib eye steaks, 1 to 1½ inches thick

Coarse salt and freshly ground
   black pepper

1 tablespoon olive oil

2 large cloves garlic, minced

½ cup beef broth

3 tablespoons unsalted butter,
   softened

In a large pan, stir together the rum, Demerara sugar, vinegar, ginger, and shallot. Add steaks, turning once to coat, and cover with plastic wrap. Refrigerate the steaks in the marinade at least 2 hours, turning the steaks every 30 minutes.

Preheat the grill; when it's hot, wipe the marinade from steaks and place them on the grill, reserving the marinade. Season the steaks well with coarse salt and freshly ground pepper and grill them 9 to 11 minutes, depending on thickness and desired degree of doneness. Turn them over halfway through cooking.

Meanwhile, heat a medium saucepan over medium-low heat; add oil and garlic. Sauté garlic 2 minutes until soft but not brown. Stir in beef broth and reserved marinade. Bring the mixture to a boil over high heat, reduce the heat to medium-high, and boil until mixture has reduced by half.

Reduce heat to low and remove ginger slices. Stir in softened butter, 1 tablespoon at a time, until it melts and the sauce thickens. Do not allow sauce to boil, because the butter will separate and the sauce will thin. Taste the sauce and season as needed with coarse salt and freshly ground pepper.

When the steaks are ready, serve with the Ginger Rum Sauce.

Recipe makes 6 to 8 servings.

The fat-basted game's tender dark meat is sweetened with apricot and balanced to an extent by the tangy gingerroot and Cognac. Tradition calls for a Chianti Classico or Rosso al Montalcino. However, we find the lighter body and sweet fruit found in the Tempernillo/Cabernet blends of Spain delightful. A Pinot Noir of concentrated flavor and extract is quite good, as well.

$+ **Abadia Returta "Rivola"**
(Sardon di Duero, Spain)

$$ **Ruffino Chianti Classico, Rufina**
(Toscano, Italy)

$$$ **Testarossa Pinot Noir "Psioni"**
(Santa Lucia Highlands, California)

Cornish Game Hens with Apricot Ginger Sauce

When dinner needs to look like you fussed all day, Cornish game hens are a perfect choice. In this simple but tasty version, game hens are stuffed with chopped onions, carrots, and celery for extra flavor and a heavenly aroma. During roasting, an elegant apricot glaze provides a glistening finale.

INGREDIENTS:

2 20-ounce Cornish game hens

½ teaspoon coarse salt

Freshly ground black pepper

Aromatics for stuffing: carrots, onion, and celery, coarsely chopped

¾ cup apricot preserves

1 tablespoon Cognac

½ teaspoon grated fresh ginger

Preheat oven to 400 degrees.

Thaw the game hens, remove the gizzards, and rinse well. Pat dry with paper towels. Season inside the cavity with salt and pepper, stuff with aromatics, and tie the cavity closed with string. Transfer the game hens to a roasting pan; set aside.

In a medium saucepan, melt apricot preserves over medium-low heat. Stir in Cognac and ginger. Reduce the heat to low and simmer 5 minutes, stirring often.

Brush the sauce over the hens and cover with a tent of foil. Roast 15 minutes; reduce temperature to 350 degrees, and roast an additional 45 minutes, basting occasionally with the apricot glaze.

Remove the foil and roast until skin is golden brown, about 15 to 20 minutes. Remove from the oven; set aside 5 minutes until Cornish hens have drawn in their juices.

Recipe makes 2 servings.

Pasta with Lemon Chicken and Vegetables

Tangy lemon juice, sweet basil, and fresh vegetables delight the palate in this easy summertime pasta dish.

INGREDIENTS:

4 split boneless, skinless chicken breasts

Juice of 2 lemons

2 tablespoons chopped fresh basil

3 cloves garlic, minced

2 tablespoons dry white wine

1½ tablespoons olive oil

2 zucchini, sliced

1 cup sliced green bell pepper

1 cup sliced red bell pepper

1 cup chopped celery

1 tablespoon cornstarch

1 cup chicken broth

1 12-ounce package pasta, cooked al dente

Rinse chicken breasts, remove skin, and pat dry with paper towels. Slice into long strips; set aside.

In a medium bowl, stir together lemon juice, garlic, and wine. Marinate the chicken strips in the lemon mixture at least 30 minutes, stirring twice.

Heat a large skillet over medium heat; add olive oil and swirl to coat pan. Add chicken strips, reserving the marinade for later use. Cook 3 to 4 minutes, stirring frequently, until the chicken is tender. Add prepared vegetables, stirring frequently until vegetables are crisp-tender, about 5 minutes.

In a small bowl, gradually whisk chicken broth into cornstarch. Add this mixture and the reserved marinade to the skillet, stirring until the sauce comes to a boil and thickens slightly. Reduce heat to medium-low and cook 5 minutes, stirring often. Serve over cooked pasta and garnish with chopped basil.

Recipe serves 4.

We enjoy wandering the Farmers' Market on Sunday morning, buying the freshest veggies and returning home to enjoy a leisurely brunch, in which wine, this sort of dish, and conversation seem to balance each other effortlessly.

In this recipe, the chicken takes on the lemon and garlic flavors in which it was marinated. The squash, sweet peppers, and juicy celery contribute mild flavors and a crisp texture. The rich, velvety sauce pulls everything together.

We have a weakness for sparkling wine on sunny, weekend mornings that leads us to suggest the simple pleasure of a Spanish Cava. A more traditional choice would be an Alsace Pinot Blanc from a producer known for its concentrated, intense wines. And, of course, that darling of the trendy crowd, an Italian Pinot Grigio.

$ Cordoneu "Cuvee Raventos" (Spain)

$+ Hugel Pinot Gris (Alsace, France)

$$ Felluga Pinot Grigio Collio (Friuli, Italy)

Growing up, we tended to measure the passing of time by which type of mango was in season. Each season lasted about six weeks, and my favorite was the fourth to ripen, an enormous, juice-drenched treasure that required a shower after eating. This dish conjures up those long-ago days, adding to my dining enjoyment. The sweet chicken breast and mangos definitely require a wine sweeter than the recipe. A Riesling is perfect, but we are fond of some of the Vouvray from Loire as well. A Moscato is fun, too!

$$ Dr. Loosen Riesling Piesporter Goldstrophkin Auslese
(Mosel, Germany)

$$ Domaine Vouvray Demi-sec
(Loire, France)

$$ Michel Chiarlo Moscato d'Asti
(Italy)

Mango-Stuffed Chicken Breasts

This Caribbean-inspired entrée is a perfect selection for an intimate alfresco dinner party under the leafy canopy of tall trees. The fresh, sweet mango, layered with the salty prosciutto and nutty fontina cheese hidden inside the chicken breasts, is elegantly highlighted by the creamy sauce with hints of nutmeg.

To create a simple but dramatic spring or summertime alfresco setting, drape a long table with several layers of pastel linens, shield candles down the center of the table with glass hurricane shades, and serve wine in thin, sparkling glassware.

INGREDIENTS:

6 chicken breasts, skinned and boned

Salt and freshly ground black pepper

6 thin slices prosciutto

1 ripe mango, peeled and thinly sliced

¼ pound fontina cheese

3 tablespoons olive oil

2 tablespoons unsalted butter

1 small shallot, minced

1 cup heavy cream

¼ cup amber rum

½ cup sour cream

¼ teaspoon freshly grated nutmeg

Rinse chicken breasts and dry with paper towels. Trim away all visible fat and flatten chicken breasts between two sheets of plastic wrap. Trim any ragged edges.

Entrées

Season the chicken with salt and pepper. Place a slice of prosciutto along the length of each chicken breast and top with several small slices of mango and thin slices of fontina cheese. Roll up each chicken breast, tucking in filling as needed; secure with several toothpicks.

Heat a large skillet over medium heat; add olive oil. Sauté chicken rolls, a few at a time, until golden brown on all sides, about 2 minutes. Transfer the chicken to an ovenproof casserole and repeat with the remaining chicken breasts.

Cover the chicken rolls with aluminum foil and refrigerate until ready to bake. Just before serving, preheat the oven to 350 degrees. Bake in a preheated oven 20 to 25 minutes, or until chicken is tender and no longer pink. Remove from the oven and keep warm.

In a medium saucepan, melt butter over low heat. Add minced shallot and sauté until translucent, about 2 minutes. Add heavy cream and rum. Increase heat to medium and bring to a simmer. Simmer rum sauce 2 to 3 minutes; remove from heat, and whisk in sour cream. Season with salt and pepper to taste.

Remove toothpicks from chicken rolls and transfer to a serving platter or individual plates. Pour the sauce into a serving dish and sprinkle with freshly grated nutmeg. To serve, pour sauce over the stuffed chicken breasts.

Recipe serves 6.

This full-tilt orchestra of flavors belting out the final movement of the "1812 Overture" is a delight when choosing wine. A Big Red. The cherries suggest a Cabernet or 1er Cru Burgundy. The rich fats require acidity. The port flavor components bring to mind an Amarone or Valpolicella Rippaso-style, fermented on the sun-dried skins and pulp from its big brother, Amarone. Another favorite would be a big, old-vine Zinfandel, with plenty of alcohol and fruit.

$+ Castaro Cellars Paso Robles Zinfandel (Paso Robles, California)

$$ Zenato Valpolicella "Ripassa" (Veneto, Italy)

$$$ Merryvale Napa Cabernet Sauvignon (Napa Valley, California)

Roasted Duck Breasts with Port Wine Cherry Sauce

When the dinner just has to be great, serve this elegant but easy dish; then sit back and enjoy the accolades. Sauté the duck early in the day and prepare the cherry sauce. Then spend time with your guests while the duck roasts in the oven.

INGREDIENTS:

6 boneless duckling breasts

Salt and freshly ground black pepper

1 15-ounce can pitted Bing cherries

3 tablespoons port wine

3 tablespoons port wine

¼ cup beef consommé or beef stock

2 teaspoons cornstarch

⅓ cup dried cherries

Juice of ½ orange

Rinse duckling breasts and dry them with paper towels. Trim the skin to the shape of the meat. Using a sharp knife, score the skin to form a diamond pattern, taking care not to pierce the meat. Season well with salt and pepper.

Drain Bing cherries, reserving syrup; set aside.

Heat a nonstick skillet over medium heat. Place the duck breasts, skin side down, in skillet. Cook 8 to 10 minutes until skin is brown and crisp, draining excess fat as needed. Turn the meat and cook 3 to 5 minutes to sear it.

Transfer the duck breasts to a roasting pan, drain the fat from skillet, and cook the remaining breasts in the skillet, draining fat as needed. Transfer the remaining duck to the roasting pan, reserving pan drippings for sauce.

Entrées

If serving the duck right away, preheat the oven to 400 degrees and continue with recipe. If the duckling is to be cooked later in the day, cover the roasting pan tightly with foil and refrigerate until 30 minutes before cooking. Make the cherry sauce (see below), cover, chill, and reheat before serving.

Roast the duckling 20 to 30 minutes in a preheated oven, depending on the size of the breasts, until the meat is pink inside.

Drain all fat from the skillet. Deglaze the hot pan with port wine and consommé, stirring to loosen brown bits from the skillet. Place cornstarch in a small bowl and whisk in a small amount of the reserved cherry syrup until smooth.

Stir the cornstarch mixture and remaining cherry syrup into the skillet. Cook, stirring constantly, 1 to 2 minutes until sauce has thickened. Stir in reserved Bing cherries, dried cherries, and juice of ½ an orange. Cook 1 to 2 minutes until cherries are hot.

Remove duckling breasts from the oven. Serve them whole or slice them at an angle. Spoon port wine cherry sauce over meat and serve.

Recipe serves 6.

Since duck breasts may need to be special-ordered, talk with your butcher at least 1 week before you plan to serve them.

At first, this dish appears so loaded with vibrant flavors and textures that selecting a wine can seem daunting. Happily, this pairing is not as complex as it appears. Any of a wide spectrum of medium to light-bodied wines will enhance this chameleon pork loin, which takes on the flavors in which it is immersed, while still having plenty of fruit to mirror the salsa flavors.

The fresh rosemary and oregano or thyme initially dominate the palate, followed by the lime-mango-cherry salsa. An unusual choice would be a Mourvedre (Mateo in Italy and at Ridge Vineyards), while the more

Roasted Pork Loin with Cherry Fruit Salsa

When summer cherries are plump and juicy it's the time to make this fabulous roast pork dish. Invite a few friends and neighbors for a casual meal or double the recipe and throw a late summer dinner party. Either way, this succulent, juicy pork roast, with its colorful, summer fruit salsa, will be a hit.

INGREDIENTS:

½ cup dry white wine

1 5- to 6-pound boneless pork loin, trimmed and tied

Coarse salt and freshly ground black pepper

5 large cloves garlic, minced

4 sprigs fresh rosemary

4 sprigs fresh oregano or thyme

2 tablespoons olive oil

¼ cup white wine or chicken broth, for deglazing

1 recipe Cherry Fruit Salsa

At least 1 hour before cooking, pour wine into a casserole dish large enough to accommodate the pork loin. If the loin is too long, slice it in half. Season pork with salt and pepper. Press minced garlic onto surface of meat. Remove herbs from stems and chop; press these onto the pork. Turn the pork to coat all sides with wine. Cover and chill until ready to cook, rotating the meat in the marinade every 30 minutes.

Preheat the oven to 325 degrees. Heat a large skillet over medium heat; add olive oil. Wipe the garlic and herbs from meat, reserving them for later use. Brown the meat on all sides, about 10 minutes.

Entrées

Transfer the pork to a roasting pan and top with the reserved garlic and herbs. Place the meat in the oven and roast it until a meat thermometer registers an internal temperature of 170 degrees, about 1½ hours.

When pork is done, transfer to a serving platter and keep warm. Place the roasting pan over medium heat and deglaze it with ¼ cup wine or chicken broth, scraping up the brown bits from the bottom. Allow the mixture to reduce by ⅓; pour it over meat. Serve with Cherry Fruit Salsa.

Recipe serves 8.

Cherry Fruit Salsa:

1 cup diced mango

1 cup diced peaches

1 cup diced cantaloupe

1 tablespoon fresh lime juice

1 tablespoon chopped fresh mint leaves

½ pound pitted fresh cherries

In a medium bowl, stir together mango, peaches, cantaloupe, lime juice, and mint. This may be done several hours ahead. Cover and refrigerate.

Just before serving, add chopped cherries and toss gently to mix. Transfer to a serving bowl and serve with the pork.

traditional, silky, cherry-bomb of top-level Cru Beaujolais or California Rhône-Clone keeps us in the realm of the familiar. When called on for a white wine, we have also paired Viognier with this dish quite successfully.

$ Chateau des Deduits Fleurie Cru Beaujolais (Burgundy, France)

$+ Cline Ancient Vines Mourvedre (Contra Costa, California)

$$ Bonny Doone Cigare Volant (Santa Cruz Mountains, California)

Braised Herbed Pork Loin

I love pork loins for entertaining because they're always tender and juicy, there is so little waste, and, most important, they require little attention from an otherwise busy host!

INGREDIENTS:

1 2½- to 3-pound boneless pork loin

¾ teaspoon salt

¼ teaspoon freshly ground black pepper

3 tablespoons olive oil (divided)

1 medium onion, sliced

2 large carrots, sliced into 2-inch pieces

3 cloves garlic, minced

¾ cup white wine

¾ cup beef broth

2 bay leaves

1 tablespoon finely chopped fresh rosemary

1 tablespoon finely chopped fresh sage

Preheat the oven to 350 degrees. Tie the pork loin with kitchen twine; season with salt and black pepper. Preheat a large skillet over medium heat; add 2 tablespoons of oil. Brown the pork on all sides, approximately 5 minutes. Transfer the meat to a roasting pan and cover it to keep it warm.

Pour the remaining oil into skillet; add onions and carrots. Sauté several minutes until the onions are translucent. Add garlic and sauté 1 more minute. Deglaze the pan with wine, scraping up any brown bits; add broth and bay leaves. Raise the heat to high and boil the mixture 5 to 10 minutes, stirring occasionally, until it is reduced by half. Pour over pork loin.

Sprinkle the top of the pork with chopped rosemary and sage. Spoon sautéed vegetables around the meat and cover the roasting pan tightly with foil.

Braise the pork loin in a preheated oven 40 to 45 minutes until tender. Remove it from the oven and allow to sit 10 to 15 minutes. Slice the pork loin and serve it with onions and carrots.

Recipe serves 6.

Braised Lamb Shanks

This classic Italian dish presents tender lamb in a rich, dark broth. Because it may be started early in the day, then left to simmer, Braised Lamb Shanks are ideal for entertaining.

INGREDIENTS:

6 lamb shanks

2 to 3 tablespoons olive oil

4 large carrots, peeled and chopped

2 turnips, peeled and diced

1 whole head garlic, separated into cloves and peeled

2 cups red wine

1 tablespoon tomato paste

2½ cups chicken broth

¼ cup Martini & Rossi Extra Dry Vermouth

1 teaspoon coarse salt

Freshly ground black pepper

3 sprigs fresh thyme

3 sprigs fresh rosemary

2 whole bay leaves

1 cup pearl onions, peeled

Preheat a large Dutch oven over medium heat until hot; add olive oil. Place lamb shanks in hot oil and cook, without turning, until brown on one side. Turn and cook shanks until dark brown on all sides, about 20 minutes. If all the lamb shanks do not fit in the Dutch oven, cook half of them, remove to a platter, and cook the remainder. Remove the lamb shanks from Dutch oven. Add chopped carrots and turnips; sauté until semisoft. Add the garlic and sauté 2 minutes.

Deglaze the pan with red wine, scraping brown bits from the bottom of the pot. Stir in tomato paste, chicken broth, and vermouth. Return the lamb shanks to the pot; season with salt and freshly ground black pepper.

Add thyme, rosemary, and bay leaves. Bring the mixture to a low boil, cover, and simmer over low heat, stirring occasionally, until meat is very tender and almost falls off the bone, about 2½ to 3 hours. If necessary, add a bit more red wine or chicken broth during cooking. Add pearl onions during the final 30 minutes of cooking.

Recipe serves 6.

Also known as Osso Bucco, this is my favorite cold-weather dish. With its savory flavors, dark velvet color, and gelatinous textures, a BIG RED is necessary. The wine needs some tannin, a bit of acidity to cut through the wondrous sauce's fat, and some ripe berry fruit to elevate all that ponderous density.

The classic pairing in Italy is a Brunello or Amarone. We are quite partial to Super-Tuscans, a blend of Sangiovese and Cabernet Sauvignon. Monsanto's Tinscvil is ideal in the under-$40 range.

While we love Brunello, they are only produced in spectacular vintages. I prefer to substitute Rosso al Montalcino, the same juice plus some younger vines, at a third of the cost. Amarone's thick, rich intensity comes from sun-drying the grapes to raisins, then gently pressing the molasses-like juice into barrels for a long, quiet fermentation. You have to try it to believe it.

$+ Casanova Di Neri Rosso di Montalcini
(Toscano, Italy)

$$$ Monsanto Tinscvil
(Toscano, Italy)

$$$ Allegrini Amarone
(Veneto, Italy)

In pairing flavors, begin with the main ingredient. Here, we begin with the delicate, rich halibut, sweetened with coconut milk and earthy sweet potatoes. The mushrooms add a meaty, savory element and act as a bridge between the tart, bitter, pungent spinach, and the slightly sweet halibut, which, after searing, retains only about 20 percent of its sweetness.

The elegance of the juxtaposed trio (Japanese bean paste) in this recipe is that the texture, color, and flavor all balance in three-part harmony. In addition, we need to consider a few bit players. The sauce is sweet and tangy. Highly aromatic gingerroot packs quite a dollop of lemony, pungent flavor, and the balsamic and sesame seed oil combination is quite powerful, with notes of bitter, tart, and burnt pungency to further complicate matters.

William Koval's Halibut with Shitake, Spinach, Sweet Potato, and Carrot Ginger Sauce

I am so honored that my good friend, William Koval, agreed to share one of his recipes for The Family Table. *William is the very gifted Executive Chef of the elegant landmark Hotel Adolphus in Dallas, Texas. His signature fresh and elegant approach to cooking, with its multilayered textures and flavors, is evident in the hotel's glorious French Room and in this delightful home-kitchen recipe.*

INGREDIENTS:

1 cup coconut milk

½ cup honey

½ pound white miso (Japanese bean paste)

6 6-ounce Alaskan halibut fillets

Salt and freshly ground black pepper

2 tablespoons vegetable oil

2 large sweet potatoes, parboiled, cooled, and diced

1 pound shiitake mushrooms, cleaned and quartered

3 tablespoons sweet black or balsamic vinegar

1 tablespoon sesame seed oil

2 pounds spinach, cleaned and stemmed

2 cups fresh carrot juice

1 cup fresh apple juice (preferably green apple)

½ cup fresh ginger juice

2 ounces butter

3 tablespoons chopped chives

Salt and freshly ground black pepper, to taste

In a medium casserole, stir together the coconut milk, honey, and white miso. Marinate the halibut overnight in the coconut milk mixture.

Entrées

Preheat the oven to 400 degrees. Remove the fish from the marinade, drain off the excess, and season it with salt and freshly ground pepper. Preheat a nonstick skillet over medium heat; add 1 table-spoon oil. Sear fillets until golden brown on each side, then transfer them to a baking pan and bake in a preheated oven 10 minutes. When the fish is done, remove it from the oven and keep it warm.

While the fish is baking, preheat a clean skillet over medium heat; add 1 tablespoon of the oil and swirl to coat pan. Sauté the sweet potatoes until golden brown. Add the mushrooms and sauté 2 minutes. In a small bowl, whisk together the sweet black vinegar and sesame seed oil; add to the skillet. Add the spinach and stir until it just begins to wilt. Season with salt and freshly ground pepper; set aside and keep warm.

In a medium saucepan, stir together carrot, apple, and ginger juices. Bring to a boil over medium-high heat, reduce the heat to medium, and reduce the mixture by ¾. When the mixture has reduced, remove from the heat and stir in the butter and chives.

To serve, place some of the vegetable mixture in the center of each plate. Place a halibut fillet on top of the vegetables and pour the carrot ginger sauce around the vegetables and fish.

Recipe makes 6 servings.

Look for white miso, or Japanese bean paste, in Japanese markets, specialty supermarkets, and natural food stores.

Our wine must be less sweet than the dish. It must be able to pull together the sweet, bit-ter, and tart, without covering up the delicacy of the halibut or the pungent chives. It must be not only aromatic, but have sufficient depth and a com-plexity that equals the recipe's layered flavors. This requires a white wine such as a dry Riesling or an Oregon Pinot Gris, or the restrained potency of a Loire Pouilly Fumé.

$ Duckpond Pinot Gris
(Willamette, Oregon)

$$ Grosset "Polish Hill" Riesling
(Clare Valley, Australia)

$$$ Pascal Joliet Pouilly Fumé
(Loire, France)

This is a dish of contrasts—crisp batter, rich oil, and juicy shrimp, versus crunchy vegetables and salty and sweet sauces. We need a wine that will contrast both the textures and flavors.

A Loire Sancerre's lime-citrus, lemongrass, and kiwifruit flavors wrap around the palate in a full-bodied, vibrant Sauvignon Blanc (Loire is where New Zealand Sauvignon Blancs go when they grow up). We also suggest the full richness of a Riesling with a few years on it. Last, a sparkling wine or Champagne is an impeccable choice and always brings a bit of celebration to the table!

$$ Chateau St. Michelle Eroica Riesling
(Washington)

$$ Pascal Jolivet Sancerre
(Loire, France)

$$$ Bollinger Brut
(Reims, France)

Shrimp and Vegetable Tempura

When I was 16 years old, I spent an entire summer in Japan as a foreign exchange student. Although Western business travelers were fairly common in Japan's larger cities then, Western tourists were more unusual. On several occasions, I was regarded with great surprise and wonder by elderly Japanese who probably hadn't seen a Westerner since the war years, particularly a young American with light blonde hair!

One of the things I loved most about being in Japan was the food. With the exception of raw octopus and jellyfish, I ate everything put before me with gusto. Yes, I ate those, too, just not with gusto. In fact, for the first and only time in my life, I had to go on a diet when I returned from Asia.

Shrimp tempura was one of my favorite food discoveries that summer: all lacy and crunchy on the outside and tender inside. I've made it at home many times since, and it's a fabulous entrée for a party. Have all the ingredients ready ahead of time, then quick-cook each ingredient at the table. Or make it a kitchen party and invite the guests to cook their own!

Set the scene by providing individual bowls of rice, decorative dishes of dipping sauces, chopsticks, and pots of fragrant oolong tea. Japanese foods are always displayed artistically, so take the time to arrange the shrimp and sliced vegetables in rows on a platter, and add a flower blossom or two, if you like. Import stores are great sources of Asian dishware and accessories at reasonable prices. Invest in a few key pieces, then supplement with your usual tableware.

Entrées

INGREDIENTS:

1½ pounds large raw shrimp

1 zucchini squash

1 onion, sliced

1 large green bell pepper

1 large red bell pepper

1 large yellow bell pepper

2 sliced Portabellini or shiitake mushrooms

1 cup flour

2 tablespoons cornstarch

¼ teaspoon baking powder

¼ teaspoon salt

1 cup ice water

1 egg, slightly beaten

Vegetable oil

Soy sauce for dipping

Plum sauce for dipping

Rinse and devein shrimp, leaving the tail on; set aside on paper towels to dry. Rinse vegetables and dry thoroughly on paper towels. Slice them and arrange them decoratively on a large platter.

Just before cooking, prepare the tempura batter. In a medium bowl, stir together flour, cornstarch, baking powder, and salt. Add ice water and the beaten egg, and stir just until mixed; the batter will be lumpy. Place the bowl inside a larger bowl filled with ice to keep the tempura batter chilled.

Heat a wok over medium heat, or an electric skillet to 350 degrees; add oil to a depth of several inches. Dip the vegetables into the batter (Chopsticks make this easy!) and drop them carefully into the hot oil. Cook the vegetables several minutes until the batter begins to brown lightly, turning once. Remove them with a slotted spoon and drain on paper towels; serve. Repeat process with shrimp and serve immediately.

Serve tempura with soy sauce and plum sauce.

Recipe serves 4 to 5.

The nut-scented, dark roux slowly envelops chopped veggies and meats, unhurriedly transforming this mixture into one of America's most magical of entrées. All we can say is that this is an unforgettable experience.

With so much going on, it is difficult to break down the exact steps and experiences that lead us to say, "We need a wine of moderate acidity and medium body; a fruit-forward red that doesn't fight for the spotlight." A Valdigue or Cru Beaujolais works well, and some Zinfandels pair ideally. In addition, a Pinot Noir with sturdy legs can handle this masterpiece without breaking a sweat.

$+ **Rancho Zabaco "Sonoma Heritage"** (Sonoma, California)

$+ **Duboeuf Morgon** (Beaujolais, France)

$$$ **Arcadian Pinot Noir** (Napa, California)

Louisiana Chicken Andouille Gumbo

This recipe is dedicated to the memory of my friend Pamela Johnson, who lived in Baton Rouge. Pam's dark eyes sparkled and danced with the joys of life, and she introduced me to Cajun food and culture. "Talk about good!"

This recipe was inspired by all the gumbo I have enjoyed, with its characteristic dark and spicy broth that originates from the careful nurturing of a roux until it turns the color of mahogany. This particular gumbo is made with chicken and andouille sausage, but it is equally delicious with crawfish, shrimp, or crab. Serve it for Mardi Gras celebrations, Super Bowl–watching parties, and casual buffets.

INGREDIENTS:

Chicken:

1 3- to 4-pound whole chicken	1 small onion, peeled and quartered
12 cups water	2 stalks celery, with leaves
3 bay leaves	2 carrots
5 sprigs fresh parsley	

Place all ingredients in a large stockpot, cover, and bring to a boil over medium-high heat. Reduce heat to low and simmer 45 minutes.

Remove the chicken from the stockpot, reserving the broth, and cool 30 minutes, or until the chicken is cool enough to handle. Remove the chicken meat from bones, chop it, and set it aside. Discard the bones.

Gumbo:

1½ cups flour	4 large stalks celery, chopped
1 cup vegetable oil	3 cups chopped onion
2 tablespoons vegetable oil, for sautéing	2 large bell peppers, coarsely chopped

Entrées

Gumbo (continued):

2 teaspoons coarse salt

2 teaspoons onion powder

1 teaspoon cayenne pepper

1 teaspoon garlic powder

¼ teaspoon paprika

2 14.5-ounce cans diced
  tomatoes with green chiles

1 pound andouille sausage links

2 16-ounce bags frozen okra,
  thawed

Tabasco, if desired

Cooked white rice

In a medium saucepan, whisk together flour and 1 cup of oil until smooth. Cook over medium-low heat, whisking constantly, until the roux turns the color of mahogany, about 25 minutes. Take care the roux does not burn. Set aside.

Strain reserved chicken broth, discarding cooked vegetables and bay leaves. Measure 10 cups of the reserved chicken broth and set aside.

Preheat a clean Dutch oven over medium heat; add the remaining oil, swirling to coat the bottom of the pot. Add celery, onion, and peppers. Sauté 10 minutes until vegetables are soft. Stir in the chopped chicken.

In a small bowl, stir together salt, onion powder, cayenne, garlic powder, and paprika. Pour this mixture over the sautéed vegetables and chicken and toss well to coat. Cook 2 minutes, stirring constantly. Stir in diced tomatoes, reserved chicken broth, and dark roux. Raise the heat to medium-high and cook, uncovered, 15 to 20 minutes.

Meanwhile, in a medium skillet over medium-low heat, sauté sausage 8 minutes, or until light brown on all sides. Slice the cooked sausage into ½-inch-thick slices and stir into the gumbo. Cook the gumbo, uncovered, 30 minutes, stirring occasionally.

Stir in okra and check seasonings; add Tabasco, if desired. Cover and cook 15 minutes, stirring occasionally, as the gumbo thickens. Serve it in large, shallow bowls over cooked rice.

Recipe makes 12 to 14 servings.

In this dish, our primary components are pungent, tender greens, creamy butterfats from the cheeses, and a silky-rich cream sauce that builds on a foundation of bland pasta. The result is a sensuous, subtle interplay of rich flavors and textures that cries for a food-friendly wine possessing sufficient acidity to slice neatly through all that richness.

The nutmeg quietly modifies the entire dish, in a hard-to-pinpoint but potent manner, in much the same way a coat of paint is a tiny portion of a house's mass, but that wee bit completely alters our perception of the structure! We need to step lightly around the baby spinach. It can wake up grumpy and loudly disrupt our plans by bringing out bitter or metallic flavors in some red wines.

One of our favorite little-known wines comes to mind. When I first tasted this white beauty, the vintage was seven years old, and it was so big and bright, it needed to breathe for 20 minutes before opening up to show an incredible graham cracker, peaches, and tangerine bombshell that wore its stony-bright, mineral-laden terroir proudly. It was a Savennieres from an old-vine Chenin Blanc vineyard in Loire.

Baby Spinach and Ricotta Lasagna with Béchamel Sauce

Casual, cozy dinners with friends, surrounded by candlelight and soft music, can keep us grounded when life moves a little too quickly. Here, a white béchamel sauce, flavored with a hint of fragrant, grated nutmeg, complements layers of fresh baby spinach in an elegantly simple six-layer lasagna. A great wine, a quick salad, and a loaf of bread with olive oil and balsamic dipping sauce, and you're all set to unwind and catch up with those dear to you.

INGREDIENTS:

Pasta:

16 ounces lasagna noodles (18 noodles)

2 teaspoons salt

1 tablespoon olive oil

Bring a large Dutch oven or stockpot of water to a boil. Add salt, olive oil, and lasagna noodles. Cook 8 minutes, or until lasagna is al dente. Drain and set aside.

Béchamel Sauce:

4¼ cups milk

10 tablespoons butter

¾ cup flour

2¼ teaspoons freshly grated nutmeg

1¼ teaspoons salt

⅜ teaspoon white pepper

In a medium saucepan, heat milk over low heat until hot; do not boil.

Entrées

In a large saucepan, melt butter over medium-low heat. When it has melted, add flour gradually, whisking quickly to blend well. Cook butter and flour mixture 2 to 3 minutes, whisking constantly so the mixture does not brown.

Remove from the heat. Quickly whisk in one third of the hot milk, taking care to incorporate all of the flour mixture. Whisk in the remaining milk, blending until smooth. Return the mixture to the heat.

Season with nutmeg, salt, and white pepper. Cook béchamel sauce 5 minutes, stirring constantly. If the mixture is too thick, heat a little more milk and whisk it into the sauce. Correct the seasonings.

Lasagna:

18 cooked lasagna noodles

1 recipe Béchamel Sauce

¼ pound fresh baby spinach

1 15-ounce container part-skim ricotta cheese

3 cups shredded mozzarella cheese

Preheat the oven to 375 degrees. Spread a scant amount béchamel sauce in the bottom of a 9- by 13-inch pan. Top with one layer of lasagna noodles, 2 layers of baby spinach, small dollops of ricotta cheese, and some mozzarella. Top with another layer of noodles, béchamel, and fillings, for a total of 5 layers.

Top with the remaining noodles, a generous amount of béchamel sauce, and the remaining mozzarella. Cover tightly with aluminum foil and bake 45 to 50 minutes in a preheated oven until lasagna is bubbly. Remove from the oven and allow to stand 10 minutes to firm.

Recipe serves 8.

This is one of the things we love so much about the world of wine. Eighty thousand wines are born anew every year! We never run out of delightful new discoveries, old dogs learn new tricks, and aging doesn't get you kicked out of Hollywood.

$ Zenato Valpolicella Classico
(Veneto, Italy)

$+ Domaine des Baumard Savennieres "Clos du Papillon"
(Loire, France)

$$ Chateau St. Michelle "Eroica" Riesling
(Washington)

Duchess Potatoes

Shaped into elegant rosettes or swirls, Duchess Potatoes look beautiful next to prime rib or lamb chops. Grated fresh nutmeg perfumes these potatoes without overpowering their delicate flavor.

INGREDIENTS:

3½ cups plain mashed potatoes

3 tablespoons unsalted butter

1 egg

3 to 4 tablespoons milk
   or half-and-half

½ teaspoon freshly
   grated nutmeg

Salt and freshly ground
   black pepper, to taste

Beat the butter and egg into warm mashed potatoes. Add milk, 1 tablespoon at a time, beating until the potatoes are smooth but still firm. Season with nutmeg, salt, and pepper.

While the potatoes are still warm, spoon them into a pastry bag fitted with a ½-inch star tip. On a lightly greased cookie sheet, pipe large rosettes or swirls of seasoned potatoes. Set aside up to 2 hours at room temperature.

Shortly before serving, preheat the oven to 450 degrees. Bake potatoes 8 to 10 minutes until potatoes are hot and edges of rosettes or swirls are browned.

Remove the piped potatoes from cookie sheet with a metal spatula and transfer to serving plates.

Recipe serves 6 to 8.

Side Dishes

Risotto Vincenzo

My good friend, restaurateur Vincenzo Savino, served this creamy risotto with asparagus. I created my own version and called it Risotto Vincenzo. Risotto must be made just before serving, so invite your guests into the kitchen while you prepare this delicacy.

INGREDIENTS:

¾ pound asparagus

5 cups chicken stock or broth

¼ cup unsalted butter

¾ cup chopped onion

1½ cups superfine arborio rice

½ cup dry white wine

Salt and freshly ground
   black pepper, to taste

Grated Parmesan cheese,
   for garnish

Trim asparagus and slice at an angle into 2-inch pieces. Place in a large skillet with ¼ inch of water, cover, and bring to a boil over high heat. When the water boils, immediately reduce the heat to low. Cook 1 to 2 minutes, until a sharp knife penetrates easily when inserted into asparagus. Drain and set aside. In a medium saucepan, heat the stock until it comes to a simmer, reduce heat, and keep it warm.

In a large saucepan, melt butter over medium-low heat, add onion, and sauté 3 to 4 minutes until soft. Pour in rice and stir until coated with butter. Cook 2 to 3 minutes, stirring constantly. Pour in wine and cook until the wine evaporates, stirring constantly.

Add ½ cup hot stock, stirring the rice mixture until the liquid is almost absorbed. Continue adding hot stock, ½ cup at a time, and stirring until the liquid is almost absorbed before adding additional stock. Cook 20 to 25 minutes, until most of the stock has been used and the rice is creamy and cooked al dente. During the final minute, stir in the asparagus and season with salt and pepper.

Serve risotto immediately in large shallow bowls; garnish with freshly grated Parmesan.

Recipe serves 6 to 8.

Composed Mixed Greens and Endive Salad with Balsamic Vinaigrette and Parmesan Wafers

The sharpness of the Belgian endive and balsamic vinegar in this salad is a wonderful contrast to the Parmesan's sweetness, and the soft greens and chewy melted cheese wafer are a delightful counterpoint to the crisp endive and onion.

INGREDIENTS:

1 small bunch green leaf lettuce

1 small bunch red leaf lettuce

1 Belgian endive

2 slices red onion, separated into rings

1 teaspoon Dijon mustard

2 teaspoons balsamic vinegar

¼ cup extra-virgin olive oil

Salt and freshly ground black pepper, to taste

1 recipe Parmesan Wafers

Wash and spin dry leaf lettuces. Arrange them in a pleasing pattern on 4 salad plates. Separate endive leaves, arrange them on top of the greens, and top with onion rings.

In a small mixing bowl, whisk mustard, vinegar, olive oil, salt, and black pepper together until the mixture begins to emulsify. Spoon over salads and garnish with Parmesan Wafers.

Recipe makes 4 salads.

Parmesan Wafers:

1 cup fresh Parmesan cheese, coarsely grated

Preheat a large nonstick skillet over medium-low heat. When it's hot, add tablespoonfuls of grated Parmesan, 2 inches apart, spreading the cheese out to an even thickness.

Cook 1 minute, or until the edges of the Parmesan wafers are dry and they can easily be lifted with a metal spatula. Turn wafers over and cook 1 minute. Transfer wafers to a cookie sheet covered with parchment paper; the wafers will firm as they cool.

Side Dishes

Orzo and Shrimp Salad

Orzo is a tiny pasta that looks like plump grains of rice. Because it is so tiny, orzo is ideal to mound on top of salads. This delightful, fresh-tasting summer salad is nestled in large, ripe tomatoes and is a colorful choice for a light luncheon. All of the preparation may be done hours before serving, so it's really easy on the host when entertaining.

INGREDIENTS:

4 large ripe tomatoes

⅓ cup uncooked orzo pasta

1 teaspoon olive oil

1 scant teaspoon Dijon mustard

1 teaspoon balsamic vinegar

2 tablespoons extra-virgin olive oil

Salt and freshly ground
   black pepper, to taste

¼ cup diced celery

¼ cup diced red bell pepper

¼ pound cooked shrimp, peeled
and deveined

4 large pieces leaf lettuce,
   for garnish

Hollow out tomatoes and drain them well upside-down on paper towels.

Cook orzo in boiling, salted water 4 minutes, or until tender. Drain, pour into a small bowl, and toss with 1 teaspoon olive oil; set aside to cool.

In a small bowl, whisk together mustard, balsamic vinegar, remaining olive oil, salt, and pepper. Pour over cooled pasta; stir in celery and peppers.

Reserve 4 shrimp for garnish. Chop the remaining shrimp and stir into the pasta. Fill the tomatoes with the orzo mixture and garnish with reserved shrimp. Place tomatoes on leaf lettuce on individual salad plates and chill until ready to serve.

Recipe makes 4 salads.

This simple yet elegant dish brings to mind a sunny afternoon outdoors in some off-the-beaten-path café in Italy, which leads us to select a Pinot Grigio, a Gavin, or even a Prosecco. Pinot Grigio's crisp acidity, apple, and lemon zest flavors contrast beautifully with this dish. Gavi's (Cortese is the grape) intensely floral nose and delicate flavors of peach, watermelon, and pineapple, cradled in a soft, sensuous body, works well here. Prosecco's sparkling melon and pear flavors, creamy texture, and lemon finish provide a fun choice.

$ Zardetto Prosecco
(Italy)

**$+ Livio Felluga
Pinot Grigio**
(Alto Adige, Italy)

$$ Villa Rosa Gavi di Gavi
(Piamonte, Italy)

Orange and Jicama Salad with Toasted Sweet Walnuts

I created this colorful winter salad for a cooking class, and everyone loved it. As a first course or side dish, it pairs the sweetness of oranges and caramelized walnuts with the tang of citrus vinaigrette.

INGREDIENTS:

1 small bunch green leaf lettuce

1½ cups julienned jicama

3 oranges, peeled and sliced crosswise

1 recipe Toasted Sweet Walnuts

1 teaspoon Dijon mustard

3 tablespoons freshly squeezed orange juice

¼ cup vegetable oil

Salt and freshly ground black pepper, to taste

Wash and spin dry leaf lettuce and arrange it on 4 salad plates. Top with jicama, sliced oranges, and Toasted Sweet Walnuts.

In a small mixing bowl, whisk together Dijon mustard, orange juice, vegetable oil, salt, and black pepper until the mixture is emulsified. Drizzle over salads.

Recipe makes 4 salads.

Toasted Sweet Walnuts:

3 tablespoons unsalted butter

3 tablespoons packed brown sugar

1½ cups walnut halves

Melt butter in a large nonstick skillet; add brown sugar and stir until it softens. Stir in walnut halves and cook, stirring occasionally, about 5 minutes until sugar begins to caramelize on walnuts.

Remove walnuts from skillet and place them on a large plate or tray to cool.

Recipe makes 1½ cups toasted walnuts.

Side Dishes

Jinx's Wilted Lettuce Salad

My mother's tangy salad of leaf lettuce, crisp bacon, red onion, and hard-cooked eggs features a warm sweet-and-sour bacon dressing. Mom has served this salad during many family gatherings and parties, because we can never get enough of it!

INGREDIENTS:

1 large head green or
  red leaf lettuce

1 red onion, sliced

1 hard-cooked egg

½ cup sliced white mushrooms

5 strips bacon

¾ cup cider vinegar

¾ cup water

2½ tablespoons sugar

Rinse and dry leaf lettuce; tear it into pieces and place in a large serving bowl. Separate onion slices into rings; add them to the salad. Slice egg in an egg slicer, turn it 90 degrees, and slice again so egg is diced. Sprinkle the egg and mushrooms on the salad.

Meanwhile, fry bacon in a medium skillet over medium-low heat until crisp. Drain on paper towels and crumble it onto salad. Pour out all but 1 tablespoon of the bacon drippings.

In a glass measure, stir cider vinegar, water, and sugar until the sugar is dissolved. Pour this mixture into the skillet and cook over medium-high heat, without stirring, until it's hot but not boiling. Do not scrape up bacon bits from pan. When the sweet-and-sour mixture is hot, pour it over the salad greens.

Toss gently and serve immediately.

Recipe serves 6 to 8.

Crème Brûlée

This popular, classic French dessert is an extra-special finale for dinner parties, and it's surprisingly easy to make at home.

INGREDIENTS:

1½ cups heavy cream

1 vanilla bean

5 egg yolks

¼ cup sugar

½ cup sugar or brown sugar, for caramelized garnish

1 teakettle hot water

Preheat oven to 350 degrees. Ready four 4-ounce ramekins.

Pour cream into a medium saucepan. Split vanilla bean with a sharp knife, scrape out the seeds, and stir them and the vanilla bean into the cream. Bring the mixture to a simmer, remove from heat, and set aside.

Whip yolks and sugar with an electric mixer until yolks are thick and pale in color.

Remove the vanilla bean from hot cream; set aside. Pour a small amount of hot cream into the egg mixture, stirring carefully to avoid forming bubbles. Add remaining hot cream, stirring carefully.

Strain the mixture into a bowl or 4-cup glass measure and skim off any bubbles. Pour the mixture into 4-ounce ramekins, leaving ¼ inch at the top for the sugar glaze.

Place the ramekins in a large baking pan and place on an oven rack. Pour hot water into the baking pan, halfway up sides of ramekins. Bake 15 to 20 minutes until custard is set. Cool; then refrigerate several hours until cold.

Just before serving, sprinkle each custard with 2 tablespoons sugar. Caramelize sugar until golden brown under the broiler or with a propane torch.

Recipe makes 4 desserts.

Desserts

Bananas Foster

My good friend and culinary colleague, Carol Ritchie, pronounced this the best Bananas Foster she had ever tasted! For added drama, cook the bananas in a large, shiny copper sauté pan. Take the copper pan to the table just before adding the warm Cognac to the sauce. Dim the lights, pour in the Cognac, and light with a long wooden match. Your guests will love it!

INGREDIENTS:

3 large bananas

3 tablespoons unsalted butter

⅓ cup packed light brown sugar

1 tablespoon freshly squeezed
orange juice

2 tablespoons light or dark rum

3 tablespoons Remy Martin
Fine Champagne Cognac VSOP

2 teaspoons orange zest

4 generous scoops vanilla
ice cream

Peel bananas and slice in half horizontally. Cut each half lengthwise; set aside.

Over medium-low heat, melt butter in a large skillet. Add brown sugar and stir to melt, about 2 minutes. Add bananas; cook 2 minutes until tender, turning once. Stir in orange juice and rum.

Gently warm Cognac in a small saucepan over low heat, pour it over the bananas, and ignite it with a long wooden match. When the flames burn out, arrange the bananas around ice cream. Spoon the sauce over the ice cream and bananas and serve immediately.

Recipe serves 4.

Saving time in the kitchen is important when preparing a last-minute dessert. For ease of serving, place scoops of ice cream in a large bowl before guests arrive. Keep bowl in the freezer until ready to use.

Panna Cotta

Panna Cotta is a light, creamy Italian custard, usually served with fresh berries. In my version, I garnish the plate with a small pool of raspberry sauce in addition to the berries for a truly spectacular-looking dessert.

INGREDIENTS:

1 package unflavored gelatin

⅓ cup granulated sugar

2 cups cold half-and-half

1 cup heavy cream

1 vanilla bean

Raspberry Coulis, for garnish

Assorted fresh berries,
  for garnish

In a medium saucepan, stir together gelatin, sugar, half-and-half, and cream. Set aside 5 minutes until the gelatin has softened.

Slice vanilla bean open using a sharp knife and scrape out the seeds with the tip of the knife. Add the seeds and vanilla bean to the saucepan; stir.

Cook mixture over medium heat, stirring occasionally, until it's hot and small bubbles form around the edges of pan; do not boil. Strain the mixture through cheesecloth into a bowl or large liquid measuring cup.

Spray 6 individual 3-inch molds with nonstick cooking spray. Ladle or pour the mixture into the prepared molds, cover, and chill 2 to 3 hours, or until set. Recipe may be made 1 day ahead.

To serve, unmold Panna Cotta by dipping the molds into a bowl of hot water for 5 to 10 seconds. Place a dessert plate over the mold, turn both over, and unmold the custard onto the plate. Repeat with the remaining molds. Garnish the plate with several spoonfuls of Raspberry Coulis and fresh berries.

Recipe makes 6 individual desserts.

Raspberry Coulis

Use this raspberry sauce when serving desserts such as panna cotta, cheesecake, and poached pears, or to create decorative designs when working with crème anglaise.

INGREDIENTS:

1 14-ounce package frozen raspberries, thawed

1 teaspoon fresh lemon juice

3 to 4 tablespoons sugar

Pour raspberries into a blender and purée. Transfer the puree to a fine sieve and set over a medium bowl. Using the back of a spoon, push the purée through sieve; discard seeds.

Stir lemon juice and sugar to taste into the Raspberry Coulis and continue to stir until the sugar is completely dissolved.

Recipe makes 1⅓ cups sauce.

Pears in Light Custard Sauce

In this dramatic dessert, fresh pears are sliced, gently formed into fans, and sautéed in butter, sugar, and a hint of freshly grated nutmeg. Just before serving, the pears are flambéed with Grand Marnier, then presented in a pool of crème anglaise.

INGREDIENTS:

4 pears, peeled, with stems intact

2 tablespoons unsalted butter

1 tablespoon sugar

¼ teaspoon freshly grated nutmeg

2 to 3 tablespoons Grand Marnier

1 recipe Crème Anglaise

Core pears from the bottom with a sharp knife. Slice them to within ½ inch of the stem, then gently fan out the slices.

In a large skillet, melt butter over medium-low heat. Add the pears and cook 4 to 5 minutes per side, carefully turning the fans with a spatula. Sprinkle with sugar and freshly grated nutmeg.

When the pears are tender, heat Grand Marnier in a small saucepan just until warm. Immediately pour the liqueur over the pears and ignite it with a long wooden match. Allow the flames to burn out.

To serve, spoon crème anglaise onto center of 4 dessert plates. Garnish with swirls of raspberry coulis, if desired. Place a pear fan in center of each plate, drizzle with Grand Marnier sauce, and serve immediately.

Recipe serves 4.

Desserts

Crème Anglaise

This sauce creates dessert magic. A thin, rich vanilla custard, it is used to garnish cakes, custards, and fruit or as a base for homemade ice cream. To transform ordinary desserts into show-stoppers, pour several tablespoons of crème anglaise on dessert plates, tilting plates to distribute sauce evenly. Drizzle small drops of chocolate sauce or raspberry coulis around the crème anglaise, then draw a knife through the chocolate or coulis to create hearts, or swirl with the tip of a knife for a marbled effect.

INGREDIENTS:

1 vanilla bean	¼ cup sugar
1¼ cups milk	2 egg yolks

Split vanilla bean lengthwise with a sharp knife, scrape out the seeds, and transfer the seeds and bean to a medium saucepan. Pour in milk and whisk the mixture together.

Cook the milk mixture over medium heat, stirring occasionally, until small bubbles form around the edges of the pan. Remove from heat; set aside.

In a small mixing bowl, beat egg yolks with sugar until the mixture is thick. Remove the vanilla bean from milk; set aside. Whisk a little of the hot milk into the egg mixture to temper the eggs, mixing well. Return the tempered egg mixture to saucepan.

Over medium heat, whisk the mixture constantly until the custard thickens and comes just to a boil. Do not allow the custard to burn on the bottom of the pan.

Pour the custard into a clean bowl, place a piece of plastic wrap directly on it, and chill until cold, about 2 hours. Stir the sauce just before using. It will keep in the refrigerator several days.

Recipes make approximately 1⅔ cups sauce.

Champagne Sabayon

When I think of sabayon (zabaglione in Italian), I always think of my sweet friend and colleague, cookbook author and restaurateur Claire Criscuolo, who graciously contributed a recipe to this book. Randy and I took Claire out to dinner at a favorite Italian bistro, and Claire ordered the sabayon with fresh berries for dessert. The look of sheer pleasure on her face inspired me to create my own version of this foamy, sweet custard sauce.

INGREDIENTS:

4 egg yolks

¼ cup plus 1 tablespoon sugar

Dash of salt

½ cup extra-dry or demisec Champagne

1 to 2 tablespoons Marsala wine

½ cup heavy cream (optional)

In the top of a double boiler, whisk together the yolks, sugar, salt, Champagne, and Marsala. Cook over simmering water, whisking vigorously, until the sauce thickens and becomes foamy, 8 to 10 minutes. Take care that the top section of the double boiler does not come in contact with water.

When the sabayon is foamy throughout, serve immediately; the mixture will not hold long without separating. To prolong serving time, place the upper portion of the double boiler on a thick pad or folded towel; do not place it on a cutting board or cold surface. Mixture will hold approximately 25 minutes if it is kept warm.

Serve sabayon over sponge cake, ladyfingers, fresh berries, or fruit tarts.

Recipe makes approximately 1½ cups.

Gently fold ½ cup softly whipped heavy cream into sabayon for an elegant, light dessert. Serve in stemmed dessert or wine glasses and garnish with shaved chocolate. Recipe serves 6 to 8.

Desserts

Strawberries Romanoff

This classic dessert, made from ripe strawberries marinated in a mixture of orange juice and Grand Marnier, looks charming with a swirl of chantilly cream.

Strawberries Romanoff is a perfect choice for those who prefer something lighter. When my friends, Marilyn and Terry McElroy, are our guests at dessert parties, Strawberries Romanoff is always Terry's first choice from the buffet.

For seated dinners, serve Strawberries Romanoff in stemmed glassware with a wide opening. Place each glass on a dessert plate, with a cookie or two. For a finishing touch, dip the rim of each glass into the orange marinade and then in a plate of sparkling or granulated sugar before filling it with strawberries.

INGREDIENTS:

1 quart ripe strawberries	½ cup heavy cream
¼ cup freshly squeezed orange juice	½ teaspoon confectioners' sugar
¼ cup Cointreau or Grand Marnier	2 tablespoons shaved chocolate (optional)

Wash berries and drain them on paper towels or in a colander. Hull them with a sharp knife, slicing very large berries in half.

Place the berries in a medium bowl. Pour orange juice and Cointreau over them; stir gently. Cover the bowl with plastic wrap and chill 2 to 3 hours, stirring occasionally.

To serve, whip cream with sugar until soft peaks form. Spoon berries and some of the marinade into each stemmed glass. Top with a swirl of cream and sprinkle with shaved chocolate.

Recipe makes 8 servings.

Strawberry Napoleon

Paris is famous for its glorious pastries. Bring a bit of Paris to your own home, no matter where you live, and treat your family to this spectacular, French-inspired strawberry custard tart. Make the pastry cream a day ahead to simplify assembly.

INGREDIENTS:

1 sheet frozen puff pastry, thawed

1 egg

1 tablespoon water

1 recipe Pastry Cream

1 cup heavy cream

1 teaspoon confectioners' sugar

1 pint fresh strawberries, washed, hulled, and halved

2 squares semisweet chocolate, melted, for garnish

1 recipe Sugar Glaze

Preheat the oven to 400 degrees. Unfold the puff pastry and slice it into thirds lengthwise. Roll out each third into a 4- by 12-inch rectangle. Place puff pastry on an ungreased cookie sheet and prick it well with a fork. In a small bowl, whisk together egg and water with a fork. Brush the egg wash over the puff pastry.

Bake in preheated oven 8 to 10 minutes, or until golden brown. If the pastry is too puffy to stack, pierce it with a knife at intervals along its length to let out steam and flatten slightly with a spatula. Transfer the pastry rectangles to a wire rack to cool.

Pastry Cream:

1¼ cups milk

1 vanilla bean

2 egg yolks

¼ cup sugar

1½ tablespoons flour

Pour milk into a medium saucepan. Split the vanilla bean open with a sharp knife, scrape out the seeds, and stir the seeds and whole vanilla bean into the milk. Scald over medium heat, stirring occasionally. Remove from the heat and set aside.

Desserts

In the medium bowl of an electric mixer, beat egg yolks with sugar and flour until the mixture is thick and pale yellow. Remove the vanilla bean from hot milk and whisk a little hot milk into the egg mixture to temper the eggs. Then pour the egg mixture into the saucepan of hot milk. Over medium heat, whisk the milk and egg mixture constantly until it thickens and comes just to a boil. Remove from heat, pour pastry cream into a bowl, and place plastic wrap directly on its surface to prevent it from forming a skin. Chill until cold.

To assemble the Napoleon:

Whip heavy cream with 1 teaspoon confectioners' sugar until soft peaks form. Place one layer of puff pastry on a serving platter. Using an offset spatula or knife, spread a layer of pastry cream over the puff pastry; then spread a layer of whipped cream over the pastry cream. Top with sliced strawberries, arranging them so their pointed ends face toward the outer edges of the Napoleon.

Top with a second layer of puff pastry, more pastry cream, whipped cream, and strawberries. Place the final layer of puff pastry on top of the strawberries and spoon Sugar Glaze over it; spread with an offset spatula until smooth.

Spoon melted chocolate into a pastry bag fitted with a narrow plain tip and pipe parallel lines at 1/2-inch intervals across the glaze with the chocolate. While the chocolate is still wet, draw a sharp knife through it to feather the lines.

Sugar Glaze:

1½ cups sifted confectioners' sugar	1 tablespoon milk

In a small bowl, whisk together sugar and milk until the glaze is smooth and thick, adding a bit more milk, if needed. It should be somewhat thick so it doesn't drip down the sides of the Napoleon.

Recipe serves 8.

New York–Style Cheesecake

I have always judged a restaurant by its cheesecake. I like it thick and dense, without sauces or toppings to mar its singular perfection, so when an eager waiter describes the house cheesecake as creamy and smooth, I always choose something else.

This New York–style cheesecake is dense and rich, so a small serving is usually sufficient. Since not everyone is as plain-Jane as I about cheesecake, feel free to garnish it with fresh berries or the sauce of your choice.

INGREDIENTS:

Graham Cracker Crust:

1¼ cups graham cracker crumbs

2 tablespoons sugar

¼ cup butter, melted

Preheat the oven to 325 degrees. Grind graham crackers in a blender or food processor until fine; transfer the crumbs to a medium bowl. Stir in sugar and melted butter until the mixture is moistened, then press it onto bottom of a 9-inch springform pan. Bake in a preheated oven 10 minutes; cool completely.

Filling:

4 8-ounce packages cream cheese, softened

1¼ cups sugar

3 tablespoons flour

4 eggs

¼ cup milk

1¼ teaspoons vanilla

Desserts

Preheat the oven to 425 degrees. In the large bowl of an electric mixer, beat cream cheese until smooth. Gradually add sugar and flour, beating just until blended. Do not overbeat.

Add eggs, one at a time, beating on low speed just until blended. Stir in milk and vanilla.

Pour the mixture into the springform pan with the crumb crust and smooth the top with a spatula. Bake in a preheated oven 10 minutes. Reduce the heat to 300 degrees and bake 50 to 55 more minutes, or until the center is set but not dry. Turn off the oven, open the door, and allow the cheesecake to sit in the oven 30 minutes. Remove the cheesecake from the oven and cool it 20 minutes on a wire rack; then gently run a sharp knife around the edge to separate it from pan. Cool 1 hour; then release the spring and remove the outer rim of the pan. Cover the cheesecake loosely with foil and refrigerate until cold.

Cheesecake will keep several days in the refrigerator, or wrap it well in foil and freeze.

Recipe makes 1 cheesecake.

Coffee Cheesecake

The heady pairing of a deep-chocolate cookie crust with dense, rich, coffee-flavored filling makes this showstopper dessert a perennial favorite at dinner parties and in dessert buffets. Each time I serve this beautiful cheesecake, I watch my guests weaken then succumb to a divine taste experience. It makes being a host such fun!

INGREDIENTS:

Chocolate Crust:

1¼ cups chocolate wafer crumbs

2 tablespoons sugar

¼ cup butter, melted

Preheat the oven to 325 degrees. Grind chocolate wafers in a blender or food processor until fine; transfer the crumbs to a medium bowl. Stir in sugar and melted butter until the mixture is moistened, then press it onto the bottom of a 9-inch springform pan. Bake in a preheated oven 10 minutes; cool completely.

Filling:

¼ cup milk

1 tablespoon instant coffee crystals

3 8-ounce packages cream cheese, softened

⅓ cup sugar

⅔ cup packed brown sugar

2 tablespoons flour

1½ teaspoons vanilla

3 eggs

Preheat the oven to 425 degrees. In a small bowl, stir together milk and coffee crystals; set aside until the coffee dissolves.

In the large bowl of an electric mixer, beat cream cheese with sugars, flour, and vanilla. Add eggs, beating on low speed just until blended. Do not overbeat. Stir in the coffee mixture, blending well.

Desserts

Pour the mixture into the springform pan with the crumb crust and smooth the top with a spatula. Bake in a preheated oven 10 minutes. Reduce the heat to 300 degrees and bake 40 to 45 more minutes, or until the center is set but not dry. Turn off the oven, open the door, and allow the cheesecake to sit in the oven 30 minutes.

Remove the cheesecake from the oven and cool it 20 minutes on a wire rack; then gently run a sharp knife around the edge to separate it from pan. Cool 1 hour; then release the spring and remove the outer rim of the pan. Cover cheesecake loosely with foil and refrigerate until cold. Several hours before serving, garnish with Coffee Whipped Cream.

Coffee Whipped Cream:

1 cup whipping cream

1 teaspoon instant coffee crystals

1½ tablespoons confectioners' sugar

In a medium bowl, stir coffee crystals into ¼ cup of the whipping cream. When the coffee has dissolved, add the remaining whipping cream to the bowl and beat at high speed with an electric mixer. When the cream begins to thicken, add confectioners' sugar and beat until soft peaks form.

Spread half the whipped cream over the top of the cheesecake. Using a pastry bag fitted with a large open-star tip (Ateco #5B or Wilton #32), pipe the remaining cream in a shell pattern along the outside edge of the cheesecake. Chill until ready to serve.

Recipe makes 1 cheesecake.

Chocolate Pots Au Crème

Traditionally served in tiny, china pots au crème cups with lids, this deep-chocolate custard is absolutely divine. Serve it at the end of an elegant meal with a swirl of whipped cream, or arrange the cups on a silver tray, and offer them as part of a chocolate dessert buffet. Either way, this sensational dessert will bring smiles to the faces of your family and guests.

INGREDIENTS:

4 ounces bittersweet chocolate

1 cup heavy cream

3 tablespoons sugar

Dash of salt

1¼ teaspoons vanilla

7 egg yolks

Whipped cream, for garnish

Chocolate shavings or sifted cocoa, for garnish

Break chocolate into small pieces. In a medium saucepan over medium heat, bring cream to a simmer; remove from heat. Add chocolate, sugar, and salt, stirring until the chocolate melts and the mixture is smooth. Stir in vanilla.

In a medium heatproof bowl, whip egg yolks at high speed until they are thick and pale in color. Pour in a small amount of the chocolate mixture to temper the eggs and stir until thoroughly blended. Whisk in the remaining chocolate mixture.

Set the bowl over a saucepan of simmering water, taking care that the bowl does not come in direct contact with the water. Cook the custard until thick, whisking constantly, about 8 minutes. The chocolate will darken in color as it thickens.

Pour mixture into pots au crème, demitasse cups, or teacups. Cover with plastic wrap and refrigerate several hours or overnight. To serve, top with a swirl of whipped cream and a dusting of cocoa or shaved chocolate, if desired.

Recipe makes 6 servings.

Desserts

Double Chocolate Fondue

Randy and I hosted a Black-Tie Valentine Dessert Party early one February to celebrate one of my favorite holidays. I served this fondue as part of a chocolate buffet. It stayed warm in a silver chafing dish, which rested on a large silver tray attractively piled with cubes of yellow pound cake, fresh pineapple chunks, whole strawberries, and slices of banana.

INGREDIENTS:

3 ounces semisweet or milk chocolate

8 ounces bittersweet chocolate

1 cup heavy cream

2 tablespoons sugar

1 tablespoon light corn syrup

1 prepared pound cake

1 16-ounce container fresh pineapple

2 bananas

1 quart fresh strawberries

Chop both chocolates into small pieces. Transfer to a large mixing bowl; set aside.

In a small saucepan, stir together cream, sugar, and corn syrup. Heat over medium-high heat, just until the cream comes to a boil, stirring often.

Pour the hot cream over the chopped chocolate, whisk until the chocolate melts completely and the mixture is smooth.

Slice pound cake, pineapple, and bananas into 1-inch cubes. Arrange whole strawberries, pineapple, bananas, and cake on a large silver tray.

Pour the chocolate sauce into a fondue pot or glass-lined silver chafing dish and set it over a low flame to keep the chocolate warm. Place the chafing dish on the silver tray with the fruit and cake. Provide decorative toothpicks or fondue forks for guests to dip cake and fruit into the fondue.

Recipe serves 20.

Cheese Blintzes
with Royal Anne Sauce

It didn't take long to observe that cheese blintzes are one of my mother-in-law's favorites. Whenever we accompanied Mom and Dad Rost to Sunday brunch, Mom would begin talking about the cheese blintzes before we even arrived at the club.

So, in honor of Mom, Patricia Rost Shilstone, here is my recipe for one of her favorite foods, Cheese Blintzes. I hope you and your guests will fall in love with them as well.

INGREDIENTS:

Crepes:

1 cup flour	Dash of salt
2 eggs	½ teaspoon oil
1 cup plus 2 tablespoons milk	Crepe filling
2 tablespoons butter, melted	1 recipe Royal Anne Sauce

Whisk flour, eggs, milk, melted butter, and salt together until the batter is smooth. Lightly oil the bottom of an 8-inch nonstick skillet and heat it over medium-low heat. Fill a ¼-cup measuring cup half full, for a total of 2 tablespoons batter.

Pour the batter into pan. Immediately tilt the pan in a circular manner to coat the bottom with a thin layer of batter. Cook until the bottom of crepe is lightly browned and the edges are dry and can be lifted easily with a fork, about 20 to 30 seconds.

Flip the pan over and transfer the crepe to a plate, cover with a towel to retain moisture, and repeat until all the batter has been used. Stack the crepes on top of each other after cooking, covering the stack with a towel to prevent them from drying out.

The crepes may be covered with plastic wrap, refrigerated, and stored overnight.

Recipe makes 16 to 18 crepes.

Desserts

Filling:

1 cup part-skim ricotta cheese

2 tablespoons cream cheese, softened

2 tablespoons sugar

½ teaspoon vanilla

1 egg yolk

Whisk all ingredients together until smooth. Cover and refrigerate until ready to fill the crepes. Filling may be stored overnight.

Royal Anne Sauce:

1 15-ounce can Royal Anne cherries, with syrup

2 teaspoons cornstarch

Drain cherries, reserving the syrup. Place cornstarch into a small bowl and whisk ¼ cup of the reserved syrup into the cornstarch until mixture is smooth.

Pour the remaining syrup and the cornstarch mixture into a medium saucepan. Cook over medium heat until the syrup thickens. Stir in cherries, heat, and serve over cheese blintzes.

Assembly: To assemble blintzes, spoon 1 heaping tablespoon of filling into center of each crepe. Fold left and right sides over the filling; then fold the edges over the filling to create a rectangular packet.

Melt 2 tablespoons of unsalted butter in a large skillet. Place the filled crepes in skillet, folded side down, cover, and heat 3 to 4 minutes over medium-low heat until the blintzes are hot and puffy. Turn blintzes over, cook 1 minute more, and transfer the finished blintzes to serving plates. Garnish with Royal Anne Sauce.

Recipe serves 8.

When serving cheese blintzes for a brunch or after-theater buffet, place the folded blintzes in a large silver service casserole dish, spoon Royal Anne Sauce over them, cover, and keep warm over a low flame.

Almond Nectarine Tart

Ground almonds added to the buttery tart pastry provide an extra flavor dimension in this pretty-as-a-picture summer dessert. Sweetened nectarine slices are overlapped in spiral fashion to create this delectable tart that every home chef can serve with pride.

INGREDIENTS:

Pastry:

⅓ cup blanched almonds

1⅓ cups flour

½ teaspoon salt

1 tablespoon sugar

½ cup cold unsalted butter

3 tablespoons ice water

¼ teaspoon almond extract

Place almonds in the bowl of a food processor and process until they are finely ground. Add flour, salt, and sugar; pulse to mix.

Slice cold butter into eight pieces; add to the flour mixture. Process until the butter is pea-size. Add ice water and almond extract and process just until the dough forms a ball. Do not overprocess. Remove the pastry from the processor, wrap in plastic wrap, and chill 30 minutes or overnight.

Desserts

Filling:

3 pounds nectarines (about 8)

¾ cup sugar

2 tablespoons flour

½ teaspoon cinnamon

¼ teaspoon freshly
  grated nutmeg

To peel nectarines, bring a saucepan of water to boil. Lower the nectarines into the boiling water, a few at a time, and cook 30 seconds. Remove the nectarines; transfer to a bowl of ice water. When cool, the skins will peel off effortlessly.

Peel, seed, and slice the nectarines into a large mixing bowl. In a small bowl, combine sugar, flour, cinnamon, and nutmeg. Pour the sugar mixture over the nectarines and stir gently to combine.

Preheat the oven to 400 degrees. Roll out chilled pastry on a floured pastry cloth and fit into a 10-inch tart pan; trim the edges. Remove 1 cup of sliced nectarines, chop, and place in bottom of tart shell.

Arrange the remaining nectarine slices in a circular pattern on top of the chopped fruit. Spoon sweetened nectarine juices over the tart.

Place the tart pan onto a baking sheet and bake in a preheated oven 40 minutes, or until pastry is golden brown and filling is bubbly.

Serve tart warm or chilled, with a scoop of vanilla ice cream, if desired.

Recipe makes one 10-inch tart.

Red Plum Buttermilk Tarts

A spiral of sliced red plums glistens atop these pretty, individual tarts. Underneath, a tangy buttermilk filling, sweetened with sugar and flavored with vanilla, nestles in flaky pastry.

This no-fuss summer dessert looks like you spent all day in the kitchen, and is a delightful finale to weekend family barbecues or a small gathering of friends. For extra ease of preparation, make the pastry a day ahead and chill in the refrigerator overnight.

INGREDIENTS:

Pastry:

1½ cups all-purpose flour

¼ cup sifted cake flour

2 tablespoons sugar

¾ teaspoon salt

½ cup chilled butter-flavored shortening

¼ cup cold unsalted butter

2 to 3 tablespoons ice water

In the bowl of a food processor, combine flours, sugar, and salt; pulse several times to mix. Add shortening and butter, slicing the butter into tablespoon-size pieces. Pulse until shortening and butter are pea-size.

Pour in ice water; then pulse just until the pastry forms a ball. Shape the pastry into a disk, wrap in plastic wrap, and chill at least 30 minutes.

Slice the chilled pastry into 6 equal wedges. On a floured pastry cloth, roll out each pastry wedge into a circle. Fit the pastry into six 4½-inch tart pans with removable bottoms. Pinch off excess pastry, or roll a rolling pin across the top of the tart pans to cut off excess.

Place the tart pans in refrigerator while preparing filling.

Desserts

Filling:

¾ cup sugar

2 tablespoons flour

1 cup buttermilk

3 eggs, slightly beaten

⅓ cup unsalted butter, melted

½ teaspoon vanilla

3 ripe red plums,
  sliced paper-thin

3 tablespoons red plum jam

Preheat the oven to 350 degrees. In a large bowl, stir together sugar and flour. Whisk in buttermilk, eggs, melted butter, and vanilla. Remove the tart pans from the refrigerator and pour in the filling.

Place the tart pans on a cookie sheet and bake 35 to 40 minutes until the filling is puffed and lightly golden brown. Take care that the cookie sheet is sturdy and does not warp during baking so the filling does not spill.

Remove the sheet from the oven—the tart centers will fall. Gently place plum slices in a spiral in the center of each tart. Return to the oven and bake 5 more minutes to soften the plums.

Meanwhile, in a small saucepan over low heat, melt jam. Brush plum slices with the jam while still warm. Cool, cover lightly with plastic wrap, and chill until ready to serve.

Recipe makes six 4½-inch tarts.

Rustic Vanilla Pear Galette

This French-countryside-inspired tart is so beautiful, but easy as pie to assemble. The spicy vanilla pear filling is mounded into the center of buttery pastry, and the pastry is simply folded up around the filling. What could be easier?

INGREDIENTS:

Pastry:

1 cup all-purpose flour

¼ cup sifted cake flour

1 tablespoon sugar

½ teaspoon salt

¼ cup cold unsalted butter

2 tablespoons shortening

2 to 3 tablespoons ice water

1 egg

1 tablespoon water

2 teaspoons sparkling or granulated sugar

Place flours, sugar, and salt in the bowl of a food processor; pulse to mix. Slice butter into 4 pieces. Add butter and shortening to flour mixture; pulse until butter is pea-size.

Add 2 tablespoons ice water and process until a soft dough is formed, adding additional ice water if the pastry appears to be dry. Remove the pastry, wrap it in plastic wrap, and chill it while preparing filling.

Filling:

3 large Bosc pears, peeled and cored

1 vanilla bean

½ cup sugar

1½ tablespoons flour

½ teaspoon cinnamon

¼ teaspoon freshly grated nutmeg

Desserts

Preheat the oven to 400 degrees. Slice pears lengthwise ¼-inch thick and place in a large mixing bowl. With the point of a sharp knife, slice the vanilla bean open lengthwise, scrape out the seeds, and add them to pears. Save the remaining vanilla bean for another use.

In a small bowl, stir together sugar, flour, cinnamon, and nutmeg. Pour sugar mixture over the pears; stir to mix well.

Roll out the pastry to a 13-inch circle on a floured surface or pastry cloth. Transfer the pastry to a baking sheet lined with parchment paper. Mound the pears in the center of the pastry.

Gently fold the pastry up over the pears, overlapping it to form a round galette. The center of galette will remain open.

Fold the edges of the parchment paper up to catch any juices that escape during the baking.

In a small bowl, whisk egg and water together with a fork to form an egg wash; brush this over pastry. Sprinkle with sparkling or granulated sugar.

Bake the galette 30 to 35 minutes, or until pastry is brown and pears are tender. Serve warm or refrigerate and serve cold.

Recipe makes 1 galette.

Springtime Garden Cupcakes

Delicate cakes topped with buttercream blossoms are just right for teas, birthdays, and Mother's Day.

INGREDIENTS:

¾ cup unsalted butter, softened

1¾ cups sugar

3 eggs

2 teaspoons vanilla

3 cups sifted cake flour

2½ teaspoons baking powder

1 teaspoon salt

1 cup milk

1 recipe Buttercream Frosting

Preheat the oven to 350 degrees. In the large bowl of an electric mixer, cream butter and sugar until the mixture is light and fluffy, about 8 minutes. Add eggs, one at a time, beating well after each addition. Stir in vanilla.

In a medium bowl, stir together cake flour, baking powder, and salt. Gradually add the flour mixture to the creamed mixture, alternately with the milk, beating well between each addition.

Line muffin tins with paper liners. Spoon the batter into the tins, filling each cup half full. Bake in a preheated oven 15 to 18 minutes until the top of each cupcake is golden and a cake tester inserted into the center of a cupcake comes out clean.

Remove the tins from the oven, and remove the cupcakes from the pans while they're still hot so they don't become soggy. Cool on a wire rack while making the Buttercream Frosting.

Desserts

Buttercream Frosting:

½ cup unsalted butter, softened

4 cups sifted confectioners' sugar

Dash of salt

5 to 7 tablespoons milk

1 teaspoon vanilla

Assorted food colorings

In the large bowl of an electric mixer, cream butter, confectioners' sugar, and salt, adding milk as needed to form a creamy consistency. Stir in vanilla.

Frost the cupcakes. Divide the remaining frosting into small bowls and tint with food coloring as desired. Spoon tinted frosting into pastry bags fitted with decorator tips and decorate the cupcakes with flowers and leaves.

Recipe makes approximately 30 decorated cupcakes.

Entrées

Sandwiches

Side Dishes

Desserts

Holidays

*E*ach year is filled with a wonderland of holidays, some big and important, others small and hardly noticeable. While some holidays have religious significance, others are noteworthy for their historical roots or because they give us a reason to pause and remember those who are dear to us. Still others are celebrated for the sheer fun they bring to our lives.

I have always loved holidays. Groundhog Day and Saint Patrick's Day provide opportunities to inject more fun into otherwise ordinary family meals, while Valentine's Day festivities provide opportunities to teach our sons lessons of love and caring for others. Randy and I share stories about honor and love for our country on Memorial Day and Independence Day with flags waving proudly outdoors and centerpieces of red, white, and blue on our family table.

We have been fortunate to share many family holidays with Timothy and Bob's loving grandparents, Patricia and Duane Rost, and after Duane passed away several years ago, Jim Shilstone. We have also spent holidays with their other grandparents, my mom and dad, Jinx and Bob Schnoes, who live in Illinois.

The common thread throughout the years has been the joy of sharing so many special days and traditions together as a family. Holidays have given us an opportunity to nurture and reinforce love of family, to appreciate family traditions and heritage, and an opportunity to worship together and recognize the importance of nurturing the spiritual side of our lives and the role friendships play in making life so much richer.

Traditional foods, which vary from culture to culture and family to family, play an important role in celebrating holidays. My earliest memories of Christmases spent at Grandmom Kathryn Hewston's home in Pittsburgh, Pennsylvania, are of the two-layered, anise-flavored springerle cookies she purchased from a nearby bakery that have inspired a tradition in my own family, and of the crisp, paper-thin gingerbread cookies she baked every year, served ice-cold from cookie tins stored in their uninsulated garage. The gingerbread cookie dough was so stiff, Grandpop Joseph had to help each year with rolling out the dough.

When we celebrated Christmas with Grandmom Henrietta and Grandad Sebastian Schnoes, Grandmom always served her delicate Eggnog Pie for dessert. Enhanced with a touch of rum, her pie was topped with a thin layer of whipped cream, and decorated with tiny flowers made from slices of red and green maraschino cherries. It wouldn't be Christmas in our home without Henrietta's Eggnog Pie, so this is a family favorite I love to recreate every year. She also baked wonderful rolled sugar cookies (we called them cut-out cookies), decorated with a thin glaze and tinted sugar. Grandmom was a gifted baker, and her influence and encouragement inspired my love for creating beautiful, delectable desserts.

In this section, traditional favorites, handed down in our families, are joined by recipes destined to become new traditions. These are complemented by wine pairings selected by friend and wine expert Eric Little to enhance each celebratory meal and to toast life's precious moments.

Although not every holiday is covered, the holidays that have the strongest significance in our family life are addressed. In this section, you will discover beautiful recipes for Christmas, New Year's, Valentine's Day, Easter, Halloween, and Thanksgiving. May they enhance your celebrations and inspire new traditions around your table.

Leg of Lamb with Whole Mint

When Randy and I lived in Paris with our two young sons, I purchased most of our meat from Monsieur Durand, the butcher just down the street from our flat. Since Americans tend to consume more meat than Parisians, Monsieur Durand's eyes would always light up when I walked in his door. While I waited, I would take note of the beautifully dressed ladies ahead of me, who would ask for one or two thin slices of ham, or perhaps two small sausage links, or a single côtes du veau. When it was my turn, Monsieur Durand would smile broadly as I requested four lamb chops, a small beef roast, or other American-sized amount.

The day I walked in and asked Monsieur Durand for a leg of lamb was a turning point in our relationship. After eagerly stepping to the cooler to bring forth his best merchandise, he proudly returned to the counter in hopes I would be pleased with his selection. Then he asked, in French, of course, how much of the leg I would like. I replied I wanted the entire leg. Not certain he had heard me correctly, Monsieur Durand proceeded to indicate varying amounts. I said again, "No, Monsieur. Je voudrais le tout," or, "I would like all of it."

Well, you would have thought I had offered to purchase everything in his shop! Monsieur's eyes widened, and I am certain he had visions of me putting his first child through college. Perhaps I did! I don't remember how much that leg of lamb cost, but I vividly remember the extra trimming and decorative scoring of the fat Monsieur did to put his personal stamp on my grand purchase. It was certainly one of the prettiest legs of lamb I ever roasted.

While my recipe for Leg of Lamb may not have all the decorative handiwork of Monsieur Durand, the artistic effect of slices of garlic wrapped in fresh mint leaves, protruding at intervals along the length of the leg, is quite beautiful. The roast glistens with

Entrées

a glaze of mint jelly, which is brushed on just before cooking, and the aroma of fresh garlic and roasted meat is intoxicating. Whether for Easter or other holidays, a birthday meal, or Sunday dinner, may serving this impressive roast to your family and guests inspire a joyful celebration around your table.

INGREDIENTS:

1 leg of lamb, approximately 4 to 5 pounds

6 large mint leaves

2 large cloves garlic, peeled and sliced

Coarse salt and freshly ground black pepper

¼ cup mint jelly

1 tablespoon chopped fresh rosemary

1 medium onion, sliced

Preheat oven to 350 degrees. Place leg of lamb on a cutting board, fat side down. With a sharp knife, cut a 2-inch slit into the lower leg and locate the large fat pocket. Keeping fat pocket intact, cut away from surrounding meat, and remove. Using butcher's string, tie the leg together.

Turn the lamb fat side up. Cut small slits ½ inch deep into lamb. Push a slice of garlic wrapped in half of mint leaf into each slit. Season the lamb with salt and freshly ground pepper, brush with mint jelly, and sprinkle with chopped rosemary.

Place the onion slices in the center of roasting pan and place the lamb on top of them. Roast in a preheated oven 1½ to 2 hours, or until a meat thermometer registers 170 degrees for medium or 180 degrees for well done.

Remove the roast from oven, cover, and set aside 10 minutes to rest before carving.

Recipe serves 8 to 10.

they can leave a negative impact as often as a positive one. They should be approached with the same caution we give the feared artichoke and–gasp–asparagus, when pairing with wine. No one likes bitter, tinny, unripe persimmon and cheap vinegar flavors.

Now that we've frightened you thoroughly, we have a no-stress solution. We find these super-herbs downright angelic in their effect on leg of lamb. And when roasted lamb is paired with the undisputed champion, Bordeaux, we enter the celestial realm.

$$ Chateau Fontenil, Fronsac
(Bordeaux, France)

$$$ d'Arenberg "The Ironstone Pressings" Grenache/Shiraz/ Mourvèdre Blend
(McLaren Vale, Australia)

$$$ Rodney Strong "Symmetry" Meritage
(Alexander Valley, California)

Rack of Lamb Dijon

Rack of lamb makes good sense on an important occasion like Valentine's Day or an anniversary. Light the hearth while the lamb roasts in the oven, then enjoy a table for two, in front of the fire, in the most romantic restaurant in town—in your home. It's a match made in heaven.

INGREDIENTS:

3 pounds rack of lamb, trimmed

1 teaspoon coarse salt

½ teaspoon freshly ground black pepper

3 tablespoons chopped fresh rosemary

3 tablespoons chopped fresh sage

2 tablespoons chopped fresh parsley

3 cloves garlic, minced

3 to 4 tablespoons Maille or other good brand Dijon mustard

½ cup bread crumbs

Mint jelly, for garnish

Ask the butcher to trim and "french" the racks.

Preheat the oven to 450 degrees. Season both sides of lamb with salt and pepper and roast it in a preheated oven approximately 15 minutes until rare.

While the lamb is roasting, stir together the herbs and garlic. Remove the lamb from oven and brush it liberally with mustard until well coated. Press the herb and garlic mixture onto lamb and sprinkle it with bread crumbs. Return the lamb, herb side up, to the roasting pan.

Cook lamb 20 to 25 minutes more, depending on thickness, until the lamb is done and herbed crust is brown. Remove from the oven and set aside 5 minutes to rest.

Carve between the ribs. Arrange 3 chops on each dinner plate and serve with mint jelly, if desired.

Recipe serves 8.

Entrées

Prime Rib of Beef

Christmas or New Year's Eve dinner is the perfect occasion to indulge in the luxury of prime rib roast, and the host can count on rave reviews.

While I was growing up, we usually dined on roast turkey for Christmas dinner because my father adores turkey, but when I spent Christmas with Randy's parents, my mother-in-law prepared a huge prime rib of beef. After one taste, I knew I had to make this dish part of my culinary repertoire. The recipe is virtually foolproof, so even if you've never cooked prime rib, you can venture into the kitchen with complete confidence. Your family will always remember this holiday delicacy.

INGREDIENTS:

- 2 tablespoons olive oil
- 1 6- to 8-pound prime rib roast
- 1 tablespoon coarse salt
- 1 teaspoon freshly ground black pepper
- 5 cloves garlic, peeled and minced

Preheat the oven to 400 degrees. Heat a large skillet over medium-low heat; add olive oil. Sear the rib roast in hot oil until all sides of meat and the fat are lightly browned. Remove from skillet and transfer to a large roasting pan, fat side up.

Rub the roast on all sides with coarse salt, pepper, and some of the minced garlic. Top the roast with remaining garlic, plus any garlic that has fallen into roasting pan.

Roast in a hot oven 25 minutes; then reduce the oven temperature to 325 degrees. Continue roasting a total of 2 to 2½ hours, or until a meat thermometer registers 140 degrees for medium rare, or 155 degrees for medium.

Remove the roast from oven, cover it loosely with foil, and set aside 10 minutes to allow it to rest before carving.

Recipe serves 8.

This fork-tender, fat-rich beef dish is understated, yet amply satisfying to the most demanding of beef lovers. An equally understated, well-balanced red wine of generous depth and character is an ideal companion.

A classic pairing would be Bordeaux with a generous portion of Merlot and a dollop of Cabernet Franc, a Pomerol, or, perhaps, one of the Petite Châteaux.

You need not venture overseas to find an ideal pairing. Such blends are far more common in this country than our wine labels lead us to believe. When you purchase a bottle labeled Cabernet Sauvignon, for instance, only 75 percent is required to actually be Cabernet Sauvignon. The wineries do not have to tell us about the other 25 percent, which often contain some Merlot or Syrah. Meritage and Claret are American versions of Bordeaux blends that do not fit the 75 percent rule. This is one of our domestic favorites!

$+ Stelzner Claret
(California)

$$ Château Tayac Prestige
(Côtes de Bourg, France)

$$$ Sinskey RSV Red
(Napa Valley, California)

This most tender of cuts is modest in both flavor and texture, that is, until it is embraced by a béarnaise sauce. As we select a wine, we need to consider the textures, both silky and firm, as well as the almost minty sting of tarragon. The sharpness of the cracked peppercorns and tartness of the citrus balance the sweet butter and beef fats. Working with such a delicious spectrum of components makes our search a pleasurable task.

We propose an Australian hillside Shiraz or the muscular, buffed body of a California Petite Sirah (Durif). With Shiraz, the white pepper, black plum, and cedar brought forth by the rocky, thin soil of a hillside vineyard differs noticeably from the ripe berry and chocolate produced by the laid-back vines of a loam-rich vineyard. Grape vines are a bit like people. Have you ever noticed that the most

Chateaubriand with Béarnaise Sauce

Béarnaise sauce is a classic pairing for the ever-opulent chateaubriand. Years ago, it was common for restaurants to offer chateaubriand for two on their menus, marketed particularly to couples celebrating romantic occasions.

Although chateaubriand is not as common in restaurants today, it continues to be an elegant suggestion for holiday meals and special occasions celebrated at home. For the busy host, beef tenderloin requires very little effort, yet always elicits oohs and aahs from those at the table. Served with a béarnaise sauce, it is a magical, melt-in-the-mouth taste experience.

INGREDIENTS:

1½ pounds beef tenderloin, tied with kitchen string

Coarse salt and freshly ground black pepper, to taste

2 tablespoons olive oil

1 recipe Béarnaise Sauce

Preheat oven to 450 degrees. Season tenderloin with salt and freshly ground pepper. Heat a large skillet over medium heat; add oil.

Carefully place the tenderloin in the hot skillet. Brown the meat on all sides, approximately 5 minutes total. Transfer the tenderloin to a roasting pan and roast it, uncovered, 15 to 25 minutes, depending on thickness and desired degree of doneness. Remove the meat from the oven, cover with foil, and set aside while making sauce.

Entrées

Béarnaise Sauce:

1 large shallot, diced

2 sprigs chopped fresh tarragon with stems

1 teaspoon cracked black peppercorns

½ cup white wine vinegar

¼ cup dry white wine

2 egg yolks

1 tablespoon water

1 tablespoon lemon juice

4 to 5 tablespoons unsalted butter, softened

1 tablespoon chopped fresh tarragon

In a small saucepan, place diced shallot, tarragon, crushed pepper-corns, wine vinegar, and white wine. Cook over medium-high heat until the mixture has reduced to ¼ cup; strain and set aside.

In a double boiler, over hot, not boiling, water, combine egg yolks, water, and lemon juice. Whisk until the egg mixture thickens and becomes lemon-colored. Gradually whisk in 4 tablespoons of the butter, 1 tablespoon at a time, to form a thick sauce. Slowly whisk in the strained tarragon reduction. If sauce is too thin, whisk in the remaining tablespoon of butter. Stir in the remaining tablespoon of chopped tarragon. Keep warm.

To serve, slice chateaubriand into ½-inch-thick slices and serve with béarnaise sauce.

Recipe serves 6.

dynamic personalities have struggled through challenges we wouldn't wish on our enemies, while the bland, complacent, and spoiled types have never really had to fight for much in life?

Durif, having masqueraded as Petite Sirah in California for over a century, and not really related to Syrah, produces a dense, elegant, big-boned beauty, with massive black-berry, dark chocolate, cedar, and the distinct perfume of violets. A natural with grilled meats, it uses every bit of its strength pairing competitively, but nicely, with chateaubriand.

$$ Chateau Reynella Shiraz (McLaren Vale, Australia)

$$ David Bruce Petite Sirah (Central Coast, California)

$$$ Rosenblum Petite Sirah, Rockpile Road Vineyard (Dry Creek, California)

Baked Easter Ham with Oven-Basted New Potatoes

My mother, Jinx Schnoes, has prepared this ham recipe for countless family holidays and celebrations. With one or two simple variations, it has been a favorite in our family, too. Years ago, I added new potatoes to the recipe when I discovered how the flavor of the basting syrup permeates them, making the potatoes a taste treat in themselves. So now, when I bake my version of my mother's Easter ham, I always serve Oven-Basted New Potatoes.

INGREDIENTS:

- 1 shank or butt portion smoked ham
- 2 tablespoons whole cloves
- 1 cup dark brown Billington's molasses sugar, packed
- 2 tablespoons dry mustard
- ½ cup cider vinegar
- ½ cup water
- 4 pineapple rings
- 4 maraschino cherries
- 1 recipe Oven-Basted New Potatoes

Rinse ham in cold water and dry with paper towels; transfer to a large roasting pan with room for potatoes. Bake at 225 degrees 30 minutes until fat has softened.

Remove the ham from the oven. With a large, sharp knife, remove the rind and discard, leaving fat in place. Score the fat with the knife to form a diamond pattern. Insert a clove into the center of each diamond. Return the ham to the oven.

In a medium saucepan, mix molasses sugar and dry mustard. Stir in vinegar and water. Cook over high heat, stirring often, until the mixture comes to a boil, being careful it does not boil over; reduce the heat to low. Cook 10 to 15 minutes until mixture forms a thin syrup.

Drain fat from the roasting pan and slowly pour the syrup over ham. Baste occasionally during the remainder of the cooking time, 2 to 3 hours.

Entrées

During the final 30 minutes of cooking, decorate the ham with pineapple rings and cherries, using toothpicks to hold the fruit in place. Baste the fruit with the syrup. Add parboiled new potatoes to the roasting pan, turning occasionally and basting with the syrup.

To serve, slice the ham and arrange it on a large platter with the basted potatoes. Garnish with roasted pineapple and cherries. Pour the remaining syrup into a gravy boat and serve with the ham.

Recipe serves 10 to 12.

Oven-Basted New Potatoes

These delicious potatoes make a simple accompaniment to most roasted meats. Simply add potatoes to a roasting pan of pork, beef, lamb, or chicken during the final 30 minutes of cooking.

INGREDIENTS:

New potatoes or small red potatoes	Water for parboiling

Rinse and gently scrub new potatoes, being careful not to rub off the skin. Using a paring knife, peel off a narrow strip of skin all around center of each potato.

Transfer the potatoes to a large saucepan or Dutch oven and add enough water to cover. Cover the saucepan and bring it to a boil over high heat. When the water comes to a boil, reduce the heat to medium-low and cook 5 to 10 minutes until a sharp knife inserts easily into potatoes, but still meets with some resistance. Do not overcook.

Drain the potatoes and set them aside until the meat is in final 30 minutes of roasting. Add them to the roasting pan, turning to coat with syrup or meat juices, and roast, turning every 10 minutes.

Two pounds of new potatoes (about 12 potatoes) serves 6.

beautiful stranger from afar, perhaps the beginning of a long relationship. But, this day we savor our all-too-few remaining traditions, and our traditions dictate that baked ham be paired with Pinot Noir.

The salty-sweet meat, basted in sour-sweet sauce, studded with pineapples—sweet and tart. You get the picture. We need a wine that has gobs of fruit—bright cherry that mirrors the maraschino. Acidity is quite important—not enough, and everything seems cloying and sugary.

We chose a Pinot Noir from the famed Santa Lucia hills, and one from the exuberant vineyards of Carneros. For fun, and a subtle taste of rose petal, jammy tart cherries and dark-chocolate mint, we suggest an old-vine Grenache/Shiraz from McLaren Vale, Australia. After all, a tradition has to start somewhere!

$+ Hill of Content Old-Vine Grenache/Shiraz
(McLaren Vale, Australia)

$$$ Acacia Pinot Noir, Carneros
(Napa, California)

$$$ Morgan Pinot Noir "Santa Lucia"
(Santa Lucia, California)

Crown Roast with Oyster Sage Dressing

Few holiday entrées are more spectacular than the showstopper crown roast. Tied to resemble a monarch's crown, and filled with an equally remarkable dressing studded with oysters, this noteworthy dish should be brought to the holiday table with great fanfare.

INGREDIENTS:

1 7- to 8-pound pork crown roast

1 teaspoon garlic salt

½ teaspoon freshly ground
   black pepper

1 recipe Oyster Sage Dressing

Order a crown roast from butcher several days before serving and ask to have it trimmed and tied.

Preheat the oven to 450 degrees. Season meat with garlic salt and freshly ground pepper and transfer to a roasting pan.

Place the roast in a preheated oven; immediately reduce temperature to 325 degrees. Roast the meat 20 minutes per pound, or 2 hours and 20 minutes for a 7-pound crown roast. One hour before the roast is done, remove it from the oven and stuff it with Oyster Sage Dressing.

Spoon dressing into the center of the crown; then roast the meat until a meat thermometer registers 160 degrees when inserted into thickest part of meat. Remove the roast from the oven, cover it, and set aside 10 minutes before carving.

Allow 2 ribs per person.

Entrées

Oyster Sage Dressing:

4 slices dry wheat bread

⅓ cup minced onion

1 stalk celery, minced

1 small apple, cored and diced

1½ tablespoons minced
   fresh sage

1½ teaspoons dried sage

Salt and freshly ground pepper

1 egg

¼ cup chicken or vegetable
   broth

½ pint oysters, drained and
   chopped

Slice bread into small cubes. Toss bread, onion, celery, apple, and seasonings together in a large bowl.

In a small bowl, whisk together the egg and broth. Stir the liquid into bread mixture, along with chopped oysters.

Spoon the dressing into the crown roast 1 hour before the roast is done. Spoon any extra dressing into a small greased casserole dish, cover, and bake at 325 degrees 45 minutes. Uncover and bake 15 more minutes.

Roasted Turkey with Pennsylvania Stuffing

This is a variation of the turkey and stuffing my mother makes. I have added dried fruit and fresh, chopped apples for flavor and texture. Even my Southern friends, who grew up on cornbread dressing, love this flavorful stuffing.

For really delicious brown gravy, I roast my turkey at a high temperature during the first 30 minutes. It browns the bottom of the turkey, resulting in richer, tastier pan juices for turkey gravy.

INGREDIENTS:

1 20-pound turkey, fresh or frozen

Salt

1 1-pound loaf wheat bread, cubed and allowed to dry 2 to 3 hours

2 cups chopped celery

1½ cups chopped onion

1 cup chopped dates

¾ cup golden raisins

¾ cup dried cranberries

⅓ cup chopped fresh parsley

2 apples, cored and chopped

3 tablespoons dried thyme

3 tablespoons dried sage

3 eggs

1 cup milk

3 tablespoons butter

If the turkey is frozen, thaw it in the refrigerator 2 to 3 days before cooking. If purchased fresh, keep it refrigerated until ready to prepare.

Early in the day, remove wrappings from the turkey and place it in a clean sink under running water. Remove all giblets and other loose turkey parts. Save the giblets for gravy, keeping them well wrapped and chilled.

Wash the turkey inside and out with plenty of water, remembering to clean inside the tail flap, where the giblets are often packaged and stored by the poultry processor. Pat the turkey dry, inside and out, with paper towels. Season the inside cavities with salt and transfer the turkey to a large roasting pan.

Entrées

Wash sink and counter areas with soap and water to remove all traces of raw turkey juices and wash your hands well with soap and water before preparing the stuffing.

For stuffing, combine bread cubes, celery, onion, dates, raisins, and cranberries in a very large mixing bowl. Add parsley, chopped apple, thyme, and sage, rubbing the herbs between your hands to release their flavor and aroma.

In a small bowl, whip eggs with a fork, and stir in milk. Pour the egg mixture into the bread mixture and toss well to moisten.

Preheat the oven to 400 degrees. Stuff the turkey's tail flap with a small amount of stuffing to create a rounded appearance, then tuck the tail flap under to secure it. Stuff the large cavity loosely with stuffing mixture.

Tie the turkey legs together; rub the skin with butter. Wash your hands thoroughly, then cover the turkey with a tent of foil, taking care the foil doesn't come in contact with the skin.

Spoon excess stuffing into a buttered casserole dish, cover with foil, and chill. One hour before serving, bake at 325 degrees 50 to 60 minutes. During the final 15 minutes of cooking, remove the cover to brown the top of the stuffing.

Roast turkey in a preheated oven 30 minutes; then reduce the temperature to 325 degrees, and continue roasting according to the time chart printed on turkey's original wrapping, or 20 minutes per pound. Roasting time for a 20-pound, stuffed turkey is approximately 5½ to 6 hours. Baste the turkey occasionally, if desired. Remove foil during final 30 minutes to brown the skin. Remove turkey from oven, cover it with foil and allow it to rest 10 minutes. Remove foil and spoon out all the stuffing from both cavities. Carve turkey.

Recipe serves 12.

For the red, we suggest a Cru Beaujolais. Note, however, that nowhere on a bottle of Cru Beaujolais does one find a reference to Beaujolais. These landed gentry prefer to identify themselves by appellation— Morgon, Chena's, St. Amour, and Brouilly. This unpretentious, silk nectar of bright cherry, raspberry, and floral notes such as lavender is a solid pairing. It is also perhaps the safest choice when entertaining friends whose wine habits are unknown.

$ Hugel Pinot Gris
(Alsace, France)

$ Berrod Fleurie
(Beaujolais, France)

**$+ Domaine Weinbach
Pinot Gris**
(Alsace, France)

Thanksgiving Turkey with Southern Cornbread Dressing

After living in the South all these years, I seem to have picked up a hint of Southern drawl. Once I started saying y'all, it was only a matter of time until I tried the traditional Southern cornbread dressing for Thanksgiving. My own recipe uses cubes of wheat bread to enhance the texture, and chopped aromatics, dried fruit, and herbs for added flavor. My Southern friends give this recipe rave reviews. Why not try it for your next Thanksgiving dinner?

INGREDIENTS:

Turkey and Dressing:

1 20-pound turkey, fresh or frozen	½ cup golden raisins
Salt	2 tablespoons minced fresh sage
1 recipe Cornbread	1½ tablespoons dried thyme
4 slices dry wheat bread, cut into ½-inch cubes	1 tablespoon dried rubbed sage
1 small onion, peeled and diced	3 cups chicken or vegetable broth
1 cup chopped celery	2 eggs
½ cup dried cherries	3 tablespoons butter

If the turkey is frozen, thaw it in the refrigerator 2 to 3 days before cooking. If purchased fresh, keep it refrigerated until ready to prepare.

Early in the day, remove wrappings from the turkey and place it in a clean sink under running water. Remove all giblets and other loose turkey parts. Save the giblets for gravy, keeping them well wrapped and chilled.

Wash the turkey inside and out with plenty of water, remembering to clean inside the tail flap, where the giblets are often packaged and stored by the poultry processor. Pat the turkey dry, inside and out, with paper towels. Season the inside cavities with salt and transfer the turkey to a large roasting pan.

Entrées

Wash sink and counter areas with soap and water to remove all traces of raw turkey juices and wash your hands well with soap and water before preparing the stuffing.

For stuffing, slice the cornbread into small cubes. In a very large mixing bowl, combine cornbread, wheat bread, onion, celery, dried cherries, and golden raisins. Add fresh and dried sage and thyme, rubbing the dry herbs between your hands to release their flavor and aroma.

In a small bowl, whip eggs with a fork, and stir in broth. Pour the egg mixture into the bread mixture and toss well to moisten.

The dressing may be used to stuff turkey, or spoon it into a large, buttered casserole dish, cover, and bake at 350 degrees 45 minutes. Uncover and bake 10 minutes more to brown top of dressing.

If using the dressing to stuff the turkey, preheat oven to 400 degrees. Stuff the turkey's tail flap with a small amount of dressing to create a rounded appearance, then tuck tail flap under to secure it. Stuff the large cavity loosely with dressing mixture. Spoon excess dressing into buttered casserole dish, and bake as directed above.

Tie the turkey legs together; rub the skin with butter. Wash your hands thoroughly, then cover the turkey with a tent of foil, taking care the foil doesn't come in contact with the skin.

Roast turkey in a preheated oven 30 minutes; then reduce the temperature to 325 degrees, and continue roasting according to the time chart printed on the turkey's original wrapping, or 20 minutes per pound. Roasting time for a 20-pound, stuffed turkey is approximately 5½ to 6 hours. Baste the turkey occasionally, if desired. Remove foil during final 30 minutes to brown the skin. Remove turkey from the oven, cover it with foil and allow it to stand 10 minutes. Remove foil and spoon out all of the stuffing from both cavities. Carve turkey.

Recipe serves 12.

aroma of Jell-O. Really! This is accomplished by placing the uncrushed, ripe grape clusters in a high-rimmed barrel; then dropping in a few blocks of dry ice, which is frozen carbon dioxide. As it evaporates, the carbon dioxide displaces the oxygen, forcing the fermentation to turn inward, producing a wild-yeast fermentation within each individual grape. However, the wine has a life shorter than a teen idol's.

As luck would have it, there is an upper level of Beaujolais, know as Cru. With names such as St. Amour, Morgon, Moulin-a-Vent, and Regnie, these age-worthy, inexpensive, upper-middle-crust-but-snubbed relatives of Burgundy are quite tasty.

$ **G. Duboeuf Fleurie, Domaine des Quatre Ventes** (Beaujolais, France)

$ **Janin Moulin-a-Ventes** (Beaujolais, France)

$$ **Domaine Zind-Humbrecht Gewürztraminer Gran Cru** (Alsace, France)

continued on next page

Cornbread:

2⅓ cups flour

1⅔ cups cornmeal

1 tablespoon plus 1 teaspoon
baking powder

¼ cup sugar

1½ teaspoons salt

2 eggs

1¾ cups milk

½ cup vegetable oil

Preheat oven to 350 degrees. In a large bowl, stir together the flour, cornmeal, baking powder, sugar, and salt; set aside. In a small bowl, beat eggs with a fork. Stir in milk and vegetable oil; mix well. Stir milk mixture into flour mixture, stirring just until mixed.

Pour cornbread batter into a greased 9- by 13-inch baking pan. Bake in preheated oven 25 minutes, or until a cake tester inserted into the middle of the bread comes out clean.

Remove from the oven and cool on a wire rack. Cornbread may be made 1 day ahead.

Side Dishes

Apple Butter

My sister, Lynn, shared this recipe with me years ago. Making apple butter is quite simple. It involves cooking apples, tart cider, and spices for many hours until the mixture mounds in a spoon. Very little work is involved, other than occasional stirring. Canning the fragrant fruit spread allows you to store it until the holidays.

INGREDIENTS:

6 pounds medium Jonathan or other tart apples (about 18)

5 cups tart apple cider

3 cups sugar

1½ teaspoons cinnamon

½ teaspoon ground cloves

Slice apples in quarters; remove the cores. Place apples in a large stockpot or Dutch oven and add cider. Cover and bring to a boil. Reduce heat to low and cook apples, stirring occasionally, until they are very soft and lose their shape, about 45 minutes.

Process the apple mixture through a food mill or strainer into a clean Dutch oven. Discard apple peels, seeds, and remaining cores. Stir in sugar, cinnamon, and cloves.

Cover the Dutch oven and cook the strained mixture over low heat, stirring occasionally. After 5 hours, adjust the lid slightly to allow steam to escape slowly. Continue cooking 2 to 3 hours, stirring frequently, until the apple butter mounds in a spoon.

Wash and sterilize canning jars, lids, and screw tops according to manufacturer's directions. Ladle hot apple butter into the jars, leaving ¼-inch headspace. Wipe the rim of each jar with a clean cloth, seal, and process them in a hot water bath 10 minutes. Remove them from the water and place them on a towel to cool.

Processed apple butter jars may be stored several months.

Recipe makes 8 to 9 half-pint jars.

French Rose and Purple Fingerling Potato Sauté

Here's a pretty way to serve potatoes for any occasion. The contrast of delicate, pink-skinned, yellow-meat potatoes and sweet, but unusual, purple-meat potatoes is eye catching and will definitely make your family and guests sit up and take notice!

This fragrant side dish, flavored with olive oil, fresh garlic, fresh tarragon, and a splash of tarragon vinegar, pairs beautifully with turkey, beef roasts, and pork. When your holiday table is crowded with family and friends, relax, knowing everyone will love this recipe.

INGREDIENTS:

1½ pounds French Rose fingerling potatoes (about 16)

1 pound purple fingerling potatoes (about 14)

1 tablespoon olive oil

2 tablespoons minced shallots

4 cloves garlic, minced

1 tablespoon olive oil, to finish

1 tablespoon tarragon vinegar

¾ teaspoon coarse salt

½ teaspoon freshly ground black pepper

2 tablespoons minced fresh tarragon

Wash and slice potatoes in half lengthwise. Place French Rose and purple potatoes in separate saucepans with enough water to cover; bring to a boil and cook 5 to 7 minutes until just tender. Drain and set aside. Potatoes may be cooked ahead, placed in separate containers, covered, and chilled.

Preheat a large skillet over medium-low heat; add oil. Sauté shallots in hot oil until soft; stir in garlic and potatoes. Sauté potatoes several minutes until hot. Add remaining olive oil and the vinegar, pouring them down the side of the skillet; tilt the skillet to mix. Toss the potatoes well to coat them with the oil and vinegar. Season the mixture with salt, freshly ground pepper, and fresh tarragon. Toss to mix.

Recipe serves 8 to 10.

Green Beans
Amandine with Roasted Garlic

My guests always love these green beans. They are elegant enough to serve on the most important occasions and have a wonderful flavor, thanks to the roasted fresh garlic.

INGREDIENTS:

½ large head garlic

1 teaspoon olive oil

1½ pounds green string beans, trimmed

2 tablespoons unsalted butter

2 tablespoons olive oil

⅓ cup sliced almonds

Coarse salt

About 1 hour before serving, preheat the oven to 400 degrees. Place half a large head, or 1 whole small head, of garlic in a square of aluminum foil. Drizzle with 1 teaspoon olive oil and gather foil together to seal in the garlic. Roast in a preheated oven 45 minutes, or until soft and fragrant.

Fifteen minutes before serving, steam green beans until crisp-tender; keep warm.

Heat a large skillet over medium-low heat; melt butter in skillet. Add olive oil and swirl to mix. Transfer the steamed green beans to the skillet and toss to coat with the butter mixture.

Remove the garlic from its foil package and squeeze the roasted cloves from their skins onto green beans. Season with salt and add almonds. Toss well to mix.

Transfer the beans to a serving platter or shallow bowl, spooning any almond slices that remain in skillet over the beans.

Recipe serves 6 to 8.

Southern Brussels Sprouts with Brown Butter

Brown butter and pecans, with a splash of fresh lemon juice, add a new twist to this traditional holiday vegetable. Even those who don't eat brussels sprouts will like this version!

INGREDIENTS:

1⅓ pounds fresh brussels sprouts (about 30 medium)

3 tablespoons unsalted butter

½ cup pecan halves

½ teaspoon coarse salt

⅛ teaspoon freshly ground black pepper

1 tablespoon freshly squeezed lemon juice

Wash and trim stem end of brussels sprouts; remove the outer leaves. Slice the brussel sprouts in half, and transfer them to a large saucepan; add water to a depth of ½ inch.

Cover, bring to a boil; then reduce the heat to medium. Steam brussels sprouts 4 to 5 minutes, or until tender when pierced with a sharp knife.

Remove from heat, drain, and set aside, keeping warm.

In a large skillet, melt butter over medium-low heat; add pecans. Cook several minutes until the butter begins to brown and the pecans are hot. Add brussels sprouts; toss to coat.

Cook brussels sprouts 5 minutes, stirring frequently to prevent the butter from burning. Season with salt, pepper, and lemon juice. Toss to mix; serve immediately.

Recipe serves 4 to 6.

Turban Squash
with Spiced Apple Compote

Every spoonful of this dramatic side dish is a perfect pairing of harvest-fresh squash and spiced apple compote.

INGREDIENTS:

1 large turban squash
(about 4 pounds)

2 tablespoons unsalted butter

1 large Granny Smith apple,
cored and diced

¼ cup Zante currants
(may substitute raisins)

¼ cup dried cranberries

1 teaspoon cornstarch

½ cup apple juice

1 tablespoon brown sugar,
packed

1 teaspoon cinnamon

¼ teaspoon freshly
grated nutmeg

Slice off about ⅓ of the upper end of the squash with a sharp knife. Scoop out seeds from the upper and lower portions with a spoon; save them for roasting, if desired. Discard pulp.

Place large lower portion face down in a skillet containing ½ inch of water. Cover the skillet tightly with a lid or foil, place it over high heat, and bring to a boil. Reduce the heat to medium-low and steam the squash 15 to 20 minutes, until tender inside. Remove and steam the upper portion.

Melt butter in a medium saucepan over low heat. Add diced apple, raise heat to medium-low, and sauté 5 minutes until it begins to soften. Stir in currants (or raisins) and cranberries. In a small bowl, whisk apple juice into cornstarch until smooth. Stir this mixture into the apples, along with brown sugar and spices. Reduce the heat to low and simmer the mixture, stirring occasionally, until the apples are soft and sauce is thickened.

Place the squash right side up on a serving dish. Fill it with apple compote, place the top of squash askew over compote, and serve immediately.

Recipe serves 8.

Baked Stuffed Onions

Onion lovers rejoice! This combination of sweet onions, stuffed with crunchy jicama and pecans, tangy cheese, sweet currants, and molasses Demerara sugar is delightful. Look for Demerara sugar near the brown sugar in the baking aisle of many supermarkets.

INGREDIENTS:

4 medium onions

2 cups chicken broth or water

½ cup diced jicama

¼ cup chopped pecans

¼ cup freshly grated pecorino Romano cheese

2 tablespoons dried currants

Salt and freshly ground black pepper, to taste

1 teaspoon Billington's or other Demerara sugar

3 tablespoons bread crumbs

Peel onions without slicing through the base. Place them in a large sauté pan or skillet and add chicken broth or water. Cover tightly; bring to a boil over high heat. Reduce the heat to medium and simmer onions until tender, turning once, about 20 minutes.

While the onions are cooking, stir together the jicama, pecans, cheese, currants, salt, pepper, and sugar in a medium bowl.

When the onions are tender, remove from heat and set aside until they are cool enough to handle. With a sharp knife, cut out the onion centers and save them for another use. Fill onions with the jicama mixture; top generously with bread crumbs.

Preheat the oven to 350 degrees. Spray a baking dish with nonstick cooking spray; transfer the onions to the dish. Bake in a preheated oven 25 to 30 minutes, or until centers are soft and bread crumbs are toasted. Serve immediately.

Recipe serves 4.

Side Dishes

Onion Soufflé

An impressive vegetable, this soufflé always gets rave reviews. It is baked in individual ramekins and goes straight from the oven to the table, golden, puffed, and still bubbling around the edges. Because most of the prep work may be done ahead, this is an ideal side dish to serve at holiday dinners. Its dramatic presentation makes onion soufflé my choice when hosting family birthday dinners or guests for any elegant seated dinner.

INGREDIENTS:

2 tablespoons butter

2 tablespoons olive oil

3 large onions, peeled and sliced

2 tablespoons flour

⅔ cup milk or half-and-half

2 eggs

Salt and freshly ground
   black pepper, to taste

½ cup grated cheddar
   cheese

In a large skillet or Dutch oven, melt butter over medium-low heat. Add oil and swirl to mix; stir in onions. Sauté onions 10 to 12 minutes until they are soft and translucent. If they begin to brown, reduce the heat to low.

Preheat the oven to 350 degrees. Sprinkle the onions with flour, stir to mix, and cook 1 minute, stirring constantly. Pour in milk or half-and-half, stir, and cook 2 minutes until mixture thickens. Remove the pan from the heat.

In a small bowl, whip eggs with a fork. Stir them into the onion mixture, mixing thoroughly, and season with salt and pepper.

Spoon onion mixture into individual 4-inch ramekins, filling each ⅔ full. Sprinkle the tops with grated cheese. Bake in a preheated oven 30 to 40 minutes until soufflés are puffed and cheese is slightly toasted. Remove them from the oven, place on small plates protected with a doily or folded napkin, and serve immediately.

Recipe serves 6.

Sweet Potato Casserole

Every Thanksgiving for years, my mother served sweet potatoes with sticky maple syrup and marshmallows melted on top. Mom was the only one who ate this overly sweet vegetable; it was too cloying for the remainder of the family.

Then I tasted a recipe Randy's mother prepared similar to this one. Pleasantly sweet and cinnamony, with apricots and maraschino cherries for color, this dish made me discover how much I enjoyed sweet potatoes. My version of Mom Rost's recipe, which she adapted from a collection of recipes from the Junior League of Americus, Georgia, has circulated throughout my entire family. All my sisters, and my mother, now prepare sweet potatoes this way. And no wonder; they're positively addictive!

INGREDIENTS:

4 large sweet potatoes

1¼ cup light brown sugar, packed

2 tablespoons butter

1 16-ounce can apricot halves, drained, juice reserved

1 cup apple juice

1½ tablespoons cornstarch

½ teaspoon cinnamon

¼ teaspoon freshly grated nutmeg

2 tablespoons dried cranberries

Place potatoes in a large Dutch oven; add enough water to cover them. Cover and bring to a boil. Cook potatoes until a sharp knife pierces them easily, but do not overcook, about 15 minutes.

Drain sweet potatoes and set aside until cool enough to handle. Peel potatoes and slice into ¾-inch thick slices. Place the slices in a large casserole dish; set aside.

Side Dishes

In a medium saucepan, stir together brown sugar, butter, and reserved apricot juice. In a small bowl, whisk a small amount of apple juice into the cornstarch to form a smooth mixture. Add the cornstarch mixture, remaining apple juice, and spices to the saucepan, stirring to combine.

Bring the mixture to a boil, stirring occasionally. Reduce heat to medium-low and cook 10 minutes, stirring occasionally, until the syrup thickens.

Top sweet potatoes with apricot halves and fill the apricot centers with dried cranberries. Pour the syrup over the potatoes. The casserole may be covered and refrigerated overnight or baked immediately.

Preheat the oven to 375 degrees. Uncover the casserole and bake 25 to 30 minutes until sweet potatoes are soft and syrup is bubbly. Serve immediately.

Recipe serves 8.

Sweet Almond Braid

This pretty yeast bread is our holiday tradition for Christmas and Easter. It's also the favorite treat of my agent Evan Fogelman. He goes absolutely weak in the knees when I take him a holiday gift basket with a loaf of Sweet Almond Braid tucked inside. I am never quite sure whether the bread makes it home to his family, or if he eats the entire loaf at the office.

Another tradition associated with this bread is very dear to me. Each year, a charity group I belong to hosts a large, spring luncheon to raise funds for the rehabilitation unit of a large, local hospital. In addition to the silent auction and other usual charity luncheon activities, all of our members bake homemade treats for the bake sale. I always bake a number of Sweet Almond Braid loaves, but no matter how many I make, they always disappear within minutes.

For the Christmas holidays, I decorate the iced loaves with cherry halves and slivered almonds, to give it a very festive appearance. For Easter, I sprinkle the still-soft icing with pastel sweet confetti, which looks like miniature dyed eggs. After the icing is dry, I wrap each loaf in a large square of clear cellophane, tie it with ribbon, and attach a gift tag.

INGREDIENTS:

1 cup milk

½ cup unsalted butter

¼ cup water

5½ to 6 cups bread flour

½ cup sugar

1½ teaspoons salt

2 packages active dry yeast

2 eggs

½ teaspoon almond extract

½ cup raisins

¼ cup slivered almonds

1 recipe Decorative Icing

4 maraschino cherries, halved and drained, for garnish

Slivered almonds, for garnish

Breads

In a medium saucepan, heat milk, butter, and water over medium heat until small bubbles form around the edges. Remove from heat and set aside until lukewarm.

Combine 2 cups of the flour, sugar, salt, and yeast in a large mixing bowl. Pour in the milk mixture and beat 2 minutes at medium speed with an electric mixer. Add eggs and almond extract; beat well.

Stir in raisins and almonds and enough of the remaining flour to form a soft dough. Turn it out onto a floured board and knead until smooth. Divide the dough in half.

Slice each half into 3 pieces and roll the first 3 into 12-inch ropes. Braid the ropes to form a long loaf, tucking edges under and transfer the loaf to a greased cookie sheet. Repeat with the remaining bread dough. Cover loaves with a towel and set aside in a warm place to rise.

When the breads have almost doubled in size, preheat the oven to 350 degrees. Bake loaves in a preheated oven 18 to 20 minutes, or until they are golden. Remove the bread from the oven and transfer it to a wire rack to cool.

When the bread is completely cool, drizzle with Decorative Icing and sprinkle with slivered almonds. Decorate with cherry halves or sprinkle still-soft icing with pastel sweet confetti. When icing has dried, serve or wrap the bread in plastic wrap and place in freezer bags. Bread may be frozen for several weeks.

Decorative Icing:

1½ cups sifted confectioners' sugar
2 to 3 tablespoons milk

Whisk together confectioners' sugar and milk until smooth.

Recipe makes 2 loaves.

Christmas Morning Bread

These large, round loaves of sweetened yeast bread are made all the more irresistible with a coating of icing and a colorful ring of cherries. Inside, candied fruit and golden raisins add a festive holiday flair. Wrapped in clear cellophane and adorned with a large bow, Christmas Morning Bread makes an attractive, thoughtful gift throughout the holiday season.

INGREDIENTS:

1½ cups milk	2 eggs
½ cup unsalted butter	⅔ cup chopped candied fruit
½ cup sugar	½ cup golden raisins
1 teaspoon salt	3 tablespoons melted butter
2 packages active dry yeast	1 recipe Decorative Icing
4½ to 5 cups bread flour	6 maraschino cherries

In a medium saucepan, stir together milk, butter, sugar, and salt. Heat over medium heat, stirring occasionally, until lukewarm and the butter begins to melt; set aside.

In a large bowl, combine yeast and 2 cups of the flour. Add warm milk mixture. Mix 2 minutes on medium speed of an electric mixer, scraping the sides of the bowl often. Add eggs; beat 1 more minute.

With a large wooden spoon, stir in candied fruit, raisins, and enough of the remaining flour to form a soft dough. Turn the dough out on a floured surface and knead until it's smooth and elastic, incorporating additional flour as needed to keep the dough from sticking to the surface.

Breads

Transfer the dough to a large greased bowl, turning it once to grease the top surface. Cover with a towel and set aside in a warm place until the dough has doubled in size, about 40 minutes.

Punch the dough down and turn out onto a lightly floured surface. Knead it just until smooth, about 1 minute, and divide it in half and shape it into 2 round loaves. Place each loaf on a greased cookie sheet, cover with a towel, and set aside in a warm place to rise.

Preheat the oven to 350 degrees. When the loaves have doubled in size, brush with melted butter. Bake in a preheated oven 18 to 20 minutes, or until breads are golden brown and sound hollow when tapped with finger. Remove them from the oven and transfer to a wire rack to cool. When the breads are cool, decorate with Decorative Icing and garnish with cherry halves.

Decorative Icing:

1½ cups sifted confectioners' sugar

2 to 3 tablespoons milk

¼ teaspoon vanilla extract

Whisk together confectioners' sugar, milk, and vanilla until smooth. Spread the icing with an offset spatula or knife.

Slice maraschino cherries in half; drain them face down on paper towels. Place the cherries face down around perimeter of breads.

Recipe makes 2 large loaves.

Panettone

For years, our family has enjoyed this fragrant Italian holiday bread while opening gifts around the Christmas tree. Its characteristic high, cylindrical shape, studded with raisins and candied citrus peel, makes an impressive holiday gift for neighbors and friends, especially when it's decoratively wrapped in clear cellophane and tied with a large, gold bow. Although traditionally baked in decorative paper forms, panettone is now easy to bake at home, thanks to the availability of these baking forms from specialty cookware stores and catalogs.

INGREDIENTS:

2 scant tablespoons active dry yeast

½ cup warm water

¼ teaspoon sugar

1 cup milk

¾ cup unsalted butter

½ cup sugar

½ teaspoon salt

¼ cup honey

1 teaspoon anise seed, crushed with a mortar and pestle

5 to 5½ cups bread flour

2 eggs

3 egg yolks

¾ cup dark raisins

¾ cup golden raisins

½ cup candied citrus peel

2 5-inch paper baking forms

Egg Wash:

1 egg

1 tablespoon water

In a very large mixing bowl, stir together yeast, warm water, and sugar. Set aside in a warm place until the mixture becomes foamy on top, about 15 minutes.

Breads

Meanwhile, heat milk, butter, sugar, and salt in a small saucepan until warm; the butter may not melt completely.

When the yeast mixture is foamy, stir in the milk mixture, honey, crushed anise, and two cups of flour. Beat 1 minute at medium speed with an electric mixer; add eggs and egg yolks and beat 2 more minutes. Stir in dark and golden raisins, citrus peel, and enough of the remaining flour to make a soft dough.

Turn the dough out onto a generously floured surface and knead 5 to 8 minutes, incorporating enough flour to prevent the dough from sticking. The dough should be smooth and spring back when pushed with a finger.

Place the dough in a large greased bowl, turning once to grease the top of it. Cover with a towel and set aside in a warm place until it has doubled in size, about 1 hour.

Punch down the dough, divide it in half, and knead each half on a lightly floured surface just until the dough is smooth. Place each round loaf into a lightly greased paper baking form. Place forms on a baking sheet, cover with a towel, and set aside in a warm place to rise, about 45 minutes. Top of the bread dough should be round and protrude 2 to 3 inches above the edge of the baking form.

Preheat the oven to 350 degrees. In a small bowl, whisk egg and water with a fork to form an egg wash. Lightly brush this over the top of the breads. Bake in a preheated oven 40 to 45 minutes, or until a long cake tester comes out clean when inserted deep into breads. If the tops brown too quickly, cover them loosely with foil.

Remove the bread from the oven and transfer with a metal spatula to a wire rack to cool. When completely cool, wrap the breads in plastic wrap for family enjoyment, or clear cellophane for gift giving. To enjoy, peel the paper form away as needed and slice the bread with a serrated knife into wedges.

Recipe makes 2 panettone.

Iced Cinnamon Rolls

The aroma of cinnamon rolls baking in the oven is unlike any other. The fragrance of hot cinnamon and yeasty dough, combined with the anticipation of that first bite, acts like a magnet, drawing everyone to the kitchen.

Cinnamon rolls make holiday mornings even more memorable, though I am quite fond of a warm cinnamon roll with a cup of tea in the evening, too. And for neighborhood gifting, a plate of homemade cinnamon rolls makes a delicious gift from the heart.

INGREDIENTS:

1¼ cups milk

½ cup unsalted butter

4½ to 5 cups bread flour

2 packages active dry yeast

½ cup sugar

1 teaspoon salt

2 eggs

½ teaspoon vanilla

2 cups dark brown sugar

2 teaspoons cinnamon

¼ cup cold unsalted butter

¼ cup butter, melted

1 recipe Icing

In a medium saucepan, heat milk and butter over medium heat until warm, about 115 degrees F. Remove from heat; set aside.

In a large mixing bowl, stir together 2 cups flour, yeast, sugar, and salt. Add the warm milk and beat 2 minutes at medium speed with an electric mixer. Add eggs and vanilla; beat 2 more minutes.

Stir in enough of the remaining flour to form a soft dough. Turn it out onto a floured surface and knead until it's smooth and springs back when pushed with a finger. Transfer the dough to a greased bowl, turning once to grease its surface. Cover with a towel and set aside in a warm place until the dough has doubled in size or cover the bowl with plastic wrap and chill overnight in the refrigerator.

Breads

When the dough has risen, preheat the oven to 375 degrees. Punch down the dough with a fist and knead 1 minute until smooth. Roll it out on a lightly floured pastry cloth to form a ½-inch-thick 12- by 21-inch rectangle.

In a small bowl, stir together brown sugar and cinnamon. Cut cold butter in with a pastry blender until it is pea-size. Sprinkle the cinnamon sugar mixture over the dough and roll it up like a jelly roll.

With a sharp knife, slice into 1-inch-thick slices and place in 9-inch greased cake pans, cut side up. Cover with a towel and set aside in a warm place to rise, about 45 minutes. Bake in a preheated oven 15 to 20 minutes until golden brown.

Remove the cinnamon rolls from oven, brush with melted butter, and set aside 10 minutes to cool. Mix the icing; spread on rolls. Serve warm, or cool and serve at room temperature.

Icing:

2 cups sifted confectioners' sugar

3 to 4 tablespoons milk

¼ teaspoon vanilla

In a medium bowl, whisk confectioners' sugar with milk and vanilla until smooth. Spread the icing on warm cinnamon rolls with an offset spatula or knife.

Recipe makes 20 to 22 rolls.

Holiday Sugar Cookies

This is one of my most-requested recipes, and no wonder. During any holiday, one of the most popular cookies is the sugar cookie. For Thanksgiving, they appear as autumn leaves, pilgrims, and turkeys, while in December, they are cut in the shapes of angels, bells, Christmas trees, and menorahs. Pink and red hearts prevail for Valentine's Day, and cute, pastel bunnies and chicks add a special touch to Easter baskets. Sugar cookies in the shape of Old Glory even make an appearance for Fourth of July celebrations.

These sugar cookies are decorated with a sweet glaze, which may be tinted or garnished with colorful sparkling sugars, but the cookies are flavorful enough to be enjoyed with a mere sprinkling of tinted sugar before baking. Since I can never have enough sugar cookies in the house, I wrote this recipe to yield more cookies than the average recipe.

Get your children, grandchildren, or neighborhood children into the act by including them in cutting out the cookie dough and decorating the cookies. The best part of asking them to help is the fun everyone has, the memories it fosters, and the fact that all mistakes taste absolutely delicious!

INGREDIENTS:

1 cup unsalted butter, softened	3½ cups flour
1½ cups sugar	1½ teaspoons baking powder
2 eggs	1½ teaspoons salt
2 teaspoons vanilla	1 recipe Glaze

In the large bowl of an electric mixer, cream butter with sugar until light, about 5 minutes. Add eggs and vanilla, beating until smooth.

Holiday Cookies & Candies

In a medium bowl, stir together flour, baking powder, and salt until well blended. Stir the flour mixture into the butter mixture in thirds, stirring with a large spoon until well combined.

Transfer cookie dough to a smaller bowl, cover tightly, and refrigerate several hours or overnight.

When cookie dough is cold, preheat oven to 375 degrees. Roll half of the dough 1/8 inch thick on a floured pastry cloth. Cut shapes with cookie cutters dipped in flour and place on ungreased cookie sheets.

Bake in preheated oven 6 to 7 minutes until edges are barely brown. Remove cookies from the cookie sheet while still hot and transfer them to wire racks to cool. When cookies are completely cool, frost them with the glaze.

Glaze:

2 cups sifted confectioners' sugar	¼ teaspoon vanilla
3 tablespoons milk	Tinted sparkling or decorator sugars

Whisk confectioners' sugar, milk, and vanilla until mixture is very smooth. Divide the glaze into several small bowls and tint with food coloring to desired shades. Spread a small amount of glaze on each cookie with a knife. Sprinkle with tinted sugars as desired.

Allow decorated cookies to dry several hours. Store in airtight containers up to 2 weeks or freeze.

Recipe makes approximately 6 dozen cookies.

Chocolate Pinwheel Cookies

A classic Christmas holiday favorite, these easy-to-make pin-wheel cookies are fun to make—and eat—any time of year. Keep the cookie dough very cold for easy slicing.

INGREDIENTS:

1 cup unsalted butter, softened

1⅓ cups sugar

2 eggs

2 teaspoons vanilla

3 cups flour

1¼ teaspoons baking powder

1 teaspoon salt

2 squares unsweetened chocolate

In the large bowl of an electric mixer, cream butter and sugar until mixture is light and fluffy, about 4 minutes. Add eggs and vanilla and beat well; set aside.

In a medium bowl, stir together flour, baking powder, and salt; set aside.

Melt chocolate in a double boiler set over simmering, not boiling, water. Or place chocolate in a small bowl and microwave at 50 percent power 2 minutes until chocolate is very soft. Stir to melt.

Holiday Cookies & Candies

With a large spoon, gradually stir the flour mixture into the creamed mixture to form a soft dough. Divide the dough in half and stir melted chocolate into one of the halves.

On a floured pastry cloth, roll white dough into a 13- by 16-inch rectangle. On a floured piece of parchment paper, roll the chocolate dough into a rectangle the same size. Lift the paper and place the chocolate dough face down on top of the white dough; peel off the parchment.

Using a pastry cloth to assist, gently roll cookie doughs together lengthwise to form a pinwheel and seal the edges. Position the parchment paper along the length of the pinwheel and roll the cookie dough into the parchment. Transfer the dough to a tray and fold the parchment paper to seal.

Chill the dough several hours until cold or overnight.

To bake the cookies, preheat the oven to 375 degrees. Using a thin, sharp knife, slice the dough into $\frac{1}{4}$-inch-thick slices and place them 1-inch apart on lightly greased cookie sheets. Return the remaining dough to the refrigerator. Bake in a preheated oven 7 to 9 minutes, or until edges of cookies are light brown.

Recipe makes 6 dozen (72) cookies.

Peppermint Pinwheel Cookies

These pastel-pink, spiral cookies, reminiscent of peppermint candy canes, are synonymous with the Christmas holidays. Kids of all ages, myself included, can't resist nibbling around the pinwheel. Best of all, the cookie dough spiral may be formed one day; then sliced and baked a day or two later—a definite advantage during the busy holiday season.

INGREDIENTS:

1 cup unsalted butter, softened	1¼ teaspoons baking powder
1⅓ cups sugar	1 teaspoon salt
2 eggs	¼ teaspoon peppermint extract
2 teaspoons vanilla	4 to 5 drops red food coloring
3 cups flour	

In the large bowl of an electric mixer, cream butter and sugar until light, about 5 minutes. Add eggs and vanilla and beat until smooth.

In a medium bowl, stir together flour, baking powder, and salt. Gradually mix dry ingredients into the creamed mixture with a large spoon to form a soft dough. Divide the dough in half and add peppermint extract and food coloring to one of the halves; set aside.

Holiday Cookies & Candies

On a floured pastry cloth, roll the plain cookie dough into a 16- by 13-inch rectangle; set aside. On lightly floured parchment paper, roll the pink cookie dough into a 16- by 13-inch rectangle. Lift the paper and place the pink dough face down on top of the plain dough; peel off the parchment paper.

Starting with long edge, roll the doughs together to form a 16-inch log. Turn the parchment paper over and place it next to the log. Roll the log onto the paper and transfer the cookie log to a cookie sheet. Cover with plastic wrap and refrigerate several hours, until cookie dough is firm, or overnight.

To bake, preheat the oven to 375 degrees. Unwrap the cookie dough, place it on cutting board, and slice it into ¼-inch-thick slices. Place pinwheel cookies on a lightly greased cookie sheet and bake in a preheated oven 8 to 9 minutes until edges of cookies barely turn brown. Cool cookies 1 minute on the cookie sheet, then transfer them to a wire rack to cool.

Recipe makes 6 dozen (72) cookies.

Linzer Tarts

Everything comes up hearts when you serve buttery Linzer Tarts. These European favorites are two-layered, heart-shaped, vanilla cookies with a strawberry filling. Enhanced by a dusting of snowy confectioners' sugar, Linzer Tarts make heartfelt gifts or a simple but romantic dessert for Valentine's Day.

INGREDIENTS:

1 cup unsalted butter, softened

1¼ cups sifted confectioners' sugar

2 eggs

1 teaspoon vanilla

3 cups flour

1 teaspoon salt

1 teaspoon baking powder

⅓ cup ground slivered almonds

1 10-ounce jar seedless strawberry jam

Cream butter with confectioners' sugar until light and fluffy. Beat in eggs and vanilla until smooth.

In a medium bowl, stir together flour, salt, baking powder, and ground almonds. Stir flour mixture into the butter mixture to form a soft dough. Cover with plastic wrap and refrigerate 1 to 2 hours until cold.

Preheat the oven to 375 degrees. Roll out the cookie dough on a floured pastry cloth to ¼-inch thickness. Cut with a 3-inch heart-shaped cookie cutter dipped in flour and place cookies on ungreased cookie sheets. Cut the centers out of half the cookies using a 1-inch heart-shaped cookie cutter.

Bake in a preheated oven for 6 to 7 minutes until edges are light brown. Remove from cookie sheets and cool on a wire rack. When cookies are completely cool, spread the solid ones with strawberry jam, mounding it in the center of each cookie; top with the remaining cookies. Sift with confectioners' sugar, which will melt over the jam, leaving a glossy center.

Recipe makes 22 to 25 Linzer Tarts.

Holiday Cookies & Candies

Pizzelles

These anise-flavored cookies are baked briefly on a patterned pizzelle iron until thin and crisp. With their lacy edges and dusting of confectioners' sugar, they remind me of snowflakes.

INGREDIENTS:

½ cup unsalted butter, softened

½ cup margarine, softened

1½ cups sugar

6 eggs

2½ teaspoons anise extract

3½ cups flour

4 teaspoons baking powder

¾ cup sifted confectioners' sugar

Cream butter and margarine with an electric mixer, gradually adding sugar, until the mixture is light and fluffy. Add eggs, beating well after each addition. Stir in the extract.

In a small bowl, sift flour and baking powder together. Gradually stir the flour mixture into the creamed mixture to form a very soft dough.

Lightly grease a pizzelle iron; heat it according to manufacturer's instructions. Drop a large teaspoonful of dough on each pizzelle design and close the lid. Bake cookies approximately 1 minute, or until pizzelles are golden in color. Do not brown.

Open the pizzelle iron and remove each cookie by lifting the edge with a fork. Transfer the cookies to a dish towel covered with paper towel to absorb moisture; cool 30 seconds. Paper towels will become damp with steam and will have to be replaced periodically. Transfer cookies to additional paper towels; dust lightly with confectioners' sugar. Transfer sugared pizzelles to wire racks to dry and finish cooling.

To store the cookies, place a small square of parchment or wax paper between each cookie and stack them in large round coffee cans or cookie tins. Cover tightly and store up to several weeks; the anise flavor develops after 24 hours.

Recipe makes 4 dozen (48) 4-cookies.

Swiss Springerle Cookies

These Swiss picture-cookies are a Christy Rost tradition. Every year, I bake several batches and package them in decorative tins to ship across the country and overseas to family members and special friends. No matter how busy I am, I always find time to make these wonderful, anise-flavored treats. It just wouldn't be Christmas without them.

My grandmother, Kathryn Hewston, purchased springerle cookies from a nearby Pittsburgh bakery every year when I was a child. Along with her ice-cold, paper-thin gingerbread cookies, she always served springerles after dinner at Christmastime. I was intrigued by the cookie's two layers–the upper one was white and had a hard shell, and the lower, softer layer was creamier in color.

That fascination, as well as a commitment to continue family traditions, led to this recipe, which I have been making for years. Along the way, it has fostered a love of collecting springerle molds, used to imprint a design on the top of each cookie. I have springerle molds from all over the country and from Europe, received as gifts and collected while living in France and during my travels in the United States.

Besides my own love of these delectable cookies, what I cherish most are the stories that trickle back to me from those who receive them as gifts. My particular favorites are stories my sisters tell of hiding the cookies to enjoy quietly at night with a cup of hot tea, or doling them out carefully to the family to make them last. When my sister, Lynn, was married, her first Christmas with her husband, Terry, inspired a note that read, "Thank you for the springerle cookies. Unfortunately, Terry loves them as much as I." I can think of no better testament to these delicious holiday confections than that.

Holiday Cookies & Candies

INGREDIENTS:

4 cups all-purpose flour

1 teaspoon baking soda

4 eggs

2 cups sugar

2 teaspoons anise extract

2 to 3 tablespoons anise seeds

1 small bowl of water to moisten rolled cookies

Grease cookie sheets. In a medium bowl, stir flour and baking soda together until well mixed; set aside. In the large bowl of an electric mixer, beat eggs with sugar until very thick and pale yellow, about 5 minutes. Stir in anise extract.

Using a large spoon, add the flour mixture, blending well. Dough will be soft and sticky. Divide the dough into thirds, shaping one portion into a ball with floured hands; cover the remaining cookie dough with plastic wrap.

On a floured pastry cloth, roll the dough ½ inch thick. Using springerle molds dipped in flour, or a floured springerle rolling pin, press firmly on the dough; then remove the mold. Dough will be about ¼ inch thick and will be imprinted.

Trim around cookies with a sharp knife or biscuit cutter and lift them with a metal spatula or knife. Using a fingertip, moisten the bottom of the cookies with a drop of water, sprinkle a few anise seeds on the cookie sheet, and place the cookies on the seeds, leaving 1 inch between each cookie. Continue with the remaining cookie dough, rerolling scraps.

Allow the cookies to stand, uncovered, overnight to dry. The next day, preheat the oven to 300 degrees and bake in a preheated oven 15 minutes until the cookies are firm and dry. They should not brown.

Remove the baked cookies from the cookie sheets while they're still hot. Cool on wire racks until completely cool. Store the cookies in an airtight container up to one month; the anise flavor develops after 2 to 3 days.

Recipe makes 40 to 45 cookies.

Holiday Madeleines

Baked in molded pans, these confections are pretty on holiday party tables, or arrange them in boxes lined with waxed tissue, tie the boxes with satin ribbons, and give them as gifts.

INGREDIENTS:

¾ cup soft butter, unsalted

1½ cups sugar

2 eggs

Grated zest of one lemon

1 tablespoon vinegar

1 cup milk

2⅔ cups flour

1½ teaspoons baking soda

1 teaspoon salt

½ teaspoon baking powder

1 teaspoon vanilla

Melted white and dark chocolate, for coating

Assorted holiday sprinkles or chopped pistachio nuts

In the large bowl of an electric mixer, cream butter and sugar until light and fluffy, about 8 minutes. Add eggs and lemon zest, beat well, and set aside. Add vinegar to milk, stir, and set aside 5 minutes to sour.

Combine flour with baking soda, salt, and baking powder. Add to the butter mixture, alternating with sour milk, beating well after each addition. Stir in vanilla.

Preheat the oven to 350 degrees. Grease madeleine pans well with butter or spray with Baker's Joy® baking spray. Fill each indentation ⅔ full. Bake in a preheated oven 8 to 10 minutes until cakes are golden brown. Cool 5 minutes, then gently remove from the pan after loosening the edges with a sharp knife. Cool cakes on wire racks.

Place white and dark chocolate into separate small bowls and microwave at 50 percent power just until soft; stir to finish melting. Dip the lower half of the madeleines into white or dark chocolate and decorate with holiday sprinkles or finely chopped nuts. Set aside on a wire rack until chocolate firms. Store in airtight containers in the refrigerator several days, or freeze up to 2 weeks.

Recipe makes 5 dozen (60) madeleines.

Holiday Cookies & Candies

Chocolate Truffles

These truffles get high marks for ease of preparation, decadent flavor, and beauty. Sweetened coconut, stirred into the melted chocolate, gives these confections a nice texture, and a splash of your favorite liqueur provides elegance. For a professional appearance, the truffles are rolled in chocolate sprinkles just before chilling. Nestle them in tiny gold paper cups before serving, or for an elegant gift from the kitchen, place them in small, white candy boxes tied with gold ribbon.

INGREDIENTS:

1 12-ounce package semisweet or bittersweet chocolate chips

¾ cup sweetened condensed milk

1 teaspoon vanilla

1 to 2 tablespoons Cognac or other liqueur, optional

Dash of salt

2 cups sweetened flaked coconut

2 cups chocolate-flavored sprinkles

1 tablespoon butter

In a double boiler over low heat, melt chocolate chips, stirring until smooth. Stir in condensed milk. Add vanilla, Cognac, and salt, stirring until thoroughly blended. Remove mixture from the heat.

Fold coconut into the chocolate mixture. Set aside 15 minutes, or until mixture is cool enough to handle.

With buttered hands, roll teaspoons of chocolate mixture into 1-inch balls; then roll them in the chocolate sprinkles. Place truffles on a tray lined with parchment or waxed paper and chill several hours until they're firm.

To serve, place truffles into paper or foil petit four cups. Store them in an airtight container in the refrigerator up to 2 weeks.

Recipe makes approximately 45 truffles.

Gourmet Caramel Apples

These awesome caramel apples are drizzled with a heavy coating of white and dark chocolate, then sprinkled with chopped nuts. Placed on a small plate and wrapped in clear cellophane with a large bow, they are an impressive holiday gift for friends.

INGREDIENTS:

6 large Red Delicious apples

6 wooden craft sticks

1 14-ounce bag caramels

2 tablespoons water

1 cup semisweet chocolate chips

1 cup white chocolate chips

½ cup chopped nuts, such as almonds, walnuts, or pistachios

Bring apples to room temperature; wash and dry them and remove the stems. Insert wooden craft sticks into the stem-end of the apples and set aside. Cover a tray with parchment or wax paper and spray it lightly with nonstick vegetable spray.

Combine caramels and water in a small nonstick saucepan. Heat over medium-low heat, stirring often, until the caramels melt and mixture is smooth. Remove the saucepan from the heat and place it on a heatproof surface.

Dip an apple into the caramel mixture, spooning the caramel over the sides until the apple is completely covered. Allow any excess caramel to drip into saucepan. Place the apple on the prepared tray and chill to set. Repeat with the remaining apples. Chill them 1 hour or until the caramel hardens.

Microwave semisweet and white chocolate in separate bowls at 50 percent power, or place the chips in separate double boilers over hot, not boiling, water; stir to melt. Drizzle dark chocolate over the apples. When that has set, drizzle white chocolate over the dark to form a lacy pattern. Dip the bottom of the apples in chopped nuts and return them to the refrigerator until the chocolate has set.

Recipe makes 6 apples.

Caramel Peanut Butter Popcorn Balls

A basket of these caramel popcorn balls is an ideal treat for Halloween parties at school or church. Peanut butter adds a tasty, unexpected surprise to these popcorn balls, and they stay fresh several days, so you can make them ahead. Wrap these treats in orange or yellow cellophane and tie them with narrow orange, yellow, or black ribbon, and there's not a ghost of a chance you will have any left after Halloween.

INGREDIENTS:

12 cups popped popcorn

1 14-ounce package caramels

3 tablespoons water

2 tablespoons peanut butter

Nonstick vegetable spray

½ teaspoon butter

1 to 2 small rolls orange or yellow cellophane

12 twist ties, to secure cellophane

15 lengths narrow orange, yellow, or black ribbon

Pop popcorn according to package directions. Pour into a large, lightly greased bowl.

Place the unwrapped caramels in a medium saucepan; add water. Cook over low heat, stirring frequently, until they are almost melted. Stir in the peanut butter until the mixture is smooth.

Pour the mixture over popcorn. Spray a large wooden spoon with nonstick vegetable spray and stir well to coat the popcorn with caramel sauce. Allow the popcorn to cool a bit until it's easy to handle.

With buttered hands, shape the popcorn into balls. Place each caramel ball in a square of yellow or orange cellophane, gather up the edges, and secure with a twist tie; then tie with ribbon.

Recipe makes 15 3-inch popcorn balls, or 12 4-inch popcorn balls.

Crispy Confetti Halloween Pops

Surprise trick-or-treaters of all ages with this variation on marshmallow crispy treats.

INGREDIENTS:

¼ cup butter or margarine

1 10.5-ounce package miniature marshmallows

5¼ cups toasted rice cereal

1 cup Froot Loops® cereal

Nonstick vegetable spray

6 ounces white chocolate

12 6-inch lollipop sticks

Halloween or autumn candy confetti

12 4- by 9-inch clear cellophane bags

12 lengths orange, yellow, or black ribbon (13 inches long)

Melt butter in a large saucepan over low heat; add marshmallows and stir to mix. Cook, stirring occasionally, until the marshmallows melt and the mixture is smooth. Remove the saucepan from the heat and add cereals, stirring well to mix completely. Spray a 9- by 13-inch pan with nonstick vegetable spray and transfer the cereal mixture to the pan. Spray your fingertips with nonstick spray and press the cereal mixture evenly into the pan. Set crispy treats aside 1 to 2 hours to cool completely; they will firm as they cool.

With a sharp knife, slice the cereal treats into 12 equal rectangles, and place them on parchment or wax paper. Insert a lollipop stick 2/3 of the way into each rectangle.

Soften white chocolate in a small microwavable bowl at 50 percent power for 2 minutes, or until chocolate is soft. Stir with a spoon until the chocolate is completely melted and smooth.

Dip crispy pops into melted chocolate and sprinkle with Halloween or autumn candy confetti. Place pops on a wire rack until the chocolate sets. They can go into the refrigerator to harden, if desired.

Wrap the pops in individual cellophane bags and tie with ribbon.

Recipe makes 12 4½-inch pops.

Halloween Treats

Meringue Ghosts

When you need to scare up a clever treat for trick-or-treaters or a Halloween party, these Meringue Ghosts are just the trick. For parties, package ghosts in small paper sacks decorated with Holloween themes, that you can find in most supermarkets or party stores. Tuck the ghosts in part way and allow the ghosts to peek out the top. Beware of making meringue ghosts on humid days; the results can be frightfully sticky!

INGREDIENTS:

3 egg whites, room temperature

½ teaspoon cream of tartar

¾ teaspoon vanilla

1 cup sugar

1 tablespoon mini chocolate chips

Preheat the oven to 225 degrees.

In the large bowl of an electric mixer, whip egg whites until foamy; add cream of tartar and vanilla. Whip until the whites form soft peaks. Add sugar, a little at a time, and whip until whites are glossy and form stiff peaks.

Transfer meringue to a piping bag fitted with a large plain tip (Ateco #4). Line two cookie sheets with parchment paper, adding a dab of meringue to each corner of the cookie sheet to secure the paper.

Pipe 4-inch ghosts, starting at the head, then arms and the body. Pipe two additional layers until ghosts are ¾ inch thick. Use mini chocolate chips to form eyes and mouths.

Bake in a preheated oven 1 hour. Turn the oven off and allow ghosts to dry 2 to 3 hours with the oven door closed. Peel off the parchment paper, cool ghosts completely on a wire rack, and store between layers of parchment paper in airtight containers.

Recipe makes 12 to 14 ghosts.

Spiderweb Caramel Apples

These spook-tacular caramel apples, covered in a web of white chocolate, will bring on shrieks of delight.

INGREDIENTS:

6 large Braeburn or
  Red Delicious apples

6 wooden craft sticks

1 14-ounce bag
  wrapped caramels

1½ tablespoons water

3 ounces white chocolate

6 small plastic spiders

Nonstick vegetable spray

Rinse and dry apples; remove stems. Insert a wooden craft stick into the stem end of each apple; set aside. Cover a tray with parchment or wax paper. Spray it lightly with nonstick vegetable spray.

Remove wrappings from caramels. In a small saucepan, combine caramels and water and cook over medium-low heat, stirring often, until the caramels melt and mixture is smooth. Remove the saucepan from the heat and place it on a heatproof surface.

Dip each apple into the caramel mixture, spooning it over the sides until each apple is completely covered. Allow any excess caramel to drip into the saucepan. Place coated apples on the prepared tray and refrigerate immediately to set the caramel.

Chop white chocolate, place into a small microwaveable bowl, and microwave 1½ minutes at 50 percent power until soft, but not melted; stir until smooth. Transfer melted chocolate into a pastry bag fitted with a small plain tip; twist top of the pastry bag to close.

Remove tray of caramel apples from the refrigerator. Pipe white chocolate vertical lines down each apple and scalloped lines around each apple between each vertical line to simulate a spider web. Place a plastic spider at the top of each apple near the craft stick. Return the apples to the refrigerator at least 30 minutes or overnight. Apples will stay fresh in the refrigerator 1 to 2 days.

Recipe makes 6 caramel apples.

Hot Spiced Cider

Our son, Timothy had a very loving fifth grade teacher, Betty Morgan. Each autumn, she made spiced cider, and the parents loved it. My version continues to garner compliments every time I serve the hot, spicy, winter beverage. It seems especially appropriate during the holidays.

A steaming cup of hot cider is particularly welcome when carolers return to the house after singing on a cold, winter night. This recipe has also been quite popular as the beverage of choice at holiday teas, and during autumn and winter cocktail parties, I have noticed that some guests prefer a pretty punch cup of hot and soothing spiced cider.

INGREDIENTS:

2 quarts apple cider	3 whole cloves
4 whole allspice berries	¼ cup red cinnamon candies
3 cinnamon sticks	

Pour cider into a large coffee percolator that has been scrubbed well to remove any trace of coffee flavor.

Place allspice, cinnamon sticks, cloves, and cinnamon candies in the percolator basket. Cover and heat; the candy melts as the spiced cider brews.

If a percolator is not available, pour cider into a Dutch oven or large saucepan and place spices and cinnamon candies directly into cider. Heat over medium heat, stirring occasionally, until the cider is hot and fragrant and the cinnamon candies have melted. Remove whole spices and serve.

Recipe makes 2 quarts.

Baked Alaska

For a festive New Year's Eve dinner with friends or a birthday surprise, Baked Alaska takes center stage every time. This dessert should be served with great fanfare, so purchase a package of tall, thin celebration candles to create a glorious blaze. Insert the candles quickly when the Baked Alaska comes out of the oven, dim the lights, and light the candles. Your dessert will arrive to appreciative gasps of surprise and delight.

This easy version starts with loaf pound cake, which is sliced horizontally and spread with raspberry jam before being layered with ice cream. Preslicing the ice cream and storing it in the freezer makes last-minute assembly of this dessert a snap.

INGREDIENTS:

1 rectangular half-gallon carton strawberry ice cream

1 rectangular half-gallon carton vanilla ice cream

1 9- by 5-inch loaf pound cake

½ cup seedless raspberry jam

3 egg whites

¼ teaspoon cream of tartar

6 tablespoons sugar

1 box 9-inch-long thin celebration candles

Several hours before serving, open the ice cream cartons until they're flat. Place them on a cutting board and slice horizontally into thirds. Place 1 vanilla ice cream slice in a 9- by 5-inch loaf pan lined with parchment paper or foil, allowing the ends of the paper to extend over the sides of the pan. Add an extra slice of vanilla ice cream if needed to cover the bottom of the loaf pan.

Desserts

Repeat with strawberry ice cream, placing a strawberry ice cream slice on top of the vanilla ice cream in loaf pan. Immediately place the pan in the freezer for several hours until firm. Return the remaining ice cream to the freezer for another use.

Shortly before serving, preheat the oven to 450 degrees. Slice the pound cake in half horizontally. Wrap the top half of cake and set it aside for another use. Place the remaining cake, cut side up, on a baking sheet and spread it with jam.

Remove the ice cream layers from the loaf pan, using parchment paper to help release them. Place the ice cream on top of the cake with the strawberry ice cream on top of the jam. Place the cake in the freezer to prevent melting while you whip the egg whites.

In the large bowl of an electric mixer, whip egg whites until foamy; add cream of tartar. Continue whipping at high speed, gradually adding sugar, until meringue is shiny and stiff peaks form.

Remove the cake from the freezer. Quickly spread meringue over it, sealing the ice cream completely.

Immediately place the cake in a preheated oven and bake 3 to 4 minutes until meringue is golden brown. Remove from the oven, carefully transfer the cake to a serving platter, and garnish with thin celebration candles.

Light the candles, dim the room lights, and serve immediately.

Recipe serves 8.

Bûche de Noël
(Swiss Mocha Cake with Chocolate Mocha Buttercream)

This impressive Yule log cake, decorated with meringue mushrooms, is traditionally served in France during the holidays. Why not make this decadent dessert part of your holiday celebration?

INGREDIENTS:

Cake:

1 cup flour

⅓ cup cocoa

½ teaspoon baking powder

2 tablespoons Swiss Mocha instant coffee powder

¼ teaspoon salt

⅔ cup milk

2 tablespoons unsalted butter

3 eggs, at room temperature

1 cup sugar

1 teaspoon vanilla

Confectioners' sugar

Preheat the oven to 350 degrees. Stir together flour, cocoa, baking powder, coffee powder, and salt; set aside. In a small saucepan, heat milk and butter over medium heat until hot and the butter has melted; set aside.

In the large bowl of an electric mixer, beat eggs until thick, about 3 minutes. Gradually add sugar, beating 4 more minutes. Fold the flour mixture into the egg mixture, just until blended. Stir in hot milk and vanilla.

Pour batter into a greased 15½- by 10½-inch jelly roll pan. Bake in a preheated oven 14 to 17 minutes, or until a cake tester inserted into the center comes out clean.

Cool cake 15 minutes, then remove from pan onto a towel covered with sifted confectioner's sugar. Roll the cake and towel together, starting at the short side of the cake. Cool the cake while it is rolled in the towel. Prepare buttercream.

Desserts

Chocolate Mocha Buttercream:

½ cup unsalted butter, softened

3 1-ounce squares semisweet chocolate

2 tablespoons Kahluaor Tia Maria

1 teaspoon powdered instant coffee

4½ cups sifted confectioners' sugar

4 to 5 tablespoons milk

Dash of salt

1 teaspoon vanilla

Meringue Mushrooms

Melt ¼ cup of the butter and chocolate in the top of a double boiler over—not in—hot water, stirring occasionally. Stir in Kahlua and instant coffee. Remove from heat; set aside.

In a large bowl, beat the remaining butter with 1 cup confectioners' sugar until smooth. Gradually beat in second cup of sugar, plus 1 tablespoon of milk. Add salt and vanilla.

Pour in reserved chocolate mixture, beating well. Beat in remaining confectioners' sugar, alternately with milk, until the buttercream is smooth.

Assembly: When the cake is cool, unroll it. Spread it with half the chocolate buttercream, then reroll it. Place it on a serving plate with the seam on the bottom.

Reserve ¼ cup buttercream for Meringue Mushrooms. Spread the remainder of the buttercream on the sides and ends of cake; Score with a fork to resemble tree bark. Decorate the cake and platter with Meringue Mushrooms.

Recipe makes 1 cake.

carbon dioxide. The carbon dioxide bubbles away harmlessly as the yeasts multiply and gobble the sugars, raising the alcohol level with increasing speed. Here is the elegance—the yeasts are bred to slow down and die as the alcohol level approaches 16 percent. A self-governing, symbiotic organism, developed millennia before DNA technology was recognized.

The winemaker uses this knowledge, artificially raising the alcohol level above 16 percent, by adding brandy to the fermenting juice before all the grape sugars are consumed. This leaves a rich, sweet, complex, sneaks-up-on-you wine that poets write of—Porto!

$$ Graham's LBV Porto
(High Douros, Portugal)

$$$ Fonseca "Quinta do Panscal" Vintage Porto
(Tavora Valley, Portugal)

$$$ Taylor Vintage Porto
(Upper Douros, Portugal)

Meringue Mushrooms

These oh-so-realistic Meringue Mushrooms are the perfect garnish for the Bûche de Noël, but they are also a sweet treat all by themselves. For gifts, package them in candy boxes and tie with a ribbon, or tuck them into small baskets and wrap in clear cellophane with a festive bow.

Meringue Mushrooms are also wonderful for entertaining. Make them a week or two ahead and store in an airtight container. Beware of humid days, though. Humidity interferes with the drying of meringue, and your mushrooms will be sticky and soft.

INGREDIENTS:

2 egg whites, room temperature

⅛ teaspoon cream of tartar

Pinch of salt

½ cup granulated sugar

2 teaspoons cocoa powder

¼ cup chocolate buttercream

In the large bowl of an electric mixer, whip egg whites and cream of tartar on high speed until soft peaks form. Add salt and continue beating, while gradually adding sugar. Whip egg whites until stiff peaks form and the surface appears glossy.

Desserts

Transfer meringue to a pastry bag fitted with a large plain tube (Ateco #8). On an ungreased cookie sheet, pipe ½-inch-wide mounds of meringue; then quickly release the pressure and bring piping bag straight up to form mushroom stems 1¼ inch high.

To form mushroom caps, pipe 1½-inch-wide domes of meringue by holding the piping bag straight up and down and exerting steady pressure. To release, move the tip of the tube in a small circular motion so the top of the mushroom cap is smooth. You can smooth the top with your fingertip, if necessary. Using a fine sieve, dust the mushroom caps lightly with cocoa.

Preheat the oven to 200 degrees. Bake meringues in a preheated oven approximately 1½ hours until meringues are very dry, but not brown. Turn off the heat and allow the meringues to dry 2 to 3 hours with oven door closed. Transfer them to a wire rack.

Slice the pointed tip from the mushroom stems with a sharp knife. Spread chocolate buttercream on the bottom of the mushroom caps; attach stems and set aside mushrooms until the buttercream is dry. Store them in an airtight container up to 2 weeks.

Do not make meringue mushrooms on humid days.

Recipe makes 16 to 18 mushrooms.

Chocolate Valentine Cake with Chocolate Ganache

This dense chocolate cake, with its smooth coating of deep chocolate ganache, will win your sweetheart's everlasting love. It's a divine showstopper dessert for parties, too, especially when you discover how easy it is to make!

INGREDIENTS:

Cake:

½ cup unsalted butter, softened

½ cup light brown sugar, packed

½ cup granulated sugar

2 eggs

1 teaspoon vanilla

1¼ cups sifted cake flour

½ cup cocoa

½ teaspoon baking powder

½ teaspoon salt

¼ teaspoon baking soda

¾ cup milk

Chocolate Ganache

White Sugar Glaze

Preheat the oven to 350 degrees. In the large bowl of an electric mixer, cream butter and sugars until light and fluffy, about 8 minutes. Add eggs and vanilla, beating well; set aside.

In a medium bowl, stir together cake flour, cocoa, baking powder, salt, and baking soda until well blended. Gradually add the flour mixture to the creamed mixture, alternating with milk, until the batter is thick and creamy.

Grease and flour a 9-inch heart-shaped cake pan. Spoon the batter into the prepared pan and bake in a preheated oven 30 to 35 minutes, or until a cake tester inserted into the center comes out clean.

Cool cake 30 minutes; remove from pan and cool completely on a wire rack. When cake is completely cool, cover with Chocolate Ganache.

Desserts

Chocolate Ganache:

8 ounces semisweet chocolate

¾ cup heavy cream

Chop chocolate until fine and transfer to a medium bowl. Pour cream into a medium saucepan and bring to a boil over medium heat. Pour the hot cream over the chocolate and whisk slowly and gently to melt the chocolate.

When the ganache is smooth, place the cake on a wire rack over a tray covered with parchment paper. Spoon ganache onto the cake and smooth it over the sides with an offset metal spatula until the cake is completely covered.

Allow ganache to dry 10 minutes, then decorate cake with white sugar glaze.

White Sugar Glaze:

½ cup sifted confectioners' sugar

1½ teaspoons milk

In a small bowl, whisk together confectioners' sugar and milk until smooth. Pour the glaze into a decorator bag fitted with a small plain tube, or pour it into a small plastic zipper bag and snip a small hole in one corner.

Pipe straight horizontal lines of glaze across the cake at 1-inch intervals. Drag a sharp knife through the glaze at ½-inch intervals from the top to the bottom of cake to create a feathered appearance.

Allow ganache to dry completely, and carefully transfer the cake to a serving platter with a wide metal spatula.

Recipe makes one 9-inch heart-shaped cake.

Cranberry Swirl Cheesecake

With a swirl of holiday red cranberry purée, this showstopper is sure to become a family tradition. Even the graham cracker crust takes on a festive flavor and appearance with the addition of finely chopped fresh cranberries mixed into it. For added convenience during the busy holiday season, bake the cheesecake a week or two before it's needed, wrap well, and freeze.

INGREDIENTS:

Cranberry Swirl:

2 tablespoons water

1 tablespoon sugar

½ cup whole fresh cranberries

In a small saucepan, stir together the water, sugar, and cranberries; bring to a boil over high heat. Reduce the heat to medium-low, stirring frequently, as the cranberries burst. When the mixture has thickened, remove it from the heat.

Transfer the mixture to a fine sieve and press it with back of a spoon, or process the mixture through a food mill; discard cranberry skins. Cover cranberry purée with plastic wrap; set aside.

Graham Cracker Crust:

1¼ cups graham cracker crumbs (about 8 crackers)

2 tablespoons sugar

¼ cup unsalted butter, melted

¼ cup chopped fresh cranberries

Preheat the oven to 325 degrees. Process graham crackers in a food processor or blender to yield 1¼ cups crumbs.

In a medium bowl, stir together graham cracker crumbs, sugar, melted butter, and chopped cranberries until crumbs are moist. Press the mixture into the bottom of a 9-inch springform pan; bake in preheated oven 10 minutes. Set aside to cool.

Desserts

Filling:

3 8-ounce packages
   cream cheese, softened

1 cup sugar

2 tablespoons flour

3 eggs

1 tablespoon milk

1 teaspoon vanilla

Preheat the oven to 375 degrees. In the large bowl of an electric mixer, blend cream cheese, sugar, and flour at medium speed until smooth. Add eggs, milk, and vanilla and beat until well combined; do not overmix. Pour into the prepared springform pan.

Stir reserved cranberry purée and spoon it onto the cheesecake in various spots. Swirl gently with a small spatula or knife.

Bake in a preheated oven 30 minutes. Reduce temperature to 300 degrees and bake 25 to 35 more minutes until the center of cheesecake is set, but still soft. Turn off the oven, open the door, and allow the cheesecake to sit in the oven 30 minutes. Remove the cheesecake from oven, cool 1 hour on a wire rack, and run a sharp knife around the edge of it. Release the outer band of the springform pan and remove it.

Transfer the cheesecake to a serving plate. Cover loosely and refrigerate several hours or overnight. With a metal spatula, gently loosen and transfer the chilled cheesecake from bottom of springform pan directly onto serving plate, if desired.

Recipe makes 1 cheesecake.

Alternately, we could go with a Barbera, a delightfully Rubenesque, silky red from Italy. While Barbera's peasant heritage brings vitality to the thinning bluebloods of more royal varietals, this wine has truly stepped onto the world stage. To play on the cranberry theme, a Valdiguié from California, known as Napa Gamay in the days before genetic testing, has intense cranberry and boysenberry essence in a voluptuous, if simple, body.

**$ Pelissero
Barbera d'Alba
"I Piani"**
(Piamonte, Italy)

**$ J. Lohr Valdiguié
"Wildflower"**
(California)

**$$ Jade Mountain
"La Provençal"**
(California)

Pumpkin Pecan Cheesecake

On Thanksgiving Day, no matter how much turkey, stuffing, and cranberries we consume, we somehow make room for dessert. You and your family will be glad you did, when you taste this holiday cheesecake. It is so rich, a small slice will do, but its light, creamy texture is perfect after a big meal. I have taken two holiday favorites, pumpkin and pecans, and combined them in this dessert, which is destined to become a Thanksgiving tradition.

INGREDIENTS:

Crust:

⅓ cup finely ground
   toasted pecans

1¼ cups graham cracker crumbs
   (about 8 crackers)

2 tablespoons sugar

5 tablespoons unsalted
   butter, melted

Preheat the oven to 275 degrees. Place pecans in a single layer on a baking sheet and toast in a preheated oven 6 to 7 minutes. Remove from the oven; cool completely. Process the cooled pecans in food processor until finely ground. Raise oven temperature to 325 degrees.

In a small bowl, combine graham cracker crumbs, sugar, ground pecans, and melted butter. Stir with a fork to moisten and mix ingredients.

Press crumbs onto the bottom of a 9-inch springform pan. Bake at 325 degrees 10 minutes. Remove from the oven; set aside to cool completely.

Desserts

Filling:

4 8-ounce packages
  cream cheese, softened

1¼ cups canned or
  fresh roasted pumpkin

1¼ cups sugar

2 tablespoons flour

1 teaspoon cinnamon

½ teaspoon freshly
  grated nutmeg

¼ teaspoon ginger

¼ teaspoon ground cloves

1½ teaspoons vanilla

4 eggs

Preheat the oven to 425 degrees. In the large bowl of an electric mixer, cream softened cream cheese, pumpkin, and sugar just until blended; do not overmix. Add flour, cinnamon, nutmeg, ginger, and cloves; beat just until mixed.

Add eggs, one at a time, mixing after each addition just until blended. Stir in vanilla.

Spoon cream cheese filling into the cooled graham cracker crust, smoothing the top with a rubber spatula. Bake in preheated oven 10 minutes; reduce heat to 300 degrees. Bake an additional 1 hour, 15 minutes, or until center is set.

Turn off the oven, open the door, and allow the cheesecake to sit in the oven 30 minutes.

Remove cheesecake from the oven; cool 1 hour on a wire rack, then run a sharp knife around the edges. Release the outer band of the springform pan and remove it.

Transfer the cheesecake to a serving platter. Cover loosely and refrigerate several hours or overnight. With a metal spatula, gently loosen and transfer the chilled cheesecake from the bottom of the springform pan directly onto serving plate, if desired.

Recipe makes one 9-inch cheesecake.

The flavor profile of this New World dessert is refreshingly different. The creamy, dense filling borders on pungent or savory, with an underlying dark molasses sweetness. When we add freshly grated nutmeg, ginger, cloves, and a hint of maple to the timeless trio of butter-flaky crust, sweetened whipped cream, and pumpkin, everything comes together beautifully in a not-too-sweet dessert that only lacks wine to be perfect.

The ginger and spice components of Gewürztraminer make for a scrumptious choice. However, there is also a royal pairing we commoners can afford. This story of rebirth and redemption began with the fall of the Soviet Union in the late twentieth century. Wine writer Hugh Johnson scoured Hungary in the chaotic, but exhilarating, days after the borders opened. He eventually tracked down more than seventy descendants of the original

Roasted Pumpkin Pie with Maple Cream

Create a sumptuous finale each Thanksgiving with this up-dated version of an old holiday favorite. You're in for a real treat with this made-from-scratch version. A pie pumpkin is roasted in the oven and used as the base for this spicy, smooth pie. The taste experience is further enhanced with a swirl of sweet, maple-flavored whipped cream.

INGREDIENTS:

Pumpkin Purée:

1 medium pie pumpkin (about 2 pounds), available in supermarket produce aisles or in farmer's markets

½ cup water

Pastry for a 10-inch pie shell

Preheat the oven to 400 degrees. Split the pie pumpkin in half; scrape out the seeds and stringy pulp, reserving the seeds to roast. Turn the halves face down in a roasting pan, add water, and cover tightly with foil. Roast in a preheated oven 40 to 45 minutes, or until the pulp is soft. Cool and spoon pulp into a food processor, discarding the skin. Process just until smooth; set aside.

Yields about 2½ cups pumpkin purée.

Pastry:

1¼ cups flour

¼ cup sifted cake flour

¾ teaspoon salt

6 tablespoons cold unsalted butter

2 tablespoons butter-flavored shortening

3 tablespoons ice water

Pulse flours and salt in a food processor to mix. Slice cold butter into 16 pieces; add to the flour mixture along with the shortening. Pulse until butter is pea-size. Add ice water; pulse just until pastry comes together and forms a ball. Wrap the pastry in plastic wrap and refrigerate at least 30 minutes.

Desserts

When the pastry is cold, roll it out on a floured pastry cloth and transfer it to a 10-inch pie plate. Flute the edges, cover with a light towel, and chill while preparing filling.

Filling:

1 recipe (2½ cups)
   pumpkin purée

1 cup sugar

1¼ teaspoons cinnamon

½ teaspoon ginger

¼ teaspoon ground cloves

¼ teaspoon freshly
   grated nutmeg

3 eggs

1 12-ounce can
   evaporated milk

Preheat the oven to 425 degrees. In a large mixing bowl, whisk together pumpkin purée, sugar, and spices until smooth. Add eggs and whisk until well blended. Gradually pour in evaporated milk, whisking constantly, until the filling is thick and smooth. Pour into the prepared pie shell.

Bake the pie in a preheated oven 15 minutes; reduce heat to 350 degrees and bake 45 to 50 more minutes until filling is set and a knife inserted into the center of the pie comes out clean. Cool; serve with Maple Cream. Cover and refrigerate leftovers.

Maple Cream:

½ pint heavy cream

1 tablespoon confectioners' sugar

1 tablespoon maple syrup

Whip cream in an electric mixer until it begins to thicken. Sprinkle in confectioners' sugar and maple syrup. Continue whipping until soft peaks are formed. Serve immediately, or cover with plastic wrap and refrigerate up to several hours.

Recipe makes one 10-inch pie.

growers and winemakers of the legendary Royal Tokai. Many remembered helping their grandfathers around the winery, and to a man, wanted to participate in the rebirth of what was once known as the "wine of Kings." Seventy years after its descent into the slow death of mediocrity, this sweet nectar of the gods shows more beautifully than when it was the exclusive property of the royal court. Love, sweat, and a worthy dream really can produce miracles in this age of technocratic neorealism. Of course, the investors' money helped quite a bit as well.

**$ Geyser Peak
Gewürztraminer**
(California)

**$$ Babich Gewürztraminer
"Winemakers Reserve"**
(Hawkes Bay, New Zealand)

**$$$ Royal Tokai
"Red Label"**
(Hungary)

Henrietta's Eggnog Pie

As far back as I can remember, my grandmother, Henrietta Schnoes, made this pie each year for Christmas. It was her signature dessert, and we all loved it. I fondly recall the time I phoned Grandmom from Houston and asked her to share her treasured recipe. She was positively delighted and asked that I let her know how it turned out.

Making Henrietta's Eggnog Pie has become a cherished tradition in our home. Our sons look forward to its creamy eggnog flavor and texture, and Randy's family is always thrilled when I arrive at holiday gatherings with an eggnog pie or two for dessert.

I always feel close to Grandmom when I make this creamy, rich dessert, and I am sharing it in memory of my sweet grandmother, who inspired my love of baking. Perhaps it will become a treasured tradition to be handed down in your own family. Grandmom would have liked that.

INGREDIENTS:

2 envelopes unflavored gelatin

¼ cup sugar

1 quart eggnog

2 teaspoons rum

2 cups whipping cream (divided)

2 baked 9-inch pie shells cooled

1 teaspoon sugar

Red and green maraschino cherries, for garnish

Desserts

In the top of a double boiler, combine gelatin and 4 cup of sugar. Stir in 1 cup cold eggnog.

Place over—not in—boiling water and stir until gelatin and sugar dissolve. Remove from the heat and stir in remaining eggnog and rum.

Pour mixture into a large bowl, cover with plastic wrap, and refrigerate until it is slightly thicker than egg white, approximately 40 minutes.

When thickened, remove the mixture from the refrigerator. In a separate bowl, whip 1 cup of cream until stiff. Whip the eggnog mixture until smooth and fold the cream into it. Pour into prepared pie shells; chill several hours or overnight.

Up to several hours before serving, whip the remaining heavy cream with 1 teaspoon sugar until soft peaks form. Spread over the pies.

Slice red and green cherries in half, then into thin slices; dry on paper towels. To decorate pies, place 1 slice of red cherry on the outer rim and place a green slice of cherry on each side of the red slice to form leaves. Garnish the outer rim with additional red and green "flowers" 4 to 5 inches apart.

Refrigerate the pies until ready to serve. After serving, leftovers may be refrigerated 2 days.

Recipe makes two 9-inch pies.

This is Christy's family heirloom recipe. The rich eggnog, sweetened cream, and maraschino cherries all tilt the scales to one side. We need good acidity and a fruit or nut component that will layer on, as opposed to cloying or muddying, the solid structure of eggy cream.

There is one style of wine particularly suited to this celebrated dish—the white Bordeaux of France. These Semillon/Sauvignon Blanc blends can be dessert wines, called Sauternes, containing the mouthwatering tangy richness of lemon and lime, with honeydew melon and floral notes.

**$$ Clos Floridene
White Graves**
(Bordeaux, France)

$$ Beringer "Alluvium"
(Knights Valley, California)

**$$$ Niebaum-Coppola
"Blancaneaux"**
(Rutherford, Napa Valley,
California)

Snowball Cake with Champagne Buttercream

This delicate, round winter cake is frosted in buttercream and topped with flaked coconut so it appears to be an icy snowball on the dessert platter, with royal icing snowflakes adorning the cake's surface.

INGREDIENTS:

Cake:

2½ cups sifted cake flour	1¼ cups sugar
2 teaspoons baking powder	¾ cup milk
¾ teaspoon salt	1 tablespoon vinegar
¼ teaspoon baking soda	2 eggs
¾ cup unsalted butter, softened	2 teaspoons vanilla

Preheat the oven to 350 degrees. Stir together cake flour, baking powder, salt, and soda; set aside.

In the large bowl of an electric mixer, cream butter and sugar until mixture is light and fluffy, about 8 minutes. Add vinegar to milk, stir, and set aside to sour, about 5 minutes. Add eggs to creamed mixture, beating well after each addition.

Mix dry ingredients into the creamed mixture, alternating with sour milk, beginning and ending with the flour mixture; the batter will be thick. Stir in vanilla.

Grease and flour a 2-quart ovenproof round bowl and line it with 2-inch-wide strips of parchment paper to make removing the cake easier. Spoon cake batter into the bowl, tapping lightly several times to remove air pockets.

Bake in a preheated oven 50 minutes, or until a cake tester inserted into the center of the cake comes out clean.

Remove the cake from the oven and cool 15 minutes; then turn it upside-down on a wire rack, remove it from the pan with the aid of the parchment strips, and cool completely. When the cake is cool, frost with Champagne Buttercream.

Desserts

Champagne Buttercream:

½ cup unsalted butter, softened

3 cups sifted confectioners' sugar

⅛ teaspoon salt

2 tablespoons milk

3 to 4 tablespoons Champagne

1½ teaspoons vanilla

1¼ cups sweetened flaked coconut

1 recipe Royal Icing Snowflakes

Cream butter with sugar and salt. Beat in milk, Champagne, and vanilla until thick and smooth.

Frost the cake and decorate it with coconut. Garnish with Royal Icing Snowflakes, if desired.

Recipe makes 1 cake.

Royal Icing Snowflakes:

3 tablespoons water

1½ tablespoons meringue powder (available in craft, cake decorating, and gourmet cookware stores)

2 cups sifted confectioners' sugar

Silver dragées, for garnish (optional)

In the large bowl of an electric mixer, beat the water, meringue powder, and confectioners' sugar at medium-low speed 8 to 10 minutes until the icing is stiff enough to form peaks.

Transfer the frosting to a decorator piping bag fitted with a plain tip (Wilton #5). To form each snowflake, pipe a 3-inch-wide cross on the parchment. Pipe a 2-inch-long X over the cross, and connect the lines with icing filigree. Garnish the snowflakes with silver dragées if you desire.

Recipes makes 12 to 14 snowflakes.

We are also quite fond of Caymus's "Conundrum." This highly-rated blend of five varietals is a dense, complex white wine, dripping with lush fruit and delicate floral notes, and the acidity is high enough to bring this exuberant beauty into elegant, crisp focus.

Of course, we seize any excuse to crack open a bottle of bubbly, preferably one with a generous amount of Chardonnay and good acidity, such as Taittinger "La Française." It is a delightful contrast to the Champagne buttercream.

$ Sokol Blosser "Evolution" (Oregon)

$$$ Caymus's "Conundrum" (California)

$$$ Taittinger Brut "La Française" (Reims, France)

Sweetheart Brownies
with Raspberry Coulis

Satisfy your heart's desire on Valentine's Day with this romantic, heart-shaped brownie dessert. Brown sugar in the batter provides an unexpected caramelized sweetness and a soft, tender texture. Each decadent Valentine brownie rests in a pool of mildly tart raspberry coulis and is garnished with cream hearts, a swirl of chantilly cream, and a sprinkling of shaved chocolate. For baking, use six 3½-inch heart pans (available at culinary cookware stores).

INGREDIENTS:

3 ounces unsweetened chocolate

½ cup unsalted butter

½ cup granulated sugar

½ cup light brown sugar, packed

1 teaspoon vanilla

2 large eggs

½ cup all-purpose flour

½ teaspoon baking powder

¼ teaspoon salt

Nonstick vegetable spray

1 recipe Raspberry Coulis

1 tablespoon confectioners' sugar, for garnish

Heavy cream, to create hearts in coulis

½ cup whipped heavy cream, for garnish

1 teaspoon sugar

1 chocolate bar, for garnish

Preheat the oven to 350 degrees. Melt chocolate and butter in a mixing bowl set over—not in—hot water, stirring until smooth. Remove the bowl from the heat. Stir in sugars and vanilla; add eggs, beating well with a spoon.

Desserts

In a small bowl, stir together flour, baking powder, and salt. Stir into the chocolate mixture, blending thoroughly. Spray the heart pans with nonstick vegetable spray. Spoon the brownie mixture into the pans, filling each one ⅔ full.

Bake in a preheated oven 22 to 25 minutes, or until a tester inserted into the center comes out clean. Remove the brownies from the oven. Serve warm or at room temperature in a pool of Raspberry Coulis.

Raspberry Coulis:

1 14-ounce package
frozen raspberries

3 to 4 tablespoons sugar

1 teaspoon freshly squeezed
lemon juice

Thaw raspberries in the package. Pour them into a blender, add sugar and lemon juice, and purée until smooth. Transfer to a fine sieve set over a medium bowl and, using the back of a spoon, push the purée through the sieve; discard seeds.

To assemble the dessert, spoon coulis onto dessert plates, tilting the plate until the coulis covers them evenly. Dust the tops of the brownies with sifted confectioners' sugar; place one brownie on each plate. With a spoon, place dots of whipping cream around the perimeter of coulis. Drag a sharp knife from the top through the bottom of each dot to form cream hearts.

Whip heavy cream with sugar to sweeten. Garnish the tops of the brownies with a dollop of whipped cream and a sprinkling of shaved chocolate.

Recipe makes 6 servings.

Upside-Down Pear Gateaux

During a black-tie Valentine party Randy and I hosted, these delicate, heart-shaped cakes, with a caramelized brown sugar and sweet pear topping, won rave reviews from our guests. My good friend, radio personality Jim White, proclaimed it to be the best pear tart he had ever tasted.

A brown sugar mixture is spooned onto the bottom of each heart-shaped pan, and sliced pears are arranged over the sugar mixture before the cake batter is poured into the pans. After baking, the cakes are turned upside-down to reveal their hidden treasure—almond gateaux garnished with pears and a glistening caramelized topping. Every bite is pure bliss.

INGREDIENTS:

Cake:

Nonstick vegetable spray with flour (Baker's Joy®)

⅓ cup unsalted butter, softened

¾ cup sugar

1 egg

1 teaspoon vanilla

¼ teaspoon almond extract

1¼ cups sifted cake flour

¾ teaspoon baking powder

½ teaspoon salt

⅔ cup milk

Brown Sugar Topping:

¼ cup unsalted butter

1 cup light brown sugar, packed

2 red pears, peeled, cored, and thinly sliced

Desserts

Preheat the oven to 350 degrees. Spray 2 8-inch heart-shaped cake pans with nonstick vegetable spray with flour, such as Baker's Joy®.

In the large bowl of an electric mixer, cream butter and sugar until light and fluffy, about 8 minutes. Add egg, vanilla, and almond extract; beat until smooth.

In a medium bowl, stir together cake flour, baking powder, and salt. Gradually add dry ingredients to the creamed mixture, alternating with milk, starting and ending with dry ingredients; set aside.

In a small saucepan over low heat, melt butter and brown sugar, stirring often. Spoon into the bottom of the cake pans just to cover. The brown sugar mixture may harden, but it will melt in the oven. Arrange sliced pears over the sugar mixture and spoon cake batter evenly over the pears.

Bake gateaux in a preheated oven 25 to 30 minutes, until the top is golden brown and the cake has pulled away from the sides of the pans. Remove from the oven, set aside 2 minutes to cool, and loosen the cake from the sides of the pans with a knife. Invert gateaux on a wire rack to cool.

Gateaux may be made 1 day ahead, covered with plastic wrap, and refrigerated.

To serve, place the cakes on serving platters and slice into small wedges.

Recipe makes 2 cakes.

Index

Index

Index

Index

Index

Index

P

Index

Index